THE TEACHING OF
CHARLES FOURIER

Charles Fourier

The Teaching of

CHARLES FOURIER

Nicholas V. Riasanovsky

UNIVERSITY OF CALIFORNIA PRESS

BERKELEY AND LOS ANGELES

1969

University of California Press
Berkeley and Los Angeles, California
University of California Press, Ltd.
London, England
Copyright © 1969, by
The Regents of the University of California
Library of Congress Catalog Card Number: 77-84043
Printed in the United States of America
SBN 520-01405-7

TO
JOSEPH R. LEVENSON
(1920–1969)

CONTENTS

PREFACE

Since childhood I have been interested in Fourier's thought. This study is, at long last, my statement of it, and it can be considered in part a reaction against the kind of summaries and expositions of Fourier's views which I have read for over thirty years. To be sure, difficult, rich, and important teachings are likely to be misinterpreted or inadequately presented. Two added considerations complicate the exposition of Fourier's ideas. As I shall try to show, his thought was all of a piece, organically united in a kind of overarching universal formula to the extent that it is impossible to do justice to a period, a part, or a significant particular aspect of Fourier's teaching without dealing with the whole. Moreover, this formula was essentially mad and encompassed most bizarre and eccentric elements. Often those intellectuals who appreciated Fourier in some particular role, such as that of a social critic, or a precursor of Marx, or a theoretician of the cooperative movement, were least prepared to admit, let alone accept, the totality of his teaching. My purpose then, is to state Fourier's system in its own terms, not in terms of its possible contribution to a different intellectual orientation. In addition, I became interested in the relation of Fourier's views to the general currents of modern thought, in the place of Fourier on the intellectual map of the modern world. The last two chapters are a small contribution to this problem of placement in a broad sense, not in regard to specific connections and influences.

My study is a modest one, and to emphasize this I should mention a few things which it does not propose to do. It is not a detailed biographical or psychological investigation of Fourier. Such an investigation would be highly desirable, although it is my guess that it would prove to be largely negative, i.e., that we should not learn much more of significance than we already know. Also, although I worked at the Archives Nationales and had access to the Fourier manuscripts, this book is based on the unpublished manuscripts only in small part. The problem was not only time but also the fact that Fourier's manuscripts combine enormous bulk with overwhelming repetitiousness. Indeed, Fourier's tight, explosive, and obsessive thought does not allow room for real variety or new departures. In other words, I came to the conclusion that for my purposes a study of Fourier's manuscripts quickly led to diminishing returns. It remains true, however, that because of Fourier's stature, his manuscripts deserve careful attention and that their value can be best assessed after such attention is given and not before. I relied mainly on Fourier's extensive published works and even then, because of the scattered nature of his writings, I cannot claim to have read quite all of them. Nor is this a book about Fourierists. I tried to use the works of Fourierists as little as possible in order to keep Fourier's own thought apart from the ideas of his disciples, although, of course, I had to turn to some of his followers, notably Pellarin, for information about Fourier.

Writing concerning Fourier's thought presents many technical difficulties. Fourier's works are bizarre in style and form as well as in content. As an example, he used more than a dozen methods, often highly unusual, to emphasize words or statements. The punctuation is eccentric and at times impossible so far as the meaning of a passage is concerned, and there are numerous errors of every sort. Fourier delighted in coining new words or new forms of existing words. All these difficulties are well known to those who are interested in Fourier. My presentation aims at achieving a certain simplification and maintaining common sense while trying to lose as little as possible of the peculiar quality of Fourier's statements. I have used italics for all kinds of emphasis utilized by Fourier (to make matters a little simpler I have never used emphasis of my own, but only as inserted by Fourier or other authors). I did change punctuation where necessary to make Fourier's statements readable. I also took the liberty of using as a rule throughout my book the most common term for a given concept of Fourier's rather than the several different terms as they replaced or overlapped each other in his writings. Thus I always mention the phalanx, never the canton. In translating Fourier, I have tried to retain something of Fourier's peculiar tone and awkward style. To help the reader who would like to go back to the original, I have added, wherever applicable, references to the new "Anthropos" edition of the works of Fourier, certainly the most readily available and the most complete. Twelve volumes of this edition have so far been published.

As I look back on my interest in Fourier and on this work, I realize that I owe much to many people. I learned some French history with Professor Gordon Wright, now of Stanford University, and some French intellectual history with the late Crane Brinton at Harvard. My first formal study of Fourierism, and my first publication in that field, resulted from a seminar with the late Professor Michael Karpovich of Harvard University. More directly in connection with the book, I wish to thank European and American specialists on Fourier or related matters who have given me much kind attention and helpful advice, notably such scholars as Emile Poulat, Henri Desroche, and Professor J. B. Duroselle in Paris, my teacher Sir Isaiah Berlin of Oxford University, Professor Frank Manuel of New York

University, and Mr. Jonathan Beecher of Harvard University. I would like to express my particular gratitude for the helpfulness and kindness of the leading Soviet specialist on Fourier, I. I. Zilberfarb. In addition to my indebtedness to the Archives Nationales, I owe thanks to many libraries, first of all to the magnificient Bibliothèque Nationale in Paris, but also to other European and American libraries, especially that of my own University. I acknowledge gratefully grants from the SSRC and Fulbright Travelling Grant which made it possible for me to spend the 1964–65 academic year in Paris. My colleagues in Berkeley, the late Professor J. R. Levenson, Professors H. F. May, Hans Rosenberg, K. M. Stampp, F. E. Wakeman, Jr., and Professor Frederick Weinstein of the State University of New York at Stony Brook read the entire manuscript and made many helpful criticisms and suggestions. I am also indebted to my research assistants Mr. Stephen Lukashevich, now professor at the University of Delaware, Mr. Vladimir Pavloff, Mr. Gerald Surh, and Mrs. Victoria King, as well as to my secretary Miss Stella Valdiviez, for help in this work, and to the Institute of International Studies of the University of California for providing the research assistantships and for aiding in the typing of this manuscript. The weaknesses of this study are, of course, my own—unless perchance some of them are Fourier's.

I am especially indebted to my wife.

Nicholas V. Riasanovsky

University of California,
Berkeley

CHAPTER I

Fourier's Life

In addition, I was distracted by commercial occupations: the work of the mind is almost nil when one has to devote one's days and one's years to occupations which are trivial and incompatible with study.[1]

The inventor of this method gives lessons in the city: he will come to the homes of those who invite him and will add other branches of learning, as needed, to the three offered above.[2]

Father Albert Lafontaine once wrote: "Fourier's life, the details of which are little known to us, seems not to have influenced in a clearly marked manner the direction taken by his ideas."[3] The statement, certainly exaggerated and strictly speaking wrong in itself, may point to several striking aspects of the utopian socialist's existence and thought, aspects noted separately or together by numerous other commentators. There was the frequently mentioned glaring contrast between bleak life and luxuriant doctrine, between cramped circumstances and unbridled imagination. There was, further, the fact that the doctrine seemed all of a piece, a most exotic mechanism obeying its own logic and detached from its environment. Then too, its author stood apart from other men, a lunatic or a prophet, but not a com-

[1] Charles Fourier, *Manuscrits* (Paris, 1851), p. 1; *Oeuvres,* Edition Anthropos, Vol. X, p. 1, first pagination.
[2] Charles Fourier, *Mnémonique géographique, ou méthode pour apprendre en peu de leçons la géographie, la statistique et la politique* (Paris, [1824]), p. 15.
[3] A. Lafontaine, *Charles Fourier* (Paris, 1911), p. 4.

1

mitted or effective participant in the affairs of the day. To be sure, such concepts of modern psychology as compensation can be invoked to turn the very poverty and isolation of Fourier's life into partial explanations of his doctrine. But these explanations should not exceed their limits. Of the many people who lead drab existences in the world, very few become Charles Fouriers. Still, although Fourier's thought often appears to bear no relation to his life, which it overshadows by far, there was a life also, and that life deserves some attention.[4]

François-Marie-Charles Fourier was born on the seventh of April, 1772 in Besançon. His father, Charles Fourier, was a well-established cloth merchant; his mother, Marie Muguet, belonged to perhaps the most prominent commercial family of the town. The boy, the youngest of four children, had three sisters. Fourier's recollections of his childhood often dwelt on discipline and on his inability to adjust to it, for example, to his being forced to eat food which he did not like. As he asserted much later, "Every father is, to a greater or a lesser extent, a domestic tyrant."[5] But it was, apparently, his

[4] Unfortunately, there is no full biography of Fourier. Most important is the study by his disciple, Charles Pellarin: *Charles Fourier, sa vie et sa théorie.* My references will be to the more complete second edition: Paris, 1843. Pellarin's work has very valuable notes, in particular a description of Charles Fourier by one of his sisters (pp. 297–301). The book has been translated into English (the translation does not include the part on the theory): *The Life of Charles Fourier* (New York, 1848). Most works on Fourier and Fourierism, including Bourgin's massive study (H. Bourgin, *Fourier, Contribution à l'étude de socialisme français,* 2 vols., Paris, 1950, pay relatively little attention to the thinker's life. Many writings on Fourier and Fourierism contain important scattered biographical information. Some of them will be mentioned in subsequent footnotes.

[5] Charles Fourier, *Manuscrits* (Paris, 1852), p. 295 and elsewhere in Fourier's writings; *Oeuvres,* Anthropos, Vol. X, p. 295, second pagination.

narrow religious upbringing by his mother that left the most harrowing memories:

At the age of seven I was thoroughly terrified by the fear of these boiling cauldrons. I was taken from sermon to sermon, from novena to novena; so much so finally that, horrified by the threats of the preachers and the dreams of boiling cauldrons which besieged me every night, I resolved to confess a mass of sins which I did not understand at all and which I feared to have committed without knowing it. I thought that it would be better to confess a few too many than to omit a single one.[6]

Bitter memories extended to the occupation of the family and its impact upon the child. One such recollection in particular has become a prized possession of Fourierist hagiography:

From that time on I noted the contrast which prevails between commerce and truth. I was taught in the catechism and at school that one must never lie; then I was taken to the store to be trained from an early age in the noble occupation of lying, that is, in *the art of selling*. Shocked by the chicanery and the fraud which I saw, I proceeded to take aside the merchants who were the victims and to reveal the deception to them. One of them in his complaint maladroitly gave me away, which cost me a thorough spanking. My parents, seeing that I had a taste for truth, cried out in a voice of reprobation: "This child will never be worth anything in commerce." And in fact I conceived a secret aversion for commerce, and at the age of seven I swore the oath which Hannibal had sworn at nine against Rome: I swore an eternal hatred of commerce.[7]

[6] *Ibid.*, pp. 78–79. A remarkable confession follows.

[7] Charles Fourier, *Analyse du mécanisme de l'agiotage [et] de la méthode mixte en étude de l'attraction.* (Extract from *La Phalange. Revue de la Science sociale*) (Paris, 1848), p. 4. Cf., for example, Pellarin, *op. cit.,* pp. 11–12, where, incidentally, five rather than seven is given as the age when Fourier swore his famous oath.

Other reminiscences by Charles Fourier of his parents and his upbringing depict other scenes of frustration and pain. Moreover, he left no record at all which could balance the picture, no memories of love, understanding, or kindness in the home.

Fourier's parents had very little education, but a greater measure of it seemed clearly appropriate for their son. The future utopian socialist attended and was graduated from "le collège de Besançon," an apparently mediocre Jesuit high school with a classical curriculum. Whereas accounts of Charles Fourier's stunning academic prowess and versatility —not to mention claims made on his behalf of having acquired a universal knowledge during those years—belong properly to the Fourier legend, young Fourier seems in reality to have done well in school and to have displayed early a number of interests and tastes. In particular, he was fascinated by geography and perhaps also by mathematics and precise counting of every kind. He enjoyed music. And he loved flowers. What little Fourier learned at school in Besançon acquired special significance for the theoretician of Harmony because it proved to be the sum total of his formal education.

Fourier's father died when the boy was nine, leaving him a considerable inheritance to be collected in installments provided that he continued to be engaged in commerce. But young Fourier, it would seem, had other ambitions than heading the family business; he wanted to pursue his education and especially to study military engineering. He claimed to have submitted to family demands only after a great struggle, but he did submit.[8]

***

[8] "I was enrolled willy-nilly. Having been brought to Lyons by the lure of a voyage and having arrived at the door of the banker Scherer to whom I was being conducted, I deserted right in the street declaring that I would never be a merchant. This was refusing

The year 1789 marked the end of Fourier's life at home in Besançon. For the first time the young man visited Paris and Rouen, and later Bordeaux and Marseilles, and even Germany and the Netherlands, but he went to live in Lyons as an apprentice in a commercial concern. Lyons thus became the first place, after Besançon, which Charles Fourier came to know well, and it was in Lyons that he spent the crucial revolutionary years through 1793.

These years were memorable ones in Fourier's life as in the lives of so many other Frenchmen. Having become twenty in 1792 and having received the first installment of his inheritance, Charles Fourier went into business on his own. In 1793 he invested his money in a variety of tropical products to be brought to Lyons through Marseilles. The goods arrived just in time to be requisitioned and perish in the counterrevolution in Lyons and the subsequent siege and capture of the city by the forces of the Convention.[9] Furthermore, Fourier himself, who had been enrolled in the counterrevolutionary forces, was imprisoned after their defeat and indeed was fortunate to escape with his life.

Even after Charles Fourier managed to leave Lyons and return to his native Besançon, his tribulations were not over. He was drafted into the army where he spent a year and a half, from June 1794 until January 1796. His stay in the army, however, was apparently peaceful, and he was dis-

Hymen at the steps of the altar. I was then taken to Rouen where I deserted for the second time. At the end I bent under the yoke, and I lost my best years in the workshops of deceit, my ears resounding everywhere with the sinister prediction: 'An honest fellow! He is worthless for commerce.'" Fourier, *op. cit.,* p. 4.

[9] In Ernest Seillère's acid words: "It is thus first in the capacity of an unfortunate speculator that he became an enemy of speculators: a rather frequent origin of convictions of that kind!" E. Seillère, *La philosophie de l'impérialisme, t. IV: Le mal romantique. Essai sur l'impérialisme irrationel. Première partie. Le romantisme des pauvres. Charles Fourier* (Paris, 1908), p. 143.

charged because of ill health. It was following this discharge
—when the rule of the Directory and later of Napoleon replaced the revolutionary years—that Fourier's life assumed
its set shape and course.

After his debacle in Lyons, the shipwreck of another consignment of goods, and the loss of his mother's fortune
through the machinations of an uncle and a repayment in
assignats, Fourier was never able again to be an independent
businessman. Instead he had to earn a living as a minor employee in the commercial world. He served as a cashier, a
bookkeeper, a *commis voyageur,* a French correspondence
clerk in an American firm, and as an "irregular" stock
broker. In his own weird manner he prepared courses and
offered to give lessons, but he had few or no pupils. In general Charles Fourier spent the first part of his adult life in
Lyons and the last in Paris, but he traveled extensively,
usually on business, in France and even in neighboring
countries. All these occupations, which the theoretician of
Harmony changed frequently, enabled him to survive, but
little more. Fourier never married, never established a home
or a family. One reads of cheap pensions in Lyons—so often
used to illustrate and in part even to prove Fourier's social
theory—and of drab apartments in Paris to be reached after
long climbs up steep staircases. Grinding poverty and his resulting inability to devote himself wholly to his mission became a constant refrain of Fourier's existence. Still, the
utopian socialist did get some help: an annual stipend after
his mother died in 1812, a long stay with his relatives which
enabled him to concentrate on his work, and even some support, as well as appreciation, from a small but growing band
of disciples. In fact, during the last ten years or so of his life,
Fourier, although his material circumstances do not seem to
have improved, no longer depended on holding a job and
could therefore devote himself entirely to the formulation

and propagation of his teaching. Charles Fourier died in Paris on the tenth of October, 1837.

Fourier's many jobs have been examined and his numerous addresses collated by disciples and by specialists because the chronologies of his employment and of his residence corresponded to another and important chronology, that of his writings. Fourier began to publish in Lyons, contributing material to the *Journal de Lyon et du Midi* in 1801–1802, the *Bulletin de Lyon* in 1803–1804, and the *Journal de Lyon. Nouvelles de la France et de l'Etranger* in 1804–1811. These occasional bad poems, strange brief articles, and early pieces of polemic represent, in spite of their scattered and seemingly slight nature, an authentic introduction and indeed more than introduction to the utopian socialist's subsequent voluminous works. It was in an article entitled "Universal Harmony" and published in the *Bulletin de Lyon* on the third of December 1803 that Charles Fourier wrote:

The calculus of Harmony . . . is a mathematical theory of the destinies of all the globes and their inhabitants, of the sixteen social orders which can be established on the various globes in the course of eternity. . . . I owe this astonishing discovery to the analytic and synthetic calculus of passionate attraction which our learned men have judged unworthy of their attention during the two thousand five hundred years that they have conducted their studies. They have discovered the laws of physical motion; this is grand, but it does not destroy poverty. The laws of social motion should have been discovered. Their invention [*sic*] will lead mankind to opulence, voluptuous life, and global unity. I repeat, this theory will be geometric and applied to the physical sciences. It will not be an arbitrary doctrine like the political and the moral sciences, which will come to a sorry end. We shall see a resounding collapse of the libraries.[10]

[10] "Harmonie universelle" in Charles Fourier, *Manuscrits* (Paris, 1851), pp. 52–53; *Oeuvres,* Anthropos, Vol. X, pp. 52–53, first pagination. This article was republished a number of times. It is generally considered to be the first statement of Fourier's teaching organically

"Universal Harmony" was the first announcement of the new teaching. Next, it had to be presented to the public. The presentation took the form of a sizable volume, *Théorie des quatre mouvements et des destinées générales. Prospectus et annonce de la découverte,* which appeared in Lyons in 1808. This original edition, however, was anonymous, and it misleadingly carried Leipzig as its place of publication.[11] *Théorie des quatre mouvements* remained the fullest statement of Fourier's doctrine until the appearance, in two volumes in 1822, in Paris of Charles Fourier's largest work, his

related to all subsequent formulations and elaborations. In Bourgin's authoritative words: "Already at that time the main lines of Fourier's doctrine are grasped and traced. . . . This first theoretical expression was not to be betrayed either in substance or in form by the vast publications which came later." (Bourgin, *Fourier,* pp. 72–74.) Or to quote Jacques Nicolai: "Subsequent works only make it more precise or develop it: they do not change it on any point." (J. Nicolai, *La conception de l'évolution sociale chez Fourier* [Paris, 1910], pp. 66.) Fourier himself apparently believed that he had "discovered" his system in 1799: Fourier, *Egarement de la raison demontré par la ridicule des sciences incertaines* and *Fragments* (Paris, 1847), p. 93; *Oeuvres,* Anthropos, Vol. XII, p. 679.

Fourier's other important early articles, also in the *Bulletin de Lyon,* include "Triumvirat continental et paix perpétuelle sous trente ans," republished in *La Phalange* and in the first volume of Fourier's collected works (*Oeuvres,* Anthropos, Vol. X, pp. 225–227) and "Lettre au Grand-Juge." The Letter, together with some other material and comments, was published as a separate booklet by Charles Pellarin in 1874 in Paris. The additional material included Fourier's letter written several months before the appearance of "Universal Harmony" where Fourier declared: "I am the inventor of the mathematical calculus of destinies, the calculus which Newton had readily at hand and which he could not even foresee; he established the laws of physical attraction, I the laws of passionate attraction, the theory of which no man before me had tackled" (pp. 14–28, especially p. 15).

[11] *Théorie des quatre mouvements* became the first volume of Fourier's collected works. Subsequent references are to the third edition, Paris, 1846; *Oeuvres,* Anthropos, Vol. I.

Traité de l'association domestique-agricole, later known as
Théorie de l'unité universelle.[12] The indefatigable theoretician offered one more general exposition of his teaching in
his third fundamental work, *Le nouveau monde industriel
et sociétaire, ou invention du procédé d'industrie attrayante
et naturelle, distribuée en séries passionnées,* published in
Paris in 1829.[13] The two volumes which Fourier put out
shortly before his death, in 1835 and in 1836 in Paris, deserve
to be considered as his last major writing. Although patchy,
even more disorganized than usual and not aiming at comprehensiveness or continuity, they present rich and varied
material, much of it central to Fourier's teaching. They also
carry one of his characteristically long titles: *La fausse industrie morcelée, répugnante, mensongère, et l'antidote,
l'industrie naturelle, combinée, attrayante, véridique, donnant quadruple produit et perfection extrème en toutes
qualités. Mosaïque des faux progrès, des ridicules et circles
vicieux de la Civilization. Parallèle des deux mondes industriels, l'ordre morcelé et l'ordre combiné.*

In addition to large books, Fourier continued to write
numerous shorter pieces. Some of these were meant as additions to or explanations of his fundamental works. *Traité de
l'association domestique-agricole* in particular received seven
or eight addenda, all published in 1823 in Paris and incorporated into subsequent editions of the *Traité.* There was
even an *Instruction pour le vendeur et l'acheteur.* Others

[12] Under the latter title the study formed the second, third, fourth,
and fifth volumes of Fourier's collected works. Subsequent references
are to the second edition, Paris, 1841–1843; *Oeuvres,* Anthropos, Vols.
II–IV.

[13] *Le nouveau monde* became the sixth and concluding volume of
the works, until, at long last, the "Anthropos" edition went beyond
the sixth volume. Subsequent references are to the third edition, Paris,
1848; *Oeuvres,* Anthropos, Vol. VI.

were independent booklets and pamphlets, such as *Sur les charlataneries commerciales* published in Lyons in 1807 or *Sur les banques rurales* which came out in Paris in 1823. Projects constituted a major, in a sense dominant, kind of Fourier's writings. Fourier emphasized that, in contrast to others, he not only criticized the present condition of the world, but invariably proposed immediate, radical, and beneficial change. His entire teaching was such a project of transforming and saving the world. Lesser projects contributed in their more modest ways to the same purpose, and they were often intrinsically linked to the great project. But, whether the issues were major or minor, whether Fourier dealt with commerce, rural banks, or simply teaching geography (*Mnémonique géographique, ou méthode pour apprendre en peu de leçons la géographie, la statistique et la politique,* published in Paris in 1824), he always castigated the existing state of affairs and urged scientific change. Characteristically, his first published piece was a prospectus, written jointly with another aspiring journalist, Martainville, and dated the eleventh of August, 1800, for the projected but never realized *Journal de Lyon et du départment du Rhône.*

Most of Fourier's proposals, to be sure, were sent directly to the powers that be and did not appear in print. As early as 1797, following his military service, Fourier advised the French minister of foreign affairs on the desirable conditions of territorial settlement with the enemies of France. At the same time he told the Directory how to reorganize the army supply system and move the army quickly across the Alps. For the rest of his life he continued to draw up projects and to appeal for their implementation in an astonishing variety of matters, ranging from different problems of government, economics, and foreign policy to musical notation and the rebuilding of Besançon.[14] These projects were closely related to the main line of Fourier's thought, and they often exhibited a certain self-winding and expansive quality. In fact, according to one view, Fourier's entire cosmological theorizing began with his interest in geography and a proposal to establish the Northern passage.[15] More generally accepted—indeed stressed by Fourier himself—is the impact on the utopian socialist's thought of such specific problems of his immediate experience as the spoiling of a large consignment of rice withheld too long from the market for reasons of speculation, and especially the famous differential in the price of an apple in Paris and in the south of France.

Polemic also occupied, from the start, a large place in Fourier's writing. The theoretician of the phalanx considered himself the destroyer of the ideas of all the "philosophes" who had preceded him, and he repeatedly gave them battle in his major and minor works. Moreover, Fourier saw false prophets appear to compete with him for public attention. Accordingly he had to attack and denounce them and their systems, while always restating the true doctrine. At times the polemical element came to occupy the dominant position. This was notably true of a little book which Fourier published in Paris in 1831: *Pièges et charlatanisme des deux sectes Saint-Simon et Owen, qui promettent l'association et le progrès. Moyen d'organiser en deux mois le progrès réel, la vraie association, ou combinaison des travaux agricoles et domestiques, donnant quadruple produit et élévant à 25 milliards le revenu de la France, borné aujourd'hui à 6 milliards un tiers.*

For many years Fourier struggled alone, and during his

[14] On embellishing Besançon see Fourier's letters in Pellarin, *op. cit.*, pp. 204–206.
[15] Seillère, *op. cit.*, p. 15.

entire life he never received much support. Still, as noted, he began gradually to acquire disciples, and toward the end of his days he became the acknowledged head of a modest movement and school of thought. Just Muiron of Besançon, who established contact with Fourier in 1816, is usually listed as the first disciple. Other early followers included Clarisse Vigoureux and the much more prominent Victor Considérant. Moreover, Fourier's following grew sufficiently strong to start a periodical press of its own, first, from 1832 to 1834, *La Reforme industrielle ou le Phalanstère,* and, soon after its demise, *La Phalange.* In spite of some difficulties with his admirers, who were often shocked by the master's unbridled fantasy, Charles Fourier published during his lifetime almost a hundred articles in this Fourierist press. In addition, after his death, *La Phalange* continued to publish his manuscripts in Paris on a large scale, as did later and to a lesser extent, in Brussels, the *Bulletin du mouvement sociétaire.* The disciples also put out Fourier's collected works which contained the three main expositions of his doctrine, published or republished separately some of the master's lesser writings, and brought out four interesting and important volumes of selections from the Fourier manuscripts.[16] Masses of manuscripts, testifying to the utopian socialist's urge to write which bordered on graphomania, remained unpublished.[17]

The disciples, or rather some of them led by a deputy

[16] All four volumes were published in Paris and were entitled *Publication des manuscrits de Charles Fourier,* followed by the respective dates: année 1851, année 1852, années 1853–1856 (published in 1856), and années 1857–1858 (published in 1858); *Oeuvres,* Anthropos, Vols. X–XI.

[17] Emile Poulat has provided an invaluable guide to the manuscripts in *Les cahiers manuscrits de Fourier. Etude historique et inventaire raisonné* (Paris, 1957). See my reference to the manuscripts in the preface above.

from Seine-et-Oise, A. F. Baudet-Dulary, mounted another effort, potentially of the greatest interest for their cause: the foundation of a trial phalanx as preached by Fourier. The attempt made in 1832 at Condé-sur-Vesgre at the edge of the Rambouillet forest promptly failed. Indeed the enthusiastic promoters did not possess either the resources or the organization and personnel to satisfy the blueprint of Fourier who was quick to criticize and even to denounce the experiment. Baudet-Dulary paid the losses out of his own pocket, and all joined in asserting that the undertaking at Condé-sur-Vesgre represented no test of Fourier's teaching.[18] Baudet-Dulary's attempt, and another in 1835–1837 in distant Rumania where a trial phalanx was disbanded as subversive, were the only two efforts to realize Fourier's doctrine during his lifetime.[19]

The disciples also contributed some of the descriptions of Fourier, his character, and his daily life which we possess, and they collected and preserved other such descriptions. Charles Fourier was apparently a slim, small man with a large forehead and piercing blue eyes. When he became old, his white, slightly curly hair provided a striking frame for his impressive head. But it was the eyes that usually attracted attention. "In the eyes of Fourier, in which there shone incessantly a fixed and abstract fire, where the despair of an unrecognized thinker pierced through the continuous preoccupations of an economist, one read so much misfortune,

[18] Fourier's violent criticism can be found in his *La fausse industrie,* Volume II, p. 25; *Oeuvres,* Anthropos, Vol. IX, p. 25. For a brief, defensive account of the painful episode see Pellarin, *op. cit.,* pp. 115–116, 244–249. Although the establishment at Condé-sur-Vesgre failed as a trial phalanx, it still exists as a kind of cooperative rest home, a remarkable monument to the staying power of Fourierism.

[19] For an up-to-date summary on Fourierism in Rumania see I.L. Zilberfarb, *Sotsialnaia filosofiia Sharlia Fure i ee mesto v istorii sotsialisticheskoi mysli pervoi poloviny XIX veka* (Moscow, 1964), pp. 309–315.

such perseverance, such nobility that well before becoming acquainted with him one could foresee his genius." [20] Fourier dressed meticulously and properly in black, "like a magistrate."

Fourier's manners and bearing were also correct and rather formal, and he lived, it would seem, according to a rigid routine and strictly on schedule. In fact, the obsessive scheduling and the often astounding precision in detail, so characteristic of the utopian socialist's writings, formed apparently also an intrinsic part of his life. Some commentators, especially hostile ones like Seillère, noted, on the basis of Fourier's own statements, a number of specific compulsions: to split matches and thus make them last longer, to preserve pins and bits of string, or to separate absolutely all the pulp of a fruit from its seed or stone so that none would be wasted.[21] As to keeping a schedule, by far the best-known story is that of Fourier's waiting for years regularly at noon each day for the invited financier who was to subsidize a trial phalanx but who never came. Fourier's volumi-

---

[20] From André Delrieu's description of Fourier in the *Siècle* of the sixteenth of October, 1837, reproduced in Pellarin, *op. cit.,* pp. 250–251.

Compare Edmund Wilson's description: "Robert Owen has the look in his portraits of a great smooth meditative hare with an assertive, independent English nose, but an elliptically oval face and deep innocent elliptical eyes that seem to stretch right around his cheeks; and Fourier's face, over its high white cravat, has something of the same odd simplification—though with the dignity of the strong old French rationalism, with its straight mouth and thin Roman nose and its lucid and religious eyes, a little too wide apart." Edmund Wilson, "Origins of Socialism. III: The Communities of Fourier and Owen," *The New Republic,* Vol. LXXXXI, No. 1178 (June 30, 1937), pp. 213–217, especially 213. For Pellarin's list of the five authentic portraits of Fourier and other related material see his section on "conservation des types authentiques," Pellarin, *op. cit.,* pp. 284–285.

[21] See especially Seillère, *op. cit.,* pp. 41–42.

nous writings and his still more voluminous unpublished manuscripts present striking, indeed almost overwhelming, evidence of this relentless drive to schedule, arrange, and organize everything.

Fourier kept apart. Isolation became a constant characteristic of his life. Unmarried, without a family of his own, the theoretician of Harmony apparently established no other lasting personal attachments. The man who wrote so insistently about love left no record of his loves. Some critics speak of *passades* and relate them to the volatile nature of love in the utopian socialist's ideal world. Others speculate that Fourier was impotent. In any case, the name of no woman has come down to us as romantically linked to that of Charles Fourier. Also, it would seem that Fourier had no close personal friends, although he did acquire disciples. These disciples, however, were kept at a certain distance; besides, the master made it unmistakably clear that his attitude to his followers depended entirely on their devoted acceptance of his teaching. The teaching always came first, not the men.

In more general terms, Fourier never ceased to denounce the human condition and humans themselves in what he considered to be the vicious and perverse stage of development known as Civilization. Much of the power of his denunciation—as we shall see in a later chapter—resided precisely in its ruthless and sweeping nature, in a refusal to make qualifications or allow for exceptions. Fourier scorned those who believed in the pristine virtues of the people as much as he disdained the champions of the existing economic order, church, and state; and he was certain that the countryside was not a whit behind the cities in vice and misery. The view had rigor and symmetry, but it could hardly offer solace. Indeed, up to the time of his final illness when he kept insisting on being left alone, the theoretician of Harmony found it difficult to address people or simply to be with them.[22] This self-imposed isolation must have been a heavy burden for Fourier. Harmony, of course, was going to dispel such isolation and in fact transform it into a perfect integration. In the meantime, one of Fourier's recurrent images was that of our sick and demented planet, whirling alone in space, quarantined, as a leper would be, by all other celestial bodies.[23]

By the usual standards Fourier lived a life of failure. Loneliness, poverty, drab work with its meager rewards, frequent changes of employment which led nowhere are all part of the record. Moreover, and not surprisingly, detailed recent

[22] Fourier's aloofness has been noted by almost all students of his life, and apparently it increased with age, although our information is far from complete. In spite of its obvious relevance to the dissemination of his teaching, Fourier avoided public speaking so successfully that at least one commentator asserted—erroneously, to be sure —that Fourier never spoke in public, G. Isambert, *Idées socialistes en France de 1815 à 1848* (Paris, 1905), p. 118, chapter IV, pp. 116–151, deals with "Charles Fourier et l'harmonie phalanstérienne"; see also M.-A. Gromier, *La vie, les oeuvres, les disciples de Charles Fourier* (Paris, 1906), pp. 24–25. For Fourier's own declaration of a desire to escape from society see Charles Fourier, "Des lymbes obscures," *La Phalange. Revue de la science sociale* (January–February 1849), Vol. IX, pp. 5–40, 97–110, p. 20.

[23] Another trend in Fourier's attitude to people has been noted, that of helping those in need. There is the story of how the boy in Besançon regularly gave away his lunch to a beggar. Later acts of kindness, related in Pellarin's biography, included Fourier's solicitations and other efforts on behalf of his early follower, Just Muiron, or war veterans "whom he did not even know personally," or a servant girl (Pellarin, *op. cit.,* pp. 147–148, 155, 264–268). Fourier's helpfulness to the needy deserves attention, all the more so because it was in perfect accord with the moral passion underlying his critique of Civilization and his preaching of Harmony, as well as with his remarkable and most perceptive championing of the underdog in his writings. But there is no reason to believe that this helpfulness broke down to any significant extent Fourier's psychological isolation. There is no evidence, for example, that the boy became a close friend of the beggar.

research tends to indicate that Fourier performed poorly even at his modest level.[24] In fact, Seillère pointed triumphantly to a recurrent figure in Fourier's writings, that of a fool in a boarding house of whom the assembled company makes constant fun, as a particularly valuable biographical insight.[25] The pattern, if indeed it existed, is not likely to have originated in a boarding house. As Fourier himself wrote about parents and children:

Fathers and mothers, following the rule that extremes meet, go from one excess to another. They spoil this child, and they torment that one. They scold, humiliate, terrify, stupefy him, they make him a servant of the family, a Cinderella. Every father is, to a greater or a lesser extent, a domestic tyrant, even though he believes that he is just; he needs among his children a favorite and a buffoon. Often the one whom he disgraces is the best.[26]

Nevertheless, however deep the misery and however sharp and frequent the blows, Fourier knew that he would ultimately triumph. In fact, the hardships themselves served a purpose:

It seems to me that fate is right in making those to whom it accords an important discovery unfortunate. By condemning them to failure in everything else it reminds them ceaselessly that they have a purpose to which they must hold and which they must fulfill. . . . Fate is right in depriving inventors as far as wealth is concerned; had they been rich they would have avoided

[24] See especially J.-J. Hémardinquer, "La 'découverte du mouvement social,'" *Le Mouvement Social,* No. 48 (July–September, 1964), pp. 49–70, especially p. 51.

[25] Seillère, *op. cit.,* pp. 112–113. Seillère criticizes and indeed denounces Fourier with passion, constantly resorting to heavy sarcasm and denigrating language. Yet his observations of the object of his hate are often acute.

[26] Fourier, *Manuscrits* (Paris, 1852), p. 295; *Oeuvres,* Anthropos, Vol. X, p. 295, second pagination.

preparatory study, that mania for investigation which carried them to success; and when I look back upon the [. . .] which led me to the discovery of the theory of universal unity, I must admit that had I had an income of ten thousand livres I would have slid by all the insights that led me to the theory, I would have slept a soft sleep, and the theory of universal unity would have remained to be discovered. . . .[27]

As it was, the insignificant and unsuccessful commercial employee stood ready to save mankind and, beyond that, to transform the universe. As early as 1802 or 1803, when Fourier had just begun writing about his teaching, he commented in a passage published after his death: "He who brings such knowledge (*telles lumières*) to mankind will be the Messiah of reason." [28] Messiahship has never been easy, but it could give content to a life. And it was this content that many saw in Fourier's arresting eyes without quite understanding their meaning. It was this that drove Fourier in his ceaseless writing and ceaseless quest, in Lyons, and in Paris, and also, in a different sense, in lands of imagination and intellect that know no boundaries. Under the surface of a proper, meticulous, awkward, and timid office employee there was a volcano, or, perhaps better, in the words of Robert Pagès, a *délire à froid,* cold delirium.[29]

[27] Fourier, *Manuscrits, Années 1853–1856* (Paris, 1856), p. 348; *Oeuvres,* Anthropos, Vol. XI, p. 348, first pagination. A word missing in the published text.

[28] Fourier, *Manuscrits* (Paris, 1852), p. 51; *Oeuvres,* Anthropos, Vol. X, p. 512, second pagination. On Fourier's conception of his mission see the next chapter and also my article: "L'emploi de citations bibliques dans l'oeuvre de Charles Fourier," *Archives de Sociologie des Religions,* No. 20 (1965), pp. 31–43.

[29] R. Pagès, "Quelques sources, notamment fouriéristes, de la sociologie expérimentale," *Archives internationales de Sociologie de la Coopération,* No. 4 (1958), pp. 127–154, especially p. 139. Cf. Erich Fromm's reference to "burning ice" as characteristic of the "psychology of the fanatic," E. Fromm, *Marx's Concept of Man* (New York, 1961), note 2, pp. 44–45.

Was Charles Fourier insane? The issue has provoked extensive comment and even acrid controversy.[30] Central to the discussion are the nature and form of Fourier's teaching as well as his attitude toward his teaching. Much of the content of the teaching—to which the next chapter will be devoted—is fantastic and bizarre to say the least. Whole parts of it, such as cosmology and analogy, seem to belong to the world of extravagant dreams. Even the more pedestrian sections contain numerous strange assertions, arguments, and prophecies. The fantastic element thus pervaded in one way or another almost all of Fourier's writings. It became, as Charles Renouvier noted, especially prominent and extreme after the theoretician of Harmony revised his original classification of "movements" to add the "aromal" to the "instinctual" or "animal," the "organic," the "material" and the "social" or "passionate." It was these mysterious aromas that accounted for such features of Fourier's system as copulation and procreation among celestial bodies, specific creations of plants and animals on one planet by other planets, and in general the cosmological links.[31] Fantasy kept expanding and becoming ever more insistent. *La fausse industrie,* published on the eve of the utopian socialist's death, was probably his most bizarre work.

While the glorious "anti-lions" and "anti-whales," to be created on our planet after it reaches the stage of Harmony,

[30] See, for example, E. Villey, "Charles Fourier, l'homme et son oeuvre," *Revue d'economie politique* (Paris), 11e année (1897), pp. 999–1017, 12e année (1898), pp. 30–59; and, Ch.-M. Limousin, *Le fouriérisme. Bref exposé. La pretendue folie de Fourier. Réponse à un article de M. Edmond Villey intitulé: "Fourier et son oeuvre"* (Paris, 1898).

[31] Ch. Renouvier, "La philosophie de Charles Fourier," *La Critique Philosophique, Scientifique, Littéraire* (Paris), (1883); No. 14 (May 5), pp. 209–220; No. 16 (May 19), pp. 241–251; No. 21 (June 23), pp. 321–333; No. 28 (August 11), pp. 23–32; No. 29 (August 18), pp. 33–40, especially p. 36.

and the solarians with their magnificent and most useful
tails attracted immediate attention and often derision, some
other aspects of Fourier's doctrine might well be considered
even more damaging to the whole than this element of pure
fantasy. The entire teaching of Charles Fourier was meant
to be a mathematical formula, and all its parts were to have
mathematical structure and precision. Yet in spite of his endless calculating and classifying, no identifiable formula
emerges. Besides, no evidence at all is adduced to indicate
why the application of Fourier's formula and model would
transform our vale of tears into Harmony. The correctness
and the resulting beneficial effects of Fourier's plan remain
entirely an assumption. Fourier was "the most absolute of all
the authors of social systems" [32]—certainly not the sanest.

Form matched content in the utopian socialist's writings. Cisambles, transambles, and postambles alternated
with intra-pauses and "arrière-propos"; queer neologisms
abounded in the text as well as in the subtitles; pagination
began at times to follow patterns of its own to achieve striking as well as most confusing results in *La fausse industrie*.
As usual with Fourier, there seemed to be both method in
the madness and madness in the method: oddly entitled
strange parts of strange books were themselves meant to
form regular series with their ascending, pivotal, and descending sections, transitions, and the like. Fourier, the author, lived his own theory.

As to the utopian socialist's attitude toward his teaching, a
subject which will have to be mentioned again later, he was
convinced that he had the secret of universal salvation and
he was obsessed by the fear of its being stolen, by the fear of
plagiarism. From the indication of Leipzig, rather than
Lyons, as the place of publication of his first major work
and to the time of his death, Fourier made use of little tricks

[32] *Ibid.;* No. 14 (May 5), p. 212.

to mislead his imaginary pursuers, and he also turned against them repeatedly in sacred rage in his writings.

Those who insist on Fourier's sanity thus have much to explain, especially if they are to deal with Fourier and his system as such rather than merely select for their own purposes this or that part of the teaching, for example, the critique of Civilization or the arguments for cooperatives. Fourierists as a group, even during their master's lifetime, as well as after his death, did their best to underplay the strikingly fantastic element in the doctrine. They excluded it from their expositions of the system and asserted that it was of secondary importance and even irrelevant. Similarly, they excused or minimized their master's paranoid tendencies and other queer personal characteristics. His fear of plagiarism in their view became a justifiable worry, for plagiarism, after all, does occur, or it was pardoned as at the worst a harmless quirk of a hard-pressed old man.

Later writers developed these arguments and found new ones. For instance, they suggested that many of Fourier's prophecies were subsequently realized, if often not exactly as he had predicted, or they argued that Fourier could not be insane because insanity meant a lack of coordination and coherence, whereas Fourier's system was perfectly consistent.[33] Charles Gide, the distinguished specialist in the history of economic theory, maintained that Fourier, like a court jester, played the fool to make the bitter truths which he enunciated more palatable. Also, the fantastic details of his teaching made his message memorable where it would otherwise have been forgotten.[34] The view that the fantastic element

[33] This last argument can be found in Limousin, *op. cit.*, p. 4.

[34] Yet Gide, a careful and sensitive scholar, felt that these explanations could at best account for only some of Fourier's fantasy. Other fantastic elements in Fourier's teaching reminded him of Don Quixote or claimed his sympathy because of their grandeur. The verdict remained ambivalent: "the best that can be said in exculpation

in Fourier was merely a matter of writing style or form received full development in the works of an outstanding contemporary Soviet specialist on Fourier, I. I. Zilberfarb. Basing his approach on Fourier's assertions that he was not properly understood—in one case at least understood literally when he should have been understood figuratively—Zilberfarb concluded that the right understanding would make Fourier rational and would relegate the fantastic element of his teaching to its outward form or, at the most, to a harmless additional play of imagination to which the utopian socialist himself assigned little or no importance. The economic and social critique and message were fundamental; other parts of the teaching were secondary and tentative at best.[35] Yet this was not at all what Fourier himself had said, even when trying—so often unsuccessfully—to limit his discussion to "reasonable" subjects. "I forbid myself to speak of transcendental harmonies, readers in the stage of Civiliza-

is that this is a simulated folly, and even here one is not certain," Ch. Gide, *Fourier, precurseur de la coopération* (Paris, 1924), pp. 7–11, quoted from p. 7. As to his playing the fool, Fourier himself claimed this, and incidentally compared himself to a court jester in regard to his *Théorie des quatre mouvements in* "Le sphinx sans Oedipe, ou l'énigme des quatre mouvements," which forms the first section (pp. 193–206) of "Manuscrits de Fourier. L'inventeur et son siècle," *La Phalange. Revue de la science sociale* (March 1849), Volume IX. It should be kept in mind, however, that in this article Fourier merely tried to explain away, by arguments such as fear of plagiarism, desire to defeat his critics, and need to take into account taboos on sex, the scattered and bizarre nature of his presentation; but he reaffirmed the absolute validity of what he had to say.

[35] See Zilberfarb, *op. cit.*, pp. 71–78, and throughout the book. See also Zilberfarb's other writings on Fourier, notably his articles: "Tvorcheskii put Sharlia Fure," *Frantsuskii Ezhegodnik, stati i materialy po istorii Frantsii* (Moscow, 1959), and "L'imagination et la réalité dans l'oeuvre de Fourier," *Le Mouvement Social*, No. 60 (July–September 1967), pp. 5–21. Emile Lehouck deals interestingly, but also unconvincingly, with the same problem throughout his *Fourier aujourd'hui* (Paris, 1966).

tion being in the condition of a man who has undergone an operation for a cataract and who must not be exposed to the brilliant light of the sun except by degrees." [36]

Fourier's character, background, and life influenced his teaching. Connections have been drawn, for instance, between his unhappiness in the parental home on the one hand, and on the other his devastating critique of the institution of the family in Civilization and his virtual abolition of it in his ideal world. Family and family upbringing played, to be sure, a crucial role both in his own life and in his judgment of the world around him. To select a more pleasant topic, Fourier's early love of music and of flowers found a rich, indeed extravagant, expression in his construction of Harmony. The utopian socialist's own character traits apparently also influenced his theorizing, in particular his original and crucially important classification of passions. Thus the *papillonne,* the passion for diversification, has been linked to Fourier's love of travel and his general restlessness. Seillère undertook a more detailed analysis to demonstrate convincingly the great extent to which Fourier's system provided for his own characteristics and even tastes and obsessions. In fact, Fourier stated that he knew only one example, namely himself, of a character type especially precious in Harmony, the *omnititre* (or *omnigyne*), and he naturally lapsed into the first person when writing about him.[37]

[36] Fourier, *Manuscrits* (Paris, 1852), p. 330; *Oeuvres,* Anthropos, Vol. X, p. 330, second pagination. After reading defenses of Fourier's sanity one acquires sympathy for Seillère's *cri de coeur:* "Perhaps there never existed a famous and influential man who was more clearly, more obviously mad than this one." Seillère, *op. cit.,* p. 3.

[37] Seillère, *op. cit.,* pp. 38–46, and throughout the entire book. Seillère bases his analysis primarily on the Fourier manuscripts published in *La Phalange* after the utopian socialist's death. See in particular: Charles Fourier, "Du clavier puissanciel des caractères," *La Phalange, revue de la science sociale,* Paris, XVIe année, Ire série, Vol. VI, pp. 5–47, 97–135 (July–August, 1847). Fourier's class-

Broader social influences played their part in shaping Charles Fourier's teaching. Linked to commerce and the world of business in general, first through his family and later through his own occupations, the utopian socialist assigned a crucial position to trade in his analysis of Civilization. We shall see, for example, that in spite of some pioneering insights into such issues as overproduction and disparities between technological advances and the structure of a society, Fourier preferred to blame the nefarious activites of the middlemen for the greater share of economic and social ills. Observation and experience in Besançon, Rouen, Paris, and other cities, but especially in Lyons, enabled the angry theoretician of Harmony to write knowingly, as well as vehemently, about such favorite topics as commercial trickery, bankruptcies, speculation, or the stock exchange. He also learned firsthand about the poverty of the masses, social tensions, and economic development which could combine technological progress with an increasing misery of the people. Fourier's Civilization turned out to be, predictably, very much the world of his own social experience.

His ideal, Harmony, also had connections with that experience. Some critics stress the impact on Fourier's thinking of the economic and social legislation of the French Revolution as well as of some projects of the period which were not translated into reality. Others point to cooperative beginnings around Fourier, for instance, the efforts of workers in Lyons to purchase food, fuel, and other items of general consumption in common, and of artisans to establish rudimentary producers' cooperatives,[38] or to the flourishing peasant cooperatives making Gruyère cheese in Fourier's na-

---

ification of passions and character types will be discussed, together with the rest of his teaching, in the next chapter.

[38] Cooperative undertakings in Lyons are given prominence, for instance, in Zilberfarb, "Tvorcheskii put Sharlia Fure," p. 303.

tive Franche-Comté. Fourier, it appears, might have even visited Hern Hutter communities during his trips abroad.[39] Paris deserves special notice as an influence. Fourier was extremely impressed, perhaps smitten, by Paris when he first saw it.[40] And it was in Paris that the idea of the architecture of the new world occurred to him,[41] with the arcades of the Palais Royal in particular reappearing almost inevitably in his subsequent discussions whenever he began to sketch the outlines of Harmony. Perhaps more importantly, it was the intense, diversified, sparkling, sensuous life of the peerless French capital that provided the closest real approximation to what Fourier wanted to achieve in his phalanxes. Fourier's ideal can thus be tied in many more ways than one to its author's social existence. Even Fourier's gastrosophy, his overwhelming emphasis on the cuisine, has been interpreted as a reflection of social trends.[42]

[39] The possible Hern Hutter connection is especially stressed in A. Ioannisian, "Istochniki proektov assotsiatsii Fure," *Istorik Marksist,* No. 1 (1939), pp. 101–124, particularly pp. 118–121.

[40] See Fourier's letter to his family of the eighth of January, 1790, in Pellarin, *op. cit.,* pp. 175–177. The opening passage reads: "You ask me whether I find Paris to my taste. Without doubt; it is magnificent, and I, who am not easily astonished, I was struck with wonder at seeing the Palais Royal. The first time one sees it, one believes he has entered a fairy palace. It is there that one finds all that one can desire, shows, magnificent buildings, promenades, fashions, in a word all that one can desire."

[41] "It was 33 years ago when I was walking for the first time the boulevards of Paris that their appearance suggested to me the idea of unitary architecture the rules of which I soon established. I owe this invention principally to the boulevard of the Invalides and above all to two small hotels situated between the streets Acacias and N. Plumet." Quoted in Pellarin, *op. cit.,* p. 261.

[42] According to Jean Gaulmier, the French Revolution deprived the chefs of the great noble houses of their employment with the result that they opened restaurants and advanced French public cooking to new heights; also, not for nothing was Fourier a contemporary of Brillat-Savarin and, more broadly, of the physiocratic

But it would be entirely wrong to interpret the utopian socialist's teaching as a series of *ad hoc* reactions to specific
events or to the changing social scene in general. Even
Marxist critics who are eager to derive Fourier's doctrine
from the "real world" around him regret that Fourier
missed important parts of that world, in particular the rise
of the proletariat.[43] Actually, if one is to use this kind of reality principle as a gauge, Fourier proved deficient on many
counts. More importantly still, he had his own way of taking
note of events and developments: from the start, that is,
from our first record of Fourier's writings, Charles Fourier
possessed his system, and everything that happened subsequently to him and around him served not to change that
system or to put it in question, but rather to illustrate it and
to provide some additional evidence for its perfect validity. In
a sense, once he had his system Fourier saw and learned
nothing.

If Fourier's teaching did not evolve from his daily experience, was it borrowed from books? The problem of intellectual influences on Fourier has given rise to some sharply
different opinions,[44] and it deserves further study. Still, the
school with its stress on agronomy (see Gaulmier's notes in André
Breton, *Ode à Charles Fourier* [Paris, 1961], pp. 83–84). By chance,
young Fourier had Brillat-Savarin as his traveling companion to
Paris.

[43] "Even after the uprisings of the Lyons workers in 1831 and in
1834 he did not abandon his former lack of faith in revolution and
did not attain an understanding of the historical role of the then
ripening proletariat as the leading force of social progress," Zilberfarb, *op. cit.*, p. 329. Zilberfarb in particular emphasizes Fourier's
social environment as determining his views. He starts from Michelet's famous dictum that Lyons, rather than any earlier theoretician,
was the sole precursor of Fourier (J. Michelet, *Histoire de la Révolu-
tion française,* Vol. VI [Paris, 1869], p. 290).

[44] One such dissenting opinion, represented by Gerald Schaeffer,
Jean Gaulmier, and others, puts Fourier squarely in the mystical,

main outlines of the matter seem reasonably clear. As Hubert Bourgin has demonstrated in his fundamental *Etude sur les sources de Fourier,*[45] and as other scholars have confirmed, Fourier did not engage in heavy or thorough reading. Apparently he never acquired the habit. Moreover, from the time of his first appearance in print he was already firmly convinced of two things: he had the true answer, and all the other writers, all the philosophes with their 400,000 volumes, were wrong, misleading, and noxious. Reading them was at best a waste of time; at the worst it could lead to perdition. No wonder that Fourier combined utter scorn for his intellectual rivals with easy admissions that he had not really read them.[46]

On the other hand, Fourier liked to keep abreast of his time and to peruse the periodical press, the *Journal des Débats,* the *Journal du Commerce,* the *Constitutionnel,* or the *Moniteur.* To quote Pellarin on Fourier's reading habits:

illuminist, masonic tradition. It is based on tenuous conjecture at best and sometimes on outright mistakes, as when Schaeffer asserts that certain of Fourier's articles were originally speeches at masonic gatherings. See Gaulmier's notes to Breton, *op. cit.;* and G. Schaeffer, "L'ode à Charles Fourier et la tradition," *André Breton. Essais et temoignages* (Neuchatel, 1950), pp. 83–109, especially p. 90, footnote 1. See also the following curious anonymous item, "A propos d'un talisman de Charles Fourier. Analyse critique et essai de reconstitution," *La Brèche* (February 4, 1963), pp. 18–23.

[45] H. Bourgin, *Etude sur les sources de Fourier* (Paris, 1905). Bourgin shows clearly and, within the limits of the materials available, almost exhaustively how little evidence there is that Fourier borrowed directly from or had even read authors suggested as possible sources of his ideas. My only criticism of Bourgin's study is that Bourgin is too concerned with the differences between Fourier's views and those of the writers in question: a particular similarity may be significant in spite of all the differences.

[46] As a highly representative instance see Fourier's treatment of Kant's thought in Fourier, *Manuscrits* (Paris, 1851), pp. 33–35; *Oeuvres,* Anthropos, Vol. X, pp. 33–35, first pagination.

During the last ten or twelve years of his life, he confined himself to spending an hour or two every day in the reading room of the Rotonde in the Palais Royal, in order to keep up with current events and the subjects brought up for discussion by the press; even then he spent much of that time with his eyes fixed on Lebrun's atlas. As to undertaking extensive reading, he was careful to avoid it; he had already given up long ago the idea of finding in the libraries evidence in support of his Theory or materials for its completion.[47]

Nor was this reading pattern, if not the exact schedule, confined to the last decade of the utopian socialist's life; in fact, in his case we know of no other.

Superficial classical education in Besançon and a persistent, if patchy and scattered, reading of periodicals—together with whatever else Fourier must have read, as well as heard, as part of the intellectual climate of the age—produced a peculiar amalgam. Fourier certainly belonged to the Age of Reason; various representatives and views of that age were mentioned frequently in his writings. Yet these references lack depth and nuance; the same quotes, occasionally incorrectly rendered, are repeated time and time again; Voltaire is frequently cited simply as an "expecting" philosophe, one who recognized the limitations of our present knowledge and social system and looked to future illumination; the longest discussion of Montesquieu deals with the material advantages which the count had as a writer over Fourier, a circumstance particularly regrettable because Fourier had so much more to say.[48] Those in search of major influences receive little help from such trivia.

It is rather a similarity in ideas that points to certain connections, and it is on the basis of such a similarity that

[47] Pellarin, *op. cit.,* p. 142.
[48] On Montesquieu see Fourier, *Manuscrits* (Paris, 1851), p. 3; *Oeuvres,* Anthropos, Vol. X, p. 3, first pagination.

Rousseau has been mentioned more often than any other writer as a predecessor of Fourier. "Fourier represents Rousseauism grown rank and luxurious."[49] "Fourier is Rousseau, only more clear, more crude, and without contradictions."[50] "He is the only philosophe who took literally and pushed to an extreme Jean-Jacques' anathema against civilization."[51] In fact, Fourier's revolt against civilization in the name of the liberation of human personality links him in a fundamental way to the Genevan thinker. Fourier himself commended Rousseau for his critique of civilization, and his depiction of love, although he also criticized Rousseau on several counts, and certainly did not consider him his master.[52]

If certain basic assumptions connected Fourier with Rousseau, some of the utopian socialist's economic views, in particular the heavy emphasis on agriculture, depended apparently on Quesnay and the physiocratic school as a whole. Again, Fourier acknowledged the link to the extent of praising Quesnay and lamenting the general turning away from

[49] E. Mason, "Fourier and Anarchism," *The Quarterly Journal of Economics,* Vol. 42, No. 2 (February 1928), pp. 228–262, especially p. 259.

[50] E. Faguet, *Politiques et moralistes du dix-neuvieme siècle* (Paris, 1898). The essay on Fourier occupies pages 43–81; quoted from page 72.

[51] P. Janet, "Le socialisme au XIXe siècle. La philosophie de Charles Fourier," *Revue des Deux Mondes,* Vol. 35 (1879), pp. 619–645, especially p. 633.

[52] See, for example, Fourier's commendation of Rousseau's critique, accompanied by criticism of Rousseau for trying to escape from Civilization back into Savagery instead of advancing to the next and higher stages in Fourier, *Pièges et charlatanisme des deux sectes Saint-Simon et Owen qui promettent l'association et le progrès* (Paris, 1831), p. 36. Rousseau is described as "one of the most skillful painters of love and worthy in this respect of a certain confidence" in Charles Fourier, *Oeuvres complètes. Vol. VII. Le nouveau monde amoureux,* Edition Anthropos (Paris, 1967), p. 33.

physiocratic ideas.[53] As a rule, however, Fourier praised no one and mentioned no preferences among his blind predecessors and contemporaries. Scholars are often reduced to indicating very general connections, as, for example, in the case of Jean Dautry when he argues that Fourier's pedagogical ideas were derived from the educational theory of the Enlightenment and beyond it from humanistic thought.[54] Very occasionally it can be established that Fourier read a work and made use of it, notably Kepler's *Harmonices mundi libri V,* which contributed to the utopian socialist's cosmology.[55] More often, as with authors like Fourier's predecessor in Lyons L'Ange and especially Rétif de la Bretonne, there are similarities, even striking similarities, to certain sections and passages in Fourier, but no direct evidence that Fourier knew the writings in question.[56]

Disregarding individual thinkers and concentrating on ideas, it becomes readily apparent that all of Fourier's basic concepts stem from the Enlightenment. These include such fundamental assumptions and principles supporting his system as optimism, a largely deistic view of God and the universe, emphasis on physics and physical and mathematical

[53] Fourier, *Manuscrits. Années 1853–1856* (Paris, 1856), pp. 84, 158; *Oeuvres,* Anthropos, Vol. XI, pp. 84, 158, first pagination.

[54] J. Dautry, "Fourier et les questions d'éducation," *Revue internationale de philosophie,* Fasc. 2, No. 60 (Bruxelles, 1962), pp. 234–260.

[55] Bourgin, *Etudes sur les sources de Fourier,* pp. 40–41. For a recent emphasis on the link between Kepler and Fourier see S. Debout Oleskiewicz, "L'analogie ou 'Le poème mathematique' de Charles Fourier," *Revue internationale de philosophie,* Fasc. 2, No. 60 (Bruxelles, 1962), pp. 176–199.

[56] Those who want to place Fourier in the mystical tradition are particularly insistent on linking him to Rétif de la Bretonne, suggesting even that he deliberately suppressed all evidence of such connections. For negative results of research see Bourgin, *Etudes sur les sources de Fourier,* and A. Ioannisian, *Genezis obshchestvennogo ideala Fure* (Moscow-Leningrad, 1939).

laws as applicable to all creation—indeed Fourier regarded Newton, as we shall see, as his one true predecessor—belief in transforming society by the use of reason, more exactly through a realization in life of a scientifically correct theoretical model, cosmopolitanism, and stress on human happiness and human passions, even on "attraction" itself. The utopian socialist's famous critique of Civilization can be considered as an extreme variant of the critique of the Age of Reason, as another attack on human ignorance and human prejudice, sparked by such theses of the Enlightenment as the relativity of man's mores and the use of religion and tradition to render people blind to their true interests. It is precisely at the deep level of basic assumptions that Charles Fourier belonged wholly to the Age of Reason, in particular to its later stage.

He was also directly affected by his environment in various details of his system. Thus he varied somewhat his appeals to different individuals and regimes, and he remained ever on the lookout for the quickest and most effective way to translate his doctrine into practice. Fourier's project of a trial phalanx for children might well have been inspired by Huard's article, "Examen impartial des nouvelles vues de M. Robert Owen par Henry Gray Macnab." [57]

But between basic assumptions and tactical detail there stood the system itself of which Fourier claimed to be—with a surprising degree of accuracy—the originator. It is to the study of Fourier's system that the next chapters will be devoted.

[57] Huard, "Examen impartial des nouvelles vues de M. Robert Owen par Henry Gray Macnab, trad. de l'anglais par M. Laffon de Ladébat," *Memorial universel de l'industrie française, des sciences et des arts,* Vol. 5 (1821), pp. 241–255.

CHAPTER II

Fourier's Teaching

Passions, so much downgraded by philosophers, are the most sublime work of God, the one to which He applied the most profound calculus. Only one kind of harmony can be seen in other branches of movement; but all are united in the mechanics of passions. This is an immense orchestra arranged for five billion instruments or characters which will inhabit our planet—not counting the animals, vegetables, aromas, and minerals all of which enter into the framework of the harmony of passions, the harmony with which everything is coordinated. This will be difficult to believe, but it will be demonstrated that God knew how to apply in his theory of the harmony of passions the means through which each one of the five billion individuals will be useful for the happiness of all the others.[1]

I am not gigantic, but you are pygmies.[2]

There is an obsessive and overwhelming repetitiousness in the writings of Fourier. In a sense, they contain only a single message, a single, almost palpable, formula which, once applied, would magically transform human society and the universe itself. Yet, whereas on the one hand the reader cannot quite grasp the formula which is to lead to palingenesis, on the other Fourier's thought expands out of its kernel to present a rationale for his views, to draw pictures of future blessedness, and to denounce the unregenerate world. An analytic exposition can proceed best from Charles Fourier's

[1] Fourier, *Manuscrits* (Paris, 1851), p. 346; *Oeuvres*, Edition Anthropos, Vol. X, p. 346, first pagination.

[2] Fourier, *La fausse industrie*, Vol. II, p. A6; *Oeuvres*, Anthropos, Vol. IX, p. A6.

main general assumptions to the particular structure which
he erected on their foundation.

1. Basic Elements

GOD, MATTER, AND MATHEMATICS . .

As Fourier wrote in the first full-scale exposition of his
doctrine:

Nature is composed of three eternal, uncreated, and indestructible principles:
(1) *God or Spirit,* the active or moving principle;
(2) *Matter,* the passive or moved principle;
(3) *Justice or Mathematics,* the principle which regulates the Movement.[3]

Elsewhere he designated mathematics as the neutral principle, parallel to his other two principles, the active and the
passive, and added *"space* or the arena of movement." Space
too was uncreated: "it could not have been created, for it
would have been impossible to put it anywhere if there had
not already existed a space."[4]

God, the first principle, occupied a crucial position in
Fourier's system, which cannot be properly understood without it. Unfortunately Fourier's views on Divinity constitute
an involved and intrinsically difficult as well as a highly controversial subject. It is certain that Fourier believed in God.
Indeed, in his case one can speak, at least in a certain sense,
of an absolute faith in God. For it was the existence of God
that formed both the foundation and the proof of Fourier's

---

[3] Fourier, *Théorie des quatre mouvements et des destinées générales,* pp. 30–31; *Oeuvres,* Anthropos, Vol. I, pp. 30–31.
[4] Charles Fourier, *Anarchie industrielle et scientifique* (Paris, 1847), p. 53.

entire system which he described as nothing else than God's
own system for men finally discovered. The major premise
of the entire edifice, the existence of Divinity, thus could
never be questioned. And Fourier never questioned it, dis-
missing atheism, and by association agnosticism, as unworthy of consideration.[5]

Yet, while those who stressed the religious element in
Fourier could readily establish the central role of God in his
teaching, their opponents were quick to point out that, once
established, that role became remarkably unobtrusive. If the
plan of Harmony belonged to God, it was up to men to discover it and work out their social salvation. Moreover, the
formation of a perfect society on earth was bound to have
cosmic repercussions making man God's partner in arranging the cosmos. But it was especially the generally abstract
quality of God, the prime mover, the carefully structured
and essentially self-contained character of the world, and the
pseudo-scientific tone of Fourier's entire teaching that made
many commentators speak of deism [6]—while a few preferred pantheism—and occasionally go so far as to claim that
Fourier's God dissolved in nature and could in fact be replaced by the concept and word "nature." Not in vain, one
could well argue, did Fourier begin the definition of his fundamental principles with that word. The five general quali-

[5] Fourier's encouraging attitude toward "composite atheism"—a
category of his own creation—and certain other forms of doubt
provides no exception, because Fourier expected all this doubt by its
very nature to raise questions which would lead to the discovery of
Fourier's God and Fourier's system.

[6] Professor Emile Faguet noted perceptively that Fourier's main
theistic argument itself, i.e., that of the impending Harmony on
earth as a consequence of the benevolent and wise nature of Divinity,
carries more conviction in the deistic, rather than the Christian,
intellectual framework, Faguet, *Politiques et moralistes du dix-neuvième siècle,* p. 58.

ties of Divinity emphasized by Fourier, namely the integrated and comprehensive direction of movement by means of attraction, the economy of means, distributive justice, universality, and the unity of the entire system, also appear to belong fully to the Age of Reason.

But one must qualify the qualifications. If stressing the deism and "naturalism" of Fourier's God constitutes a legitimate counterargument aimed at those who present the utopian socialist as essentially a religious thinker in either the traditional or the mystic sense, it can be carried, in its turn, too far. Fourier, for example, insisted that God, like man, had both body and soul.[7] Furthermore, while this God usually limited himself to the functions of the prime mover, the active principle, he did sometimes appear as a personality, and a sharply pronounced and peculiar personality at that. The misfortunes of our wayward planet which would not follow the divine law of attraction satisfied God's sense of irony, one of His 810 passions. Fourier even assured his contemporaries: "God laughs at your misfortunes which guarantee his vengeance, God rejoices when He sees your battlefields piled high with corpses and your empires ravaged by indigence and revolutions under the auspices of philosophy which you take as your guide while you disdain attraction."[8] Willful blindness, as long as it lasted, clearly did not deserve any other response. God's benevolence consisted in making a perfect order possible and in giving man every opportunity for discovering it, not in commiserating with man in his criminal folly. In the last analysis Fourier's religious views, like his other views, constituted a peculiar

[7] See, e.g., an extended discussion of this subject in Fourier, *Manuscrits. Années 1857–1858* (Paris, 1858), pp. 316–318; *Oeuvres,* Anthropos, Vol. XI, pp. 316–318, second pagination. God's body, Fourier decided, was fire, and it was associated with light.

[8] Fourier, *Egarement de la raison,* p. 22.

amalgam of his own making. Yet the emphasis remained constant: whether in His fundamental role as the God of deism or during His occasional appearances as a personality, for example, as the God of Wrath, Divinity seemed to exist for and be concerned with only one thing, Fourier's message.[9]

Fourier wrote less about his other two principles, matter and mathematics, in part because he apparently believed that their nature and definition could be taken for granted. He did insist that matter has always existed and will always exist, arguing elaborately that any other formulation would prevent God at some time from enjoying matter.[10] Mathematics too remained eternal as the regulating principle of the world. To sum up Fourier's views in his own words:

The system of nature is composed of nothing but the diverse movements and modifications of the two principles, the material and the spiritual, which compose the universe. One of these principles is called matter in its totality, and body or product in its subdivisions. The other is called God in its totality, and soul, instinct, in its subdivisions. These two principles are modified and united according to invariable laws which are called mathematics, laws which constitute in the movement of the universe the third, regulating or arbitrating, principle, because God submits his creative activities to these laws and subordinates to them the properties of bodies and souls. There are thus three constitutive principles in the universe. A search for the complete system of nature must include the theory of all the movements produced by the combined action of the three principles.[11]

[9] Fourier's doctrine of the transmigration of souls and his relationship to Christianity will be discussed later in this chapter, his criticism of the established churches in the next.

[10] Fourier, *op. cit.,* pp. 92–94; *Oeuvres,* Anthropos, Vol. XII, pp. 678–680.

[11] Fourier, *Manuscrits. Années 1853–1856* (Paris, 1856), p. 338; *Oeuvres,* Anthropos, Vol. XI, p. 338, first pagination.

THE MOVEMENTS AND ATTRACTION

Fourier believed originally that there were four kinds of movements, hence the title of his first major work, *Théorie des quatre mouvements et des destinées générales.*

Universal movement divides into four principal branches: *the social, the animal, the organic,* and *the material.*

(1) *The social movement.* Its theory must explain the laws following which God orders the structure and the succession of different social mechanisms on all the inhabited celestial bodies.

(2) *The animal movement.* Its theory must explain the laws following which God distributes passions and instincts to all the created beings, past or future, on all the celestial bodies.

(3) *The organic movement.* Its theory must explain the laws following which God distributes the properties, forms, colors, tastes, etc. to all the substances, created or to be created, on all the celestial bodies.

(4) *The material movement.* Its theory, already explained by modern geometricians, made known the laws following which God regulates the gravity of matter on the diverse celestial bodies.[12]

In the second full-scale exposition of his doctrine Fourier added a fifth kind of movement: "The aromal or the distribution of known and unknown aromas which affect actively or passively the animal, vegetal, and mineral creatures." [13] According to the new arrangement, the social movement, called this time also "passional," was promoted to a special

[12] Fourier, *Théorie des quatre mouvements et des destinées générales,* pp. 29–30; *Oeuvres,* Anthropos, Vol. I, pp. 29–30.

[13] Fourier, *Theorie de l'unité universelle,* Vol. I, p. 32 of the Avant-Propos; *Oeuvres,* Anthropos, Vol. II, p. 32 of the Avant-Propos. "Creatures" is the exact translation, but Fourier most probably also meant "creations." He believed in repeated creations, and it was these creations that were especially affected by the aromas.

"pivotal" position, while the aromal joined the other three in a reconstituted group of four.

Thus, of the four, or five, kinds of movements composing the universe, the laws of one, the material, were already known. This was the achievement of scientists, and above all of Newton. Fourier considered Newton to be a virtually unique genius in the history of humanity, as in effect his only true predecessor, and he referred over and over again to Newton and Newton's discovery. It was Fourier's self-appointed task and accomplishment to complete Newton's work, that is, to establish the laws of all the other movements and thus obtain complete knowledge of the universe.

At this point it may be best to differentiate between the broad and the narrow compass of Fourier's sweeping claim, although the line between the two is sometimes impossible to draw, and although Fourier himself would have objected to the distinction. In a broad sense, Fourier's views certainly had a cosmic scope. In fact, the theoretician of Harmony repeatedly declared that even the material movement had been merely opened for study rather than properly studied, that, in particular, so far only effects, not causes, had been elucidated in the material world, and he proceeded to speculate in his own fantastic kind of astronomy all his life. Fourier's intellectual constructions, the movements themselves for that matter, were not restricted to our planet. Moreover, as we shall see, Fourier's projected reconstruction of life on earth led beyond our globe into the cosmos. Nor is there serious reason to doubt the sincerity, the madness if you will, of this entire aspect of the utopian socialist's teaching.

Still, it is important to emphasize the narrow sense which was more immediately related to Fourier's obsessive message and mission. In the narrow context Fourier aimed at translating the already-discovered physical laws of the universe into social laws, of creating in this manner a science of the social movement parallel to the physical sciences, and of regenerating humanity through an application of the new science. This last goal went, to be sure, beyond Newton, but the difference was in the very nature of things dealt with. As Fourier explained, Newton and the other scientists happened to work with a useless kind of movements, all the useful ones remaining untouched until Fourier. [Fourier's all-important formula was thus an attempt at transmutation of Newton's laws into a social context.]

Was such a formula possible? Did the discovery of material laws in the universe imply the presence of similar social laws? It was here that Fourier's God performed his main function. [For it was the fundamental characteristics of Divinity, such as universality, the integrated and comprehensive direction of movement by means of attraction, and the unity of the entire system [14] that promised success to the daring father of the phalanx. Indeed, a powerful, wise, and benevolent divinity could not help but provide a perfect social formula for men.] Fourier proceeded to establish this important point in a characteristically elaborate, pseudo-scholastic, and pseudo-scientific manner:

. . . there are six alternatives:

(1) *He did not know* how to give us a code guaranteeing justice, truth, and industrial attraction. In this case it is unfair of Him to create in us the need without the means of satisfaction, a

[14] In dealing with the unity of the universe and the resulting analogies among its constituent parts Fourier occasionally approvingly mentioned and even quoted Schelling, although it is extremely unlikely that he had read the German philosopher. A particularly curious reference states: "In fact *Schelling,* when he said that the universe is a mirror of itself, did not at all prove this truth in detail —he ventured it. A friend of mine went to visit him in Munich and questioned him about this thesis. He did not know what to say: it was by chance that he had spoken well" (Fourier, *La fausse industrie,* Vol. I, p. 444; *Oeuvres,* Anthropos, Vol. VIII, p. 444).

satisfaction which the animals have for whom He has composed social codes which are based on attraction and regulate their industrial system.

(2) *Or He did not want* to give us this code. In this case He is a wilful persecutor, creating at His pleasure needs in us which we cannot satisfy, because none of our codes can extirpate the well-known misfortunes.

(3) *Or He knew and did not want.* In this case He vies with the devil, knowing how to do good and preferring to do evil.

(4) *Or He wanted and did not know.* In this case He is incapable of ruling us, recognizing and wishing the good which He can not produce and which we shall be even less able to put into operation.

(5) *Or He neither knew nor wanted.* In this case He is below the devil who can well be accused of viciousness but not of stupidity.

(6) *Or He knew and wanted.* In this case the code exists, and He must reveal it to us, for of what good would a code be if it were to remain hidden from men for whom it is destined.[15]

The sixth alternative then was the obvious answer. God had to provide for men as He had provided for the stars and the planets. The divine attribute of directing movement by means of attraction expressed itself in gravitational attraction, in gravity, among celestial bodies. Among men, Fourier decided—in what was probably the most important leap of imagination in his entire teaching—this divine quality of attraction became passional attraction, a system of human passions and their interplay.

THE PASSIONS

Fourier postulated twelve passions in man, plus the overarching and synthesizing passion of unityism which resulted

---

[15] Fourier, *Le nouveau monde industriel et sociétaire*, p. 373; *Oeuvres,* Anthropos, Vol. VI, p. 373. Cf. Fourier, *Théorie de l'unité universelle*, Vol. II, pp. 250–271; *Oeuvres,* Anthropos, Vol. III, pp. 250–271.

from an unrestricted and full exercise of these twelve. The twelve passions were divided into three categories. The first consisted of the five senses, that is, of sight, hearing, taste, smell, and touch. It was directly related to luxisme, i.e., to the human desire of "internal and external luxury," represented by health and wealth with the ensuing satisfaction of the sensual appetites. Next came the four "group," or affective, passions, the function of which was to minister to the spiritual appetites of man. These were ambition, friendship, love, and family feeling. Fourier classified the first two as the major group passions and the last two as the minor ones.

The third category constituted Fourier's special discovery. It contained the three directing, distributing, or regulating passions which organized the others and led to the formation of "series." The cabalist (*cabaliste*) was the passion for intrigue. The butterfly (*papillonne*) stood for the urge for diversification. Finally, the composite (*composite*), the only passion the definition of which is not entirely clear, represented both the human desire for a simultaneous satisfaction of more than a single passion, with the added condition that the passions so satisfied must include at least one "passion of the senses" and another of the spirit, a desire also described as "a thirst for enthusiasm," and the rapturous enthusiasm itself resulting from such satisfaction. In the last sense, the composite has also been interpreted by commentators as the creative passion. While the cabalist underlay the complicated system of discords in Fourier's plan for humanity, the composite served as the foundation for the equally complicated system of accords.[16] In full and unfettered play the twelve

[16] Fourier defined the composite as "a thirst for enthusiasm" in Fourier, *Manuscrits* (Paris, 1852), p. 188; *Oeuvres,* Anthropos, Vol. X, p. 188, second pagination. See Fourier's various descriptions and uses of the composite in E. Silberling, "Composite," *Dictionnaire de sociologie phalanstérienne. Guide des oeuvres complètes de Charles Fourier* (Paris, 1911), pp. 93–94. Silberling, however, does not do

passions culminated in the passion for unityism, the drive toward unity which combined and integrated the happiness of the individual with the happiness of all.

2. The Phalanx

THE PHALANX

In Civilization, however, unityism could not develop. In fact, Civilization mismanaged, frustrated, and suppressed all the passions, with the resultant inevitable misery of mankind.[17] Salvation lay in the scientific organization of passions according to the divine plan which Fourier had discovered. Finely graded passions had to be correctly combined in groups and series so they could obtain free expression and satisfaction. A rich variety of characters was necessary to produce the proper interplay of passions. Never hesitant in using numbers, the theoretician of Harmony asserted: "The twelve fundamental passions are divided into a multitude of nuances which are more or less dominant in every individual; there results an infinite variety of characters, which nevertheless can be reduced to eight hundred and ten principal ones." [18] Fourier next took these 810 characters, multi-

justice in his selections to the numerous instances when the composite refers simply to the desire for a combined satisfaction of passions in two different categories. Cf. Lehouck, *Fourier aujourd'hui,* p. 27.

[17] See the next chapter devoted to Fourier's critique of Civilization.

[18] Fourier, *Théorie des quatre mouvements et des déstinées générales,* pp. 83–84; *Oeuvres,* Anthropos, Vol. I, pp. 83–84. Like the number 12 for passions, the number 810 for characters is presented by Fourier as a scientific discovery, and it defies further analysis. (For an attempted analysis which appears defective on a number of counts see Renouvier, *op. cit.,* p. 248.) Nor could I establish here any borrowing by Fourier from earlier writers. Again as with the passions, the characters are precisely subdivided. They consist of 576

plied the figure by two to allow for the very young and the very old, the sick, the substitutes, and certain other categories, and came up with the ideal number of 1,620—or roughly speaking 1,600 to 2,000—men, women, and children, who, scientifically organized, were to form the basic social unit of the regenerated world, the phalanx.[19]

THE PHALANSTERY

All members of a phalanx were to live in one huge building known as the phalanstery, which served both as their residence and as the locale for most of their indoor activities. In fact, except for the phalanstery itself, Fourier's plans provided for only a few supplementary constructions, such as stables, storehouses, and certain workshops, located in a reg-

solitones, or monogynes, that is, people dominated by a single passion, 80 dominated by two passions, one spiritual and one sensual, 96 dominated by two spiritual passions, 16 dominated by one spiritual and two sensual passions, 24 dominated by three spiritual passions, 8 dominated by four spiritual passions, 8 dominated by two spiritual and three sensual passions, and 2 dominated by five spiritual passions (Fourier, *Le nouveau monde industriel et sociétaire*, pp. 340–341; *Oeuvres*, Anthropos, Vol. VI, pp. 340–341). The 576 solitones, in turn, are divided as follows: of those dominated by a sensual passion, 24 are dominated by smell, 36 by hearing, 48 by sight, 60 by touch, and 72 by taste; of the others, 40 are dominated by friendship, 56 by ambition, 32 by family feeling, 64 by love, and 32 by the composite, 48 by the butterfly, and 64 by the cabalist (Fourier, "Du clavier puissanciel des caractères," p. 38). Other divisions, combinations, and classifications ensue. The 810 characters by no means exhausted human possibilities. Notably they took no account of the rare but highly precious individuals with more than five dominant passions.

[19] For the multiplication by two see Fourier, *Théorie de l'unité universelle*, Vol. III, pp. 440–441; *Oeuvres*, Anthropos, Vol. IV, pp. 440–441. Male members were to have a slight numerical advantage over the female ones in the composition of the phalanx: 415 as against 395 of the 810 characters, or roughly the proportion of 21 to 20.

ular and symmetric pattern in its immediate vicinity.[20] As usual, everything had to be scientifically arranged and nothing could be left to chance.

> It is very important to forestall arbitrariness in building. . . . It is necessary to apply a method adapted at every point to the play of passional series: our architects who do not know these series would not be able to find an appropriate method; and at the same time it remains true that if the material side becomes falsified in the process of arranging, the same will happen to the passional.[21]

In this case, as in so many others, Fourier remained acutely aware of the interaction of factors in society. Not only was "societary" architecture to have a crucial role in the harmonious new society, but even in Civilization a certain kind

[20] See, for example, charts of a phalanstery between pages 122 and 123 of Fourier, *Le nouveau monde industriel et sociétaire; Oeuvres,* Anthropos, Vol. VI, between pp. 122 and 123. Pages 123–129 are devoted to the phalanstery. See also the single very large sheet with a drawing of a phalanstery and a description entitled: *L'avenir. Perspective d'un phalanstère ou palais sociétaire dédié à l'humanité* (d'après le plan de Ch. Fourier. Accompagné d'une description signée: Victor Considérant) (Bordeaux, n.d.).

As already mentioned in the preceding chapter, it was in Paris that Fourier, according to his own words, found inspiration for "unitary architecture." The arcades of the Palais-Royal, Parisian boulevards, and the palaces of the French capital and its environs recur in one form or another whenever Fourier turns to architecture. Interestingly, the closest antecedent in appearance to the phalanstery that I have been able to find is "a project for the restoration of the palace of Versailles" drawn by Etienne-Louis Boullée a few years before the Revolution and never executed. The Project is now at the Bibliothèque Nationale. The point here is not that of a specific direct influence on Fourier—it is unlikely that Fourier ever saw Boullée's project, nor was that project unique—but of the type of architecture which dominated Fourier's thought.

[21] Fourier, *Le nouveau monde industriel et sociétaire,* p. 123; *Oeuvres, Anthropos,* Vol. VI, p. 123.

of building could serve as a beacon and a spur toward the happy future.

Correct building called for a huge phalanstery, some six stories high, with a long main body and two wings. Its form was to be characteristically symmetrical and rectangular, providing also for inner courtyards and a spacious parade ground immediately in front, with the main body of the phalanstery and the two wings adjoining it on three of its four sides. The central part of the main body of the building, culminating in a tower, would contain among other things the grand entrance and the grand staircase, and a central hall or halls, as well as a carillon and postal pigeons. A large hothouse would serve as its inner court. An opera and a church would also be in the same vicinity or they might be erected as separate buildings behind the projecting wings and connected to the phalanstery proper by subterranean passages. All noisy occupations would be confined to one wing and its inner court. A circumventing "street-gallery" would constitute a special feature of the harmonious architecture of the future. Protected and heated, it would shelter the members of the phalanx from inclement weather and make all communication within a phalanstery a pleasure. In fact, the full development of this concept called for two street-galleries, one on the first-story and another on the second-story level, the former composed of "arcades which stretch parallel to the building as at the Palais-Royal." [22]

The bulk of the phalanstery was to be occupied by the private apartments of its members and by rooms serving more general purposes, such as working or dining in common. Of course, they too had to be arranged according to a scientific plan. Thus in locating people it was important not only to make particular provisions for such categories as children

[22] *L'avenir. Perspective d'un phalanstère ou palais sociétaire dédié à l'humanité.*

and old men and women, but also and especially to obtain the proper mix of apartments of different quality rather than simply to separate the better from the worse. Common rooms also had to conform to the new society of passional series, abandoning the uniformity and the lumping together characteristic of Civilization. Dining quarters, for example, would consist not of a single hall but of nine rooms—1 for old people, 2 for children, 3 for the poor, 2 for the middle class, and 1 for the rich—plus rooms for visitors and for various small gatherings of those who wanted to eat more privately.[23]

THE SERIES

Activities in a phalanx were to be based on the series. In other words, almost always individuals were not to engage in their occupations or pastimes alone or as part of a haphazard gathering, but rather as members of scientifically operating series. More exactly, individuals with the same interest would voluntarily form a small group, and groups with like occupations would naturally combine into a series.[24]

[23] Fourier, *Le nouveau monde industriel et sociétaire*, p. 126; *Oeuvres*, Anthropos, Vol. VI, p. 126. Members of a phalanx were divided into three classes according to wealth. (The dining arrangements remind one irresistibly of those of the Student Union of the University of California in Berkeley.)

[24] "A passional series is a league of diverse groups echeloned in ascending and descending order, passionally united by the identity of taste for some function, such as the culture of a certain fruit, and providing a special group for each variety of work included in the object which occupies it. If it cultivates hyacinths or potatoes it must form as many groups as there are varieties of hyacinths which can be cultivated on its soil, and the same goes for the varieties of potatoes" (Fourier, *Le nouveau monde industriel et sociétaire*, p. 52; *Oeuvres,* Anthropos, Vol. VI, p. 52). Cf. an early "mathematical" formulation of the structure of a series. "The main characteristic of a series in regard to interest is the same as in geometry: the product of the extreme elements equals the square of the middle element." Charles

This organization would lead to the full play of "the two sympathies of the soul which consist of the accords of identity and of contrast": of identity, because each group would be made of volunteers passionately devoted to the purpose of the group; of contrast, because contiguous groups would compete with each other while forming alliances with more distant groups within the series. In addition, each group would be spurred to greater effort by the excellent results of its work in new conditions and by the praise of others, as well as "by the charm of collective perfection and the luxury of the whole which reigns in the works and products of the entire series." The serial passions of the composite and the cabalist would thus find a natural field for their expression. The third serial passion, the butterfly, no less important than the other two, would be provided for by the brevity of sessions, by the choice of new pleasures presented in quick succession before one becomes satiated with the old ones.[25]

In a somewhat different summary Fourier wrote:

A passional series is not regular and does not acquire the above-mentioned properties, except by fulfilling three conditions.

(1) *Compactness,* or bringing together the cultivated varieties by means of contiguous groups. Seven groups cultivating seven very different kinds of pears . . . could not form a passional series; these groups would not have either sympathy or antipathy among them, either rivalry or emulation, because of the lack of rapprochement or compactness of the cultivated kinds. . . . The passion called *the cabalist* would not have free play, and it is one of the three passions that must direct every passional series.

Fourier, "Les trois noeuds du mouvement," *La Phalange. Revue de la science sociale,* Vol. IX (February 1849), pp. 111–169, quoted from p. 135; *Oeuvres,* Anthropos, Vol. XII, p. 440.

[25] Fourier, *Le nouveau monde industriel et sociétaire,* pp. 73–74; *Oeuvres,* Anthropos, Vol. VI, pp. 73–74. See also *ibid.,* pp. 60–65, 86–91; *Oeuvres,* Anthropos, Vol. VI, pp. 60–65, 86–91.

(2) *Brief sessions:* the longest limited to two hours. Without this arrangement, an individual would not be able to enagage in some thirty series; and from that point the accords of repartition and the mechanism of industrial attraction would be destroyed. Long sessions would ensnare the passion called *the butterfly,* the mania to flit from pleasure to pleasure, one of the three that must direct every passional series and provide a counterweight to excess by offering the option of a double pleasure each hour of the day.

(3) *Partial work:* the work of every individual must be limited to a certain part of the total functions. If the cultivation of the Rose-Mousseuse provides five or six different functions, the group in charge must appoint five or six subgroups which would divide the functions according to the taste of each. The Civilized way which forces a man to fulfill all the functions of a job hinders the play of the passion called *the composite,* or the enthusiastic, one of the three that must direct every passional series.

In sum, the mechanism of the series is reducible to a precise, set rule, which is to develop the three distributive passions, the 10th, the 11th, the 12th, by means of the three methods, compactness, brief sessions, and partial work; and these methods are nothing but passion itself, the natural effect of the passion.[26]

An orchestra or a choir indicated well the nature of a series.

LIFE IN A PHALANX

Fourier mentioned repeatedly that a member of a phalanx would belong on the average to some thirty series. In a more detailed discussion of the matter he concluded that a Harmonian with his normal life of 144 years would participate

[26] Fourier, *Le nouveau monde industriel et sociétaire,* p. 54; *Oeuvres,* Anthropos, Vol. VI, p. 54. The glorious properties possessed by a regular series and referred to in the first sentence were: emulation, justice, truth, direct accord, inverse or indirect accord, and unity of action (*ibid.,* p. 53; *Oeuvres,* Anthropos, Vol. VI, p. 53). Cf. Fourier, *Théorie de l'unité universelle,* Vol. II, pp. 19–26; *Oeuvres,* Anthropos, Vol. III, pp. 19–26.

in all, or almost all, series of his phalanx by the time of his death, although he would engage in only one-eighth of them, or about 12, continuously.[27] Moreover his frequent meals, public meetings, notably the remarkable *bourse* held every day, and personal encounters were also to be devoted in large part to the activities of the series.

Fourier believed in precise scheduling. For example, he furnished the following outline:

Time	Lucas's day in the month of June
at 3½	rise, preparation for the day
at 4	a session in a group in the stables
at 5	a session in a group of gardeners
at 7	*lunch*
at 7½	a session in a group of harvesters
at 9½	a session in a tent in a group of vegetable gardeners
at 11	a session in the barn series
at 1	*dinner*
at 2	a session in a group of foresters
at 4	a session in a manufacturing group
at 6	a session in the watering series
at 8	a session at the bourse
at 8½	*supper*
at 9	amusements
at 10	*going to bed.*[28]

Although he was poor and belonged to the third class of Harmonians, Lucas obviously had a varied and full life based on the series. The rich Mondor could afford an even more exquisite existence.

[27] Fourier, *Manuscrits* (Paris, 1851), pp. 100–101; *Oeuvres,* Anthropos, Vol. X, pp. 100–101, first pagination. The discussion assumes that there would be one hundred series in a phalanx, but, apparently because of a slip, gives their total as one hundred and fifty. One-eighth is another major recurrent number in Fourier's writings: his allowance for exceptions. Man is changeable, rather than constant, hence the changing of series, but provision must also always be made for the exception.

[28] Fourier, *Le nouveau monde industriel et sociétaire,* p. 67; *Oeuvres,* Anthropos, Vol. VI, p. 67.

Time	Mondor's day in summer
	Sleep from 10½ in the evening until 3 in the morning
at 3½	rise, preparation for the day
at 4	"cour du lever public," news chronicle
at 4½	breakfast, the first meal, followed by a parade of workers
at 5½	a session in a hunting group
at 7	a session in a fishing group
at 8	*lunch,* newspapers
at 9	a session in a group for cultivation under tent
at 10	a session at the Mass
at 10½	a session in a group at the pheasant house
at 10½ [*sic*]	a session at the library
at 1	*dinner*
at 2½	a session in a group for plant cultivation in a glass house
at 4	a session in a group for exotic plants
at 5	a session in a group for the live-fish tanks
at 6	*a snack* outdoors
at 6½	a session in a group for merinos
at 4 [*sic*]	a session at the bourse
at 9	*supper,* the fifth meal
at 9½	"cour des arts," concerts, balls, performances, receptions
at 10½	*going to bed.*[29]

A brief description of a day of a participant could render better than mere listing the spirit of activity, excitement, and

[29] *Ibid.,* p. 68; *Oeuvres,* Anthropos, Vol. VI, p. 68. The difference between the rich and the poor in the phalanx, exemplified by these two famous schedules, has been studied by a number of scholars, for instance by the Soviet Academician V. P. Volgin ("Sistema Fure," in *Sharl Fure, Izbrannye sochineniia,* Vol. I [Moscow-Leningrad, 1951], pp. 5–79, especially page 50; Volgin published an earlier and somewhat different version of this article in *Pod Znamenem Marksizma,* Nos. 7–8 [July–August, 1929], pp. 102–126). It will be discussed later in this chapter. Here the schedules are meant to serve as illustrations of life in a phalanx.

intrigue that prevailed in a phalanx. Thus, Lucile, age seven, after the usual early rise and meal worked until six thirty in her "groupe des pigeons" and after that, until seven forty-five, in the kitchen. She had lunch with her ballet group and then a rehearsal until ten when refreshments were served. Next she worked in a group of maids cleaning rooms, and after that went to the bourse where she negotiated "au parquet des enfants." She had a lively dinner as a member of a group engaged in looking after the fowl, and in fact stayed too long at the table and missed a session with her group for "strawberries of the Orient." Members of another group tried promptly, although unsuccessfully, to recruit her. In the afternoon Lucile engaged in shepherding, but was sought out during the refreshment time at four by officers of her strawberry group and told by them of the danger of their group being eclipsed and also of her promotion.[30] Fortunately, very shortly afterward the venerable Frédégonde came to feed her favorite carp and, after being helped by Lucile, promised to support the group for "strawberries of the Orient" against their rivals. The shepherding ended at six and was followed by a snack and two more jobs: cleaning rooms with a group of maids until seven thirty, and preparing in a group of "fruitiers" baskets of fruit decorated with leaves until eight thirty. The evening brought more pleasures. The usual family supper at nine was cancelled because a caravan of visitors had arrived from other phalanxes.

[30] Groups would be "eclipsed" in Harmony for producing a distinctly inferior product. An eclipsed group would have to carry a black banner, and its prestige and attractiveness would certainly decline. If it could not remedy the situation it might well go out of existence for sheer lack of appeal. In this manner, Fourier maintained, uneconomic production would be eliminated without resort to compulsion. See, for example, Fourier, *Manuscrits* (Paris, 1851), the note at the bottom of pp. 149–150; *Oeuvres,* Anthropos, Vol. X, pp. 149–150, first pagination.

Therefore, all ate in public dining rooms where they formed "some impromptu groups." [31] While we find Lucile well set in her series, poor little Zoë rose to full participation in the life of a phalanx and the resulting happiness simply because she had a sweet tooth, something that would have brought her only punishment in Civilization where she would have kept asking for sweets and delicacies unobtainable to her.[32]

In fact, it was a salient characteristic of the phalanx that everyone, from little Zoë to a Nero—about whom more later —found fulfillment in it while contributing to the happiness of others. Fourier's discovery of the divine formula for the correct arrangement of human passions permitted all to follow exactly and entirely the inclinations of their natures and yet in the process add their share to a perfect social harmony. Whereas hostile critics and other outsiders accused Fourier of a minute, petty, and at the same time overwhelming tyranny, of regulating every second of a person's life and every step he took in any direction, the theoretician of Harmony and his true followers remained convinced that they meant to impose nothing on anyone: their only intention was to provide arrangements which would enable human nature to attain its full expression. As Abel Transon, a follower who left Saint-Simon and joined Fourier, put it, the system was that of "absolute order by means of absolute freedom." [33] Everything depended, to be sure, on the efficacy of Fourier's formula.

Members of a phalanx would join only those groups and series which attracted them. And within each group they

[31] *Ibid.,* pp. 148–153; *Oeuvres,* Anthropos, Vol. X, pp. 148–153, first pagination.

[32] *Ibid.,* pp. 121–125; *Oeuvres,* Anthropos, Vol. X, pp. 121–125, first pagination.

[33] Quoted from Henri Louvancour, *De Henri de Saint-Simon à Charles Fourier. Etude sur le socialisme romantique français de 1830* (Chartres, 1913), p. 72.

would perform only that part of work which appealed to them. Those who enjoyed watering yellow roses might not enjoy pruning them. In fact, there emerged the following fundamental contrast between Civilization and Harmony: "In the former a man or a woman performs twenty different functions belonging to a single kind of work. In the latter a man performs a single function in twenty kinds of work, and he chooses the function which he likes while rejecting the other nineteen." [34]

The inhabitants of a phalanx would select their groups and series for the following day at the daily meeting of the bourse, the nerve center of a phalanx. Fourier wrote enthusiastically about the bourse in his first major work:

In every phalanx there are negotiated every day at the bourse at least eight hundred meetings for work, meals, gallantry, journeys and other purposes. Each of these meetings requires debate among ten, twenty, and sometimes a hundred persons; there are at least twenty thousand intrigues to disentangle in a bourse within one hour. To reconcile them there are officials of every kind, and arrangements by means of which every individual can follow some thirty intrigues at the same time; with the result that the bourse of the smallest phalanx is more animated than those of London and Amsterdam. . . . Women and children, as well as men, negotiate to set their meetings of every kind, and the struggles that arise over this issue among the series, the groups, and the individuals constitute the most piquant game, the most complicated and active intrigue that can possibly exist; the bourse is thus a great entertainment in the combined order. [35]

The new system would not only give full opportunity for self-expression, but where necessary help the individual to

[34] Fourier, *Manuscrits* (Paris, 1851), p. 97; *Oeuvres*, Anthropos, Vol. X, p. 97, first pagination. In the second sentence Fourier certainly meant women—indeed also children!—as well as men.

[35] Fourier, *Théorie des quatre mouvements et des destinées générales*, pp. 171–172; *Oeuvres*, Anthropos, Vol. I, pp. 171–172.

make his choices. For that purpose each phalanx would contain very rigorously trained and highly esteemed female and male confessors. These confessors would have to be at least sixty years old, not an advanced age in Harmony to be sure but nevertheless indicative of the extent of studies which they would have to undergo before they could practice their scientific profession, studies which would involve "algebraic formulas and minutely graded tables of psychological attributes." They would offer, for a small fee, expert advice to fellow members of a phalanx concerning "sympathetic" relations with people and more especially concerning the most gratifying kind and sequence of amorous liaisons. The confessors would be particularly helpful when emotion might make it difficult for individuals themselves to make the correct choice, and also in the case of visitors when interpersonal arrangements would have to be made quickly. Members of another group of special assistants, the *fées,* would rush to carry out the instructions of the confessors and match promptly the right people. While the very structure of the phalanx was predicated on everyone naturally and spontaneously occupying his exact and clearly identifiable psychological niche, the functions of the confessors apparently served Fourier as an added guarantee that the horrible psychological waste, mismatching, and general frustration characteristic of Civilization would be eliminated from the world of the future.[36]

Fourier admitted counseling into Harmony, but he consistently excluded compulsion. To repeat, the magic formula would enable mankind to attain absolute order through absolute freedom. The already-mentioned practice of "eclipsing" represented almost the limit of coercion in the world of phalanxes. And it bears repeating that eclipsing itself

[36] Fourier, *Manuscrits. Années 1857–1858* (Paris, 1858), pp. 19–45; *Oeuvres,* Anthropos, Vol. XI, pp. 19–45, second pagination.

would operate indirectly, by making unprofitable work less attractive, not directly, by forbidding anyone to engage in the work of his choice. Each phalanx would be guided by an "Areopagus," consisting of elected representatives from the series and other prominent members of the phalanx, and by a council, or regency, established by the Areopagus. The role of these two institutions, however, would be purely advisory. They would have nothing to establish or promulgate, because a phalanx, once set, would operate spontaneously by attraction. And they would have no coercive power.[37] Authorities outside a phalanx, essentially merely honorific in nature, would be even more nebulous than those in it. They would in no sense restrict the freedom of the Harmonians. Fourier envisaged a world without soldiers, without policemen, and, of course, without crime.

It can be argued, to be sure, that whereas the new system would reduce the weight of state, government, or any other public power upon the individual to a vanishing point, it would establish an enormous social pressure. Indeed education, work, social classification, advancement of every kind, and life itself in Harmony would consist of little else but coordination and competition with as well as judgment by one's peers or immediate superiors. But again everything depends on the point of view. While outsiders accused Fourier's system of tyranny, the father of the phalanx remained convinced that his entire scientific blueprint provided perfectly and exclusively for full satisfaction of every single individual's passions and desires, for a full flowering of his personality. Far from being crushed or deformed by social pressure—a common enough occurrence in Civilization—a Harmonian would experience this pressure only as a helpful and rewarding aid and spur to his natural development. The

[37] Fourier, *Le nouveau monde industriel et sociétaire*, pp. 113–114; *Oeuvres*, Anthropos, Vol. VI, pp. 113–114.

ways of the future world could not be judged by those of the
present one which constituted its vicious opposite.

Fourier never tired of repeating that all human passions
were suppressed in Civilization and that all of them must be
released and allowed full play in Harmony. The social system was a single whole, and, depending on its nature, it led
logically either to total misery or complete blessedness. Ultimately there could be no such thing as a little suppression or
a bit of freedom. Still, commentators have long debated the
issue whether in Fourier's view of equal passions some passions were more equal than others. Fourier's own definitions
and classifications greatly complicated the matter. As we
have seen, the twelve passions, not even counting that of
unityism, were divided into three different groups, or, in another sense, into two major groups, the last three "organizing" the first nine. If the nine appeared more immediate or
real, the three were sometimes presented as if belonging to a
"higher" order as well as constituting Fourier's particular
contribution to our knowledge of man. They were, after all,
the "serial" passions and thus the foundation of the entire
system. Again, Fourier carefully subdivided his four "group"
passions into major and minor ones for reasons that are not
entirely apparent.[38]

A somewhat different argument concerning Fourier and
the passions relates to whether Fourier meant what he said
and, especially, said what he meant. In particular, it has been
maintained that Fourier based his entire system really on a
single passion, love, and on the organization of love; because
he dared not express his views fully in print, much of his
writing assumed the character of double-talk and even of
downright camouflage. Seillère, who urged this opinion in
its extreme form, even produced the exact date, 1819, when

---

[38] Fourier's theory of passions will be discussed in greater detail
in Chapter V.

in his judgment Fourier succeeded in substituting taste for love, gastronomy for love-making, and thus was enabled to present an acceptable, if camouflaged, version of his system.[39]

There are certainly two sides to this issue, and a good argument can be made for the claim that love was indeed "more equal" than Fourier's other passions. Fourier used love extensively as a motive force in Harmony, for example, as a force of attraction into the industrial armies which were to perform large and important assignments in the new world. More important still, and in spite of the denial of this by most Fourierists, love in its various aspects and manifestations was apparently meant, according to Fourier, to suffuse the series and the entire life of the Harmonians. Occasionally Fourier would even concede that it was certain that "life, after the end of love affairs, is nothing but a prison to which one becomes more or less adjusted according to the favors of fortune."[40] No wonder that the theoretician of the phalanx did his best to prolong sexual love in Harmony until a very old age, with such added attractions as a system of liaisons between the very old and the young. Fourier's general views of history and society went well together with this emphasis on love. Thus the utopian socialist believed that humanity had enjoyed free love in its happy original condition and that the progressive character of a society could be best judged by the extent of the freedom of women, correlated happy psychological development with sexual freedom as in Tahiti or Japan, and asserted that the Great French

[39] Seillère, *op. cit.,* p. 109. Cf. Edmond Villey, "Charles Fourier, l'homme et son oeuvre."

[40] Fourier, *Manuscrits. Années 1857–1858* (Paris, 1858), p. 55; *Oeuvres,* Anthropos, Vol. XI, p. 55, second pagination. See also, e.g., "Textes inédits de Charles Fourier présenté par Simone Debout Oleszkiewicz," *Revue internationale de philosophie,* Vol. XVI, No. 60 (1962), pp. 147–175, especially pp. 156–160.

Revolution and more especially the National Convention failed solely and decisively because they dared not abolish marriage and the family.[41] Critics are also correct in pointing out that Fourier stressed love more in his earlier than in his later writings. Moreover, he changed at least in part consciously, explaining that he did not want to shock his unprepared contemporaries and would, therefore, use illustrations related to another passion, such as taste. In fact, Fourier came to believe that initially the phalanx itself would have to be established without the proper organization of love, since this would be unacceptable to men and women brought up in Civilization. But he never gave up this organization as an ultimate goal.

And yet Seillère and those of his persuasion who believe that Fourier's system was centered exclusively on love are more wrong than right. For one thing, taste represented more than a mere *pis-aller* to Fourier. The theoretician of the phalanx made a most wonderful and extensive use of gastronomy, or rather to use his terminology, "gastrosophy," as a compelling force and a *leitmotiv* of existence in Harmony. The urge to eat was quite as real to him as the urge to make love, and hunger in contrast to sex knew no limitation of age or stage of physical development. If Fourier's views of society made a great allowance for love, they also took taste and satisfaction of taste into account. In fact, emphasis on

---

[41] For the Tahitians and Japanese, see Fourier, *Théorie des quatre mouvements et des destinées générales*, pp. 131–132 (*Oeuvres*, Anthropos, Vol. I, pp. 131–132); and Fourier, *Manuscrits. Années 1853–1856* (Paris, 1856), pp. 311–312 (*Oeuvres*, Anthropos, Vol. XI, pp. 311–312, first pagination); and Fourier, *La fausse industrie*, Vol. II, pp. 812 (P9)–813 (Q9) (*Oeuvres*, Anthropos, Vol. IX, pp. 812 [P9]–813 [Q9]). Love is heavily emphasized in Fourier, *Le nouveau monde amoureux*. For the last assertion see, for instance, Fourier, *Manuscrits* (Paris, 1851), p. 314 (*Oeuvres*, Anthropos, Vol. X, p. 314, first pagination); and Fourier, *Egarement de la raison* . . . and *Fragments*, p. 36 (*Oeuvres*, Anthropos, Vol. XII, p. 622).

hunger went particularly well with a certain crude realism in Fourier's thought. Nor was the human being limited to love and taste. Fourier noted, for example, that in men, in contrast to women, ambition and friendship were on the whole stronger than love and family feeling. Using a different approach, he related friendship to childhood in particular, love to youth, ambition to maturity, and lastly family sentiment to old age. As we have seen, he showed little favoritism for love, by comparison with other passions, in the crucial issue of character classification. Besides, the father of Harmony delighted especially in combinations of passions and in complex arrangements to satisfy such combinations. For that reason he assigned to the opera a central position in the society of the future: opera indeed served a variety of passions and desires, which, it might be added, did not include love or taste. In general it would be most incorrect to consider Fourier's very complex system, with all its coordinated cogs and devices, the series, and the over-all fundamental formula itself as a camouflage for sexual license rather than as what was to him the ultimate revelation. Fourier himself had nothing but scorn for those who sought to find in free love *per se* a shortcut to blessedness.[42]

[42] Fourier gave preference to ambition, or honor, and friendship over love and family feeling as motivation of men, e.g., in Fourier, *Manuscrits* (Paris, 1852), p. 236; *Oeuvres*, Anthropos, Vol. X, p. 236, second pagination, and he related affective passions to age, e.g., in Fourier, *Théorie de l'unité universelle*, Vol. III, pp. 339–340; *Oeuvres*, Anthropos, Vol. IV, p. 339–340. See footnote 18 above for Fourier's view of the domination of different passions among human beings. Opera in Harmony will be discussed later in this chapter. On sexual license see, for instance, Fourier's criticism of Saint-Simon and Owen in Fourier, *Piège et charlatanisme des deux sectes Saint-Simon et Owen*, pp. 53–55. It should be added that the recent publication of Fourier's *Le nouveau monde amoureux*, with an interesting introductory study by Mrs. S. Debout-Oleszkiewicz (pp. VII–CXII), does not essentially change the picture. In the newly published material, Fourier emphasizes the value of love as a vital link in Harmony and

Because the phalanx would give free and full play to all the passions, life in it would become a series of delights. Its tempo would accelerate to reach a continuous crescendo. Fourier decreased the sleep of his Harmonians to allow them more time for enjoyment, and he left them as their only regret the fact that the day contained twenty-four hours and not forty-eight. Nor, in spite of their long lives, would there ever be enough days. Instead at breakneck speed days would change into weeks, months, seasons, and years. Life itself would pass as a single moment, as one many-faceted and kaleidoscopic explosion of rapturous joy.[43]

CLASSES AND REMUNERATION IN A PHALANX

A phalanx would contain three classes, the rich, the middle class, and the poor. Characteristically, Fourier emphasized the difference in food, the point that the harmonious society of the future would provide three main categories of meals. But, as already noted, there would also be differences in apartments and in other material elements of life. Sometimes, as in the cases of his characters Lucas and Mondor, the theoretician of the phalanx sketched distinct occupations for the poor and the rich in their daily rounds of activities in Harmony. Two main reasons seem to explain Fourier's maintenance of this class stratification which has provoked strong criticism from egalitarian commentators. On the one hand, Fourier was constantly concerned with making a phalanx attractive to all humans, and especially to the rich and the privileged who could substantially contribute to the transformation of his dream into reality. Obviously every-

sketches various, at times quite bizarre, erotic arrangements, but he does not at all deny the importance of other passions, notably taste, nor, of course, of his total formula and system. Indeed the new material substantially confirms what Fourier had written elsewhere.

[43] E.g., Fourier, *Manuscrits* (Paris, 1851), p. 95; *Oeuvres,* Anthropos, Vol. X, p. 90, first pagination.

thing had to be done to satisfy them. On the other hand, and more fundamentally, Fourier believed in the necessary and beneficial role of differences among individuals. In this respect, the disparities in income joined such other variations as those of character, ability, desire, and taste to create the precisely correct mixture for human intercourse to be seized in Fourier's formula.

The father of the phalanx believed that one of his greatest discoveries was that of the right principle of remuneration. The gain was to be divided as follows: five-twelfths to labor, four-twelfths to capital, and three-twelfths to talent.[44] Labor's part was to be distributed among all the working series, but by no means evenly. Instead Fourier favored a system which would increase reward for labor in direct proportion to the unpleasantness of that labor, to its relative unattractiveness, and to its social significance in holding a phalanx together. Within each series remuneration again differed, more experienced and highly regarded members receiving a greater recompense than newcomers. The inhabitants of a phalanx could thus be rewarded in three categories with that of capital enjoying full consideration. It has even been suggested that capital would fare at least as well in Harmony as in the unreformed world, all the more so because Fourier was confident that shares would bring exceptionally high interest in a phalanx. The Harmonians would

[44] On the whole, and with some variations, Fourier upheld this formula to the end of his days. Perhaps his greatest departure from it was his decision that in a small-scale and incomplete phalanx of only some three hundred members there would be no need for a separate part for talent with the result that two-thirds of the gain there should go to labor and one-third to capital. Fourier, "De la sérisophie ou épreuve réduite," *La Phalange. Revue de la science sociale* (May–June, July–August, September–October 1849), pp. 386–450, 5–64, 161–183, especially p. 416; *Oeuvres*, Anthropos, Vol. XII, p. 248. "Talent," never systematically discussed by Fourier, is certainly the vaguest of his three components in remuneration.

pay a single tax as they received their annual remuneration, and would be free to use as they deemed best, save, donate, or bequeath the remainder. Full freedom of inheritance would join the other freedoms in the happy world of the future.

Even though he delighted in distinctions, Fourier always insisted on integration and harmony. Therefore, in contrast to Civilization, that crooked mirror of what human society was meant to be, classes in a phalanx would come together instead of tearing apart. To begin with, the poor in Harmony, while they could still be so designated in relation to their rich fellows, would be in effect better off materially and certainly happier than the wealthy in Civilization. Fourier postulated this high minimum of well-being as a prerequisite for any successful society of the future. In addition, the poor, as well as all other members of a phalanx, would be proprietors. Even as workers they would receive, as we have seen, a proportion of total gain rather than a set wage, and they would develop a lively proprietary interest in the development and success of all their activities and enterprises. Moreover, they would not remain merely workers for long. The high standard of life and the easy savings would enable them to purchase shares and join the capitalists of the phalanx. Fourier eventually projected three categories of shares, with "workers'" shares yielding up to 40 per cent interest and limited to one or two per member of a phalanx. By contrast, the third and largest category of shares would bring only a 5 or 7 per cent interest. The road of talent would also presumably be completely open to the poor, and it would not even require the original saving.

But the poor did not even have to rise economically and socially in a phalanx to be fully accepted by and integrated with the middle class and the rich. Fourier was much concerned with the perfect blending of his three classes to produce the ideal harmonious society. He insisted, for example, that initially only the proper and polite poor should be admitted into a phalanx, so that the wealthy would not be deterred from associating with them. Education in Harmony had as one of its main tasks the spreading of good manners and general refinement among all people. Again, Fourier insisted, it would be a dreadful mistake to judge the poor in Harmony by the condition and the standards of the masses in Civilization.

As always, the series served as the most important integrating force. The theoretician of the phalanx believed that the classes would first begin to mix through the children, who are free of the prejudices of their elders, and through the interest of the parents in the welfare and activities of their offspring.[45] Once the series were properly organized and went into full operation, a new harmonious system would replace the isolation and hostility of Civilization. Working passionately together men and women would quickly forget social distinctions and devote themselves entirely to the novel life of competing and cooperating groups and series. Typically, the poor would be admiringly followed by the rich in the occupations which the poor knew best, or for which they demonstrated more talent; the same person, regardless of his class, would occupy a great variety of positions in his many series, associating on different terms with different people. The rich would hasten to promote the spirit and the cause of their series by such means as financing luxurious banquets for the entire series or building ele-

---

[45] In his usual pseudo-scientific manner Fourier declared that: "the neuter being the principal source of links, it is by means of the neuter sex, by means of the children, that affection will begin to emerge among the different classes, the classes which are today so full of hate, so careful to isolate themselves from one another . . ." Fourier, *op. cit.*, p. 5; *Oeuvres*, Anthropos, Vol. XII, p. 283. I shall refer to Fourier's view of children as the neuter sex in the fifth chapter.

gant pavilions at the place of its activities. In this manner
they would forge further links between themselves and the
less prosperous members of the series.

More important and personal connections would also be
established.

A father in Harmony, being passionately engaged in "forty or
fifty" kinds of work, becomes as a result passionately interested in
his most intelligent collaborators, and above all in the poor children whom he sees excel in his favorite occupations in which his
son does not participate at all. From this fact arise adoptions of
industrial association, adoptions of continuators. They would not
take place in Civilization where the rich do not develop a passion
for work, or, if they are devoted to it, they have to face everywhere a company of intriguers and scoundrels and never that of
intelligent and enthusiastic children, worthy of the rank of titular
continuators.[46]

In the course of his long life and his many series a rich Harmonian would adopt at least a hundred such children as his
heirs. Moreover, when after several generations, the new system of human relations became fully established, this Harmonian would have even more relatives by blood and marriage. Indeed, because of such developments as "polygamy
extended to women as well as men" and longevity which
would enable members of a phalanx to see their descendants
of the seventh generation, he would acquire the total of
more than three hundred heirs. Allowing for the fact that
many of these heirs would in turn have heirs, the fortune of
our Harmonian would eventually benefit all members of his
phalanx, excluding perhaps the usual exception of one
eighth of the total number. Cohesion would surely prevail
over separateness, sympathy over hostility. The theoretician

[46] Fourier, *Théorie de l'unité universelle,* Vol. IV, pp. 445–446;
Oeuvres, Anthropos, Vol. V, pp. 445–446.

of Harmony calculated that legacies would be divided as follows: one-third or one-half to children "of all degrees," one quarter to adopted children, and one quarter to friends, wives, and collateral relatives.[47]

In effect Fourier proposed to replace the class rivalries and antagonisms of Civilization, together with many other rivalries and antagonisms of the unregenerate world, by the constant intrigue and competition of his groups and series. The new rivalry would be keener and more exciting than the old, but constructive rather than destructive. Vigorously competing groups would be linked by the interest of their common series. Rival series would all work for the good of the phalanx. Most important, antagonisms would not center on people. A bitter rival in one occupation would be an eager partner in another, a venerated teacher in a third, and a useful assistant in a fourth. He might well be also a relative by blood or adoption, a friend, or a lover.

To sum up, sects are natural enemies to one another. But in the combined order the links of friendship which exist among their members are infinitely stronger than the collective rivalries of the sects. In the combined order individual friendships have seven times more influence than collective rivalries. On the contrary, in the Civilized order the rivalries have seven times more power than the individual friendships.[48]

[47] *Ibid.*, pp. 452–454; *Oeuvres,* Anthropos, Vol. V, pp. 452–454. Moreover, these legacies would be "progressive," that is, paying 8 or 10 per cent interest, so that the heirs would have no reason to desire an early death of the testator. Fourier, *La fausse industrie,* Vol. II, p. M4; *Oeuvres,* Anthropos, Vol. IX, p. M4.

[48] Fourier, *Manuscrits* (Paris, 1851), p. 129; *Oeuvres,* Anthropos, Vol. X, p. 129, first pagination. See also Fourier, "Des trois groupes d'ambition, d'amour et de familisme," *La Phalange. Revue de la science sociale* (January, February, March 1846), especially pp. 149–154.

THE PHALANX ECONOMY

Fourier's phalanx had as its purpose such an organization of relations among human beings that all passions of every individual would find full expression. Everything had to be bent to that great end. And yet the phalanx had also to meet another need: to provide the economic basis for the new society, to produce enough goods and services to satisfy the extremely high standards of material enjoyment characteristic of Harmony. Without economic success, the world of the future would remain a chimera. Fortunately Fourier again rose to the occasion.

The father of the phalanx concentrated so effectively on the economic arrangements and advantages in Harmony that some commentators even took this to be his main theoretical argument rather than a subsidiary and supporting line of reasoning. Many others, while recognizing Fourier's primary allegiance to the doctrine of passions, themselves found his economic views more valuable. In any case, in the utopian socialist's teaching, economics took second place only to psychology.

Fourier developed several arguments in support of the economic superiority of the new order. To begin with, there was the fact of association itself. The father of the phalanx, and his disciples, and the disciples of his disciples went through uncounted calculations proving the enormous saving of labor and material achieved by such practices as common kitchens, common dining rooms, or common nurseries for children. Boarding houses, Fourier asserted, provided cheap meals with a variety of foods beyond the reach of a single family. How much more then could the kitchen of a phalanx accomplish! Indeed low cost and variety would go together in this as in so many other undertakings of a correctly organized society. As to the labor force, some seven-eighths of the total number of women alone would be released from domestic tasks to be profitably employed in other series. Children would be productive in a phalanx. And whole classes of parasites such as soldiers, policemen, and customs officials would disappear in Harmony.[49] It is noteworthy that Fourier retained parsimoniousness and minute saving for all future time, in a society of full abundance and happiness. All Harmonians, including those of the highest standing, would save matches, eat entirely the edible part of fruits, and carefully wear their clothes as long as possible. The father of the phalanx argued boldly that this too corresponded to the theory of passions: there would be only a strictly limited number of people eager to produce certain items, and therefore it would be especially wise not to be wasteful of these items.[50]

Association would permit full application of reason and science to economic activities. Fourier liked to emphasize the superiority of cultivation and production in Harmony to those in Civilization. His examples of that superiority, however, dealt as a rule not with any technological breakthroughs, but rather with a more careful organization and again, in a sense, saving. In perhaps the most celebrated instance Fourier began by declaring that no savings would be small in a system applied to the entire globe and proceeded to demonstrate how a modest increase in the production of eggs each day, in every phalanx, obtained by a better care and choice of hen and multiplied all over the planet, would prove more than sufficient in a year to pay off the entire national debts of England and France.[51]

[49] See the next chapter for a more detailed treatment of parasites in Civilization and of its other weaknesses.

[50] Fourier, *Manuscrits* (Paris, 1852), pp. 87–92; *Oeuvres,* Anthropos, Vol. X, pp. 87–92, second pagination.

[51] Fourier, *Manuscrits* (Paris, 1851), pp. 176–177; *Oeuvres,* Anthropos, Vol. X, pp. 176–177, first pagination. See also Fourier, "La

The motivation of its workers was another great advantage of the phalanx economy.[52] All Harmonians, to repeat, would engage only in those occupations, and those specific parts of the occupations in question, to which they were passionately devoted. Thus not only would the new system relieve seven-eighths of the women of domestic work, but the remaining eighth would exclusively consist of individuals enthusiastically dedicated to the kitchen and the nursery. They would organize appropriate groups and series and transform the drudgery of Civilization into the sparkling dance of the phalanx. Fourier went far indeed in stressing the enthusiasm of the Harmonians for their work. Relying on the composite passion, he even pictured it as sheer ecstasy, as an explosive burst of energy comparable to the superhuman efforts of soldiers scaling a rock in the heat of battle or miners digging to rescue trapped comrades.

The new system would offer many special assets. Instead of having to hire lazy and frequently incompetent servants, the Harmonians would have servant work performed by the usual competing groups and series which would guarantee both the abundance and the excellence of personal services. Moreover, Fourier devised a scheme according to which half the children would be employed in dirty work which would fit their natural preferences and enable them to play the delicious role of knights-errant of the new world, while the other half, those of softer and sweeter tastes, would be engaged in such pleasant tasks as beautifying the countryside.[53] Once the new order was established, nature itself

dette d'Angleterre payée en six mois par les oeufs de poule," *Théorie de l'unité universelle,* Vol. III, pp. 206–211, which includes a discussion of saving in general in the phalanxes, with a table on p. 208.

[52] One is tempted to think of the Soviet collective farms, the *kolkhozes,* as Fourier's phalanxes, or caricatures of Fourier's phalanxes, without the motivation.

[53] These Little Hordes and Little Bands will be discussed in the next section of the present chapter.

would change to benefit mankind. Mild climate would replace the bitter cold, the entire earth becoming a garden for
cultivation. New creations would produce animals and other
creatures beneficial to mankind, instead of the destructive
enemies of the present. These new beings, anti-lions and anti-
whales among others, would prove of inestimable value in
transportation as well as in other branches of the economy.[54] But these last considerations take us beyond the
phalanx proper; nor have they been much stressed by the
followers and admirers of Charles Fourier's economic
theories.

Everything considered, Fourier could well regard his frequently made assertion that the establishment of phalanxes
would result in a "quadruple product" as highly conserva-
tive. He emphasized that there would be no risk involved.
And he was perfectly willing to promise more than a fourfold increase when he noticed that others projected big rises
in production even without the benefit of his system.

The economic life of a phalanx would center on agriculture. Fourier established an appropriate ratio, three to one
for agriculture as against industry, and assured his readers
that this ratio would correspond to the wishes of men,
women, and children in selecting their occupations.[55] If it
would place manufactured goods at the short end of the
total economic output of the phalanx, their relative paucity
would be compensated by their high and durable quality as
well as by the usual thriftiness and meticulous care with
which the Harmonians would treat them. By contrast, there
would always be an abundance and an enormous variety of
products for the table. Agriculture for Fourier included a
considerable emphasis on the raising of domestic animals

[54] See below, in this chapter, a summary of climatic, and indeed
cosmic, results of the establishment of the new order.

[55] Fourier's devotion to agriculture and neglect of industry will be
discussed in Chapter IV dealing with the nature of Fourier's
socialism.

and birds, but a devaluation of the production of grain. The Harmonians would consume much less bread than people in Civilization, concentrating instead on such foods as sugar and fruits, a taste displayed unerringly by children to the consternation of their near-sighted parents. Orchards, vegetable gardens, and gardens proper would be the natural setting for the happy groups and series of the new world.

Industry in Harmony would apparently consist almost entirely of arts and crafts practiced in well-appointed ateliers conducive in every way to emulation and intrigue. Much of it would be of a service nature. Fourier left almost no references to any large-scale or mechanized industry. As to commerce, which the utopian socialist criticized so bitterly in Civilization,[56] it would constitute a monopoly of the phalanx and would be organized, as usual, in groups and series. While it would expand twentyfold compared to its present extent, it would occupy only one-twentieth, or even one-fiftieth, of the personnel engaged in it in Civilization.

EDUCATION, CHILDHOOD, AND YOUTH IN A PHALANX

Education, free and embracing all the young in a phalanx, would prepare the rising generations of Harmonians for the fullest and most fruitful participation in the life of the new world. More than that, in contrast to Civilization, this education would be no mere apprenticeship, but already an integral part of the organization and the daily activities of the entire community. Like everything else in Harmony, the problem of education demanded care and precision.

Fourier subdivided the pupils and hence the educational system of a phalanx into two "vibrations," and four phases. As he was growing up, each Harmonian would go through the choirs of the *Bambins* or *Bambines* in the first phase of the lower vibration, and successively the choirs of the

[56] See Chapter III.

Chérubins or *Chérubines* and the *Séraphins* or *Séraphines* in the second phase. The Harmonian would then be graduated to the higher vibration, consisting again of two phases: the third, composed in succession of the choirs of the *Lycéens* or *Lycéennes* and of the *Gymnasiens* or *Gymnasiennes,* and, finally, the fourth containing the choirs of the *Jouvenceaux* or *Jouvencelles.*[57] A child would enter the choirs of the bambini at the age of three, and move from the lower to the higher vibration at the age of nine. He would be graduated into the final phase, that of the youths, at about fifteen and a half, and might continue in that phase until the age of nineteen or twenty.

To be sure, Fourier also classified children before the age of three, into the *Nourrissons,* from zero to eighteen months, and the *Poupons,* from eighteen to thirty-six months —introducing elsewhere also the category of the *Lutins*— and he emphasized that health and a full physical development should be the main goals in their upbringing. To achieve these purposes best, they would be in the care of the groups and series of *bonnes.* Mothers would come to feed infants from the breast, and both fathers and mothers would enjoy playing with their children and even "spoiling" them while bearing no responsibility for their upbringing. But, as Fourier put it, it would be the bambini alone, rather than the younger children, "who would start to frequent as members the workshops and the industrial gatherings,"[58] in

[57] Fourier, *Théorie de l'unité universelle,* Vol. IV, p. 7; *Oeuvres,* Anthropos, Vol. V, p. 7. For Fourier's views on education in Harmony see especially the first two hundred or so pages of that volume, Fourier, *Manuscrits* (Paris, 1852), pp. 73–314; *Oeuvres,* Anthropos, Vol. X, pp. 73–314, second pagination and Fourier, *Le nouveau monde industriel et sociétaire,* pp. 166–244; *Oeuvres,* Anthropos, Vol. VI, pp. 166–244.

[58] Fourier, *Théorie de l'unité universelle,* Vol. IV, p. 13; *Oeuvres,* Anthropos, Vol. V, p. 13. Actually, in the celebrated example of separating peas by size children perform useful work from the age of

other words, participate in the groups and series of their phalanx.

Physical development enhanced by work in appropriate groups and series would constitute the main emphasis in education until the age of nine, that is, the end of the lower vibration. Fourier proposed, for example, an examination in dexterity, consisting of seven parts, one for each of the four members, one for the two arms, one for the two legs, and one for the four members together, as a requirement for admission to the next educational level.[59] At the same extremely young age children would also be taught one of the three properties of God, the economy of means, which in

25 months. Fourier, *Le nouveau monde industriel et sociétaire,* pp. 182–183; *Oeuvres,* Anthropos, Vol. VI, pp. 182–183.

[59] Fourier, *Théorie de l'unité universelle,* Vol. IV, p. 9; *Oeuvres,* Anthropos, Vol. V, p. 9. Fourier was especially critical that people in civilization use as a rule one and not both arms, neglect their toes, and in general fail to develop their physical potential. It was apparently an extension of the same kind of preoccupation that made the father of Harmony assign an additional powerful, useful, and magnificent member to the Solarians, to the hilarious delight of his critics. For a discussion of this additional member see Fourier, *La fausse industrie,* Vol. I, pp. 442–443; *Oeuvres,* Anthropos, Vol. VIII, pp. 442–443. Recently Jonathan Beecher demonstrated that, according to Fourier, after 16 generations, that is, some 400 years, of the existence of Harmony, Harmonians would also acquire this splendid additional member, "archibras" or tail. The relevant passage had been excised by Fourier's disciples. Jonathan Beecher, "L'archibras de Fourier. Un manuscrit censuré," *La Brèche,* No. 7 (December 1964), pp. 66–71.

For a fuller account of the examination to be taken at the age of four and a half for promotion from the bambini to the cherubs, which would also include such tests as washing 120 dishes in half an hour without breaking a single one of them, and peeling a demi-quintal of apples in a proper manner and within the prescribed time, as well as music, dancing, and the presentation of certificates of various degrees of proficiency in 21 different activities, see Fourier, *Le nouveau monde industriel et sociétaire,* pp. 196–197; *Oeuvres,* Anthropos, Vol. VI, pp. 196–197.

terms of their activities would signify parsimonious saving of all the little items and bits they could save in a phalanx. Later they would be required to know the second property of God, distributive justice, to move from the category of the cherubs to that of the seraphs, and the third, the universality of Providence, to be graduated from the lower vibration and join the *lycéens*. As to groups and series, children of three would be engaged in some twenty or thirty occupations developing interests and tastes which they would joyously pursue throughout life. In contrast to the unfortunate young in Civilization, they would have the fascinating world of passionate series open to them. Special efforts would be made to entice them into this world by such means as tools and entire workshops scaled to their size, and a complicated system of ranks, distinctions, and awards so attractive to children. Fourier emphasized that children would work with, learn from, and be judged by their peers and especially by their natural models and mentors, the children immediately ahead of them. They would, however, also profit from the guidance and the companionship of the very old whom they would repay by veneration.

Although children in Harmony would have a tremendous variety of choices among ways of developing their inclinations and talents, they would concentrate on two activities: opera and cuisine. These two subjects, Fourier believed, should form the core of general education in the world of the future. For one thing, they were superb for the training of the senses. While touch, according to Fourier, did not really develop until puberty, the other four dominated childhood and would find their best application in the opera and the cuisine. The opera would serve sight and hearing, the cuisine taste and smell. The opera would also be of inestimable value in teaching Harmonians the dexterity which they could use so well in their tireless work in groups and series. In a more detailed analysis the father of the phalanx emphasized seven elements in an opera: singing or measured human voice, instruments or measured artificial sound, poetry or measured word, gesture or measured expression, dance or measured march, gymnastics or measured bodily movements, and painting, decorations and costumes or measured ornament.[60] Altogether the opera constituted a mechanism of measured geometric distribution, "the active emblem of the spirit of God or the spirit of measured unity." [61] Combination or grafting of independent elements, and measure, two of Fourier's favorite principles, found a splendid embodiment in the opera.

The results of operatic training would be equally splendid, and they would extend beyond the extremely important subject matter itself, and even beyond the general development of the senses and of dexterity:

Considered from the point of view of a moral influence on the child, it is there that youth is taught to look with horror at everything that wounds truth, justice and unity. At the opera no favor can excuse him who is false in voice, measure, gesture, or step. The child of a prince participating in troupes or choirs is forced to suffer the truth and the motivated criticisms of the crowd. It is at the opera that he learns to subordinate himself in every movement to the unitary coordination, to the general accord. The opera is thus the school of material unity, of justice, and of truth: it is, in these respects, the image of the divine spirit, the true road of "the ways of Harmony." [62]

The cuisine remained Fourier's special concern throughout his life. Not only did he consider the sensual passion of

[60] Fourier, *Théorie de l'unité universelle,* Vol. IV, pp. 76–77; *Oeuvres,* Anthropos, Vol. V, pp. 76–77 and Fourier, *Manuscrits* (Paris 1852), p. 142; *Oeuvres,* Anthropos, Vol. X, p. 142, second pagination.
[61] Fourier, *Théorie de l'unité universelle,* Vol. IV, p. 77; *Oeuvres,* Anthropos, Vol. V, p. 77.
[62] *Ibid.,* pp. 82–83; *Oeuvres,* Anthropos, Vol. V, pp. 82–83.

taste, with hunger resulting from a denial of its claims and gastronomy developed to minister to its needs, as a fundamental factor in human life and history, he also exhibited a particular attraction to that factor. Fourier's writings are full of groups and series devoted to such matters as different variants of soups, of competitions on a tremendous scale to produce the best *paté,* of brilliant careers made in the field of pastries and jams. In Harmony, where the true science of gastrosophy would replace our weak and corrupt gastronomy, people would eat enormously and yet retain, because of the scientific cuisine and the general nature of life in the new society, perfect health. A humble fare would consist of a choice of some 30 or 40 dishes, as well as beverages, of a quality surpassing the delicacies of present-day gastronomes. And the Harmonians would always innovate. "A Harmonian has each day two gastrosophic cabals regarding festive dishes . . . the poorest third-class table does not pass a day without enjoying some gastronomic novelties." [63] Sugary confections and fruits would replace bread as staple food. Leading cooks would acquire the importance and prestige of ministers of state.[64] Children in particular would find "a thousand sources of industrial intrigue in the products of the children's kitchen, in the sugared creams, compotes, pastry, sweets, herbs and fruits." [65] Their education by means of the cuisine would thus be the most natural kind

[63] Fourier, "Des lymbes obscures ou périodes d'enfer social et de labyrinthe passionnel," *La Phalange. Revue de la science sociale* (January–February 1849), pp. 5–40, 97–110, quoted from pp. 104–105. Fourier must have meant "gastrosophic novelties."
See also the section on "Combined gastronomy [gastrosophy] considered in the political, material, and passional sense" in Fourier, *Théorie des quatre mouvements et des destinées générales,* pp. 159–172; *Oeuvres,* Anthropos, Vol. I, pp. 159–172.

[64] Fourier, *Manuscrits* (Paris, 1852), p. 148, footnote 1; *Oeuvres,* Anthropos, Vol. X, p. 148, footnote 1, second pagination.

[65] Fourier, *Théorie de l'unité universelle,* Vol. IV, p. 112; *Oeuvres,* Anthropos, Vol. V, p. 112.

imaginable, the most likely to attract them and to satisfy their passions, and at the same time it would prepare them for an extremely important aspect of human life. Moreover, the cuisine, like the opera, led beyond itself.

It is in the kitchen and at the table that children in Harmony learn at an early age to appreciate animals and vegetables, and the mistakes committed in their education and cultivation. The more refined they become as gourmets, the more interest they take in the preparation. The two arts of the cook and the gastronome become for them a way to hygiene, then to chemistry, then to agronomy and other sciences. Frequenting the kitchens is thus to a child in Harmony a key to all studies.[66]

No wonder that cooks in Harmony would be "scientists of the first order," [67] "pivots of education and enjoyments." [68]

At the age of nine a child in Harmony would move into the second or higher "vibration" and the third phase of his or her education. Where the first phase, that of the bambini, concentrated on physical development, and the second phase, that of the cherubs and the seraphs, on "the industrial faculties," the third, encompassing the *lycéens* and the *gymnasiens* together with their female counterparts, nine to fifteen or sixteen years old, would shift the attention to the soul. "Noble means will be put into play, heroic acts of friendship, honor, patriotism." [69] To accomplish his purpose, Fourier devised for this third phase of education two of his more remarkable inventions, the Little Hordes and the Little Bands.

Selected as always on the basis of inclination, two-thirds of

[66] See footnote 64.

[67] Fourier, *Theorie de l'unité universelle,* Vol. IV, p. 115; *Oeuvres,* Anthropos, Vol. V, p. 115.

[68] See footnote 64.

[69] Fourier, *Théorie de l'unité universelle,* Vol. IV, p. 131; *Oeuvres,* Anthropos, Vol. V, p. 131.

the boys in Harmony and one-third of the girls would belong to the Little Hordes. Satisfying the widespread childhood tastes for dirt and danger and the equally strong penchants for friendship and honor, the Little Hordes would form the quasi-savage knighthood of Harmony devoted to rapid and enthusiastic execution of repugnant and sometimes perilous work. The Little Hordes would keep Harmony clean of all filth and refuse, repair roads, look after the well-being of animals, and, incidentally, bring to account anyone mistreating animals, do the dirtier jobs in butcheries and kitchens, and perform numerous other tasks such as killing poisonous snakes. First to rise at 3 a.m., these new knights would exhibit fanatical devotion and self-sacrifice in all their activities. "They run frenetically to work which they perform as a pious deed, an act of charity towards the phalanx, a service to God and unity." [70] In return they would ask for little or no pecuniary recompense, willingly assuming the last place in the annual division of earnings. Indeed, those joining a Horde would donate an eighth of the money they might have to their new organization to be used to satisfy and at the same time shame those series which would argue for a larger share for themselves at the annual division. By performing splendidly the generally repugnant tasks which have to be carried out in any society, and to a lesser extent by their spirit of abnegation and idealism at the time of the division of earnings, the Little Hordes would make a major, even an indispensable, contribution to Harmony.

And this most valuable contribution would be obtained at a very low price. To repeat, the members of the Little Hordes would be merely exercising to the full their childhood passions for filth and for heroism. Interestingly enough, they would be led not only by their own male and

[70] *Ibid.*, p. 149; *Oeuvres*, Anthropos, Vol. V, p. 149.

female khans and other officers, but also by bonzes or druids, that is, by grown-up people who had retained the childhood inclinations characteristic of the Hordes. Harmony would provide its Hordes with ponies, which they would ride in the Mongol manner and formation, surpassing before long the Tartars, the Mameluks, and the Arabs, with a profusion of appropriate musical instruments, and with strikingly colorful, rich, and distinctive clothing of oriental design. Finally, the Little Hordes would receive for their services all the honor and respect imaginable:

They are repaid by honors without limit. The Argot [another name for the Little Hordes derived from their clipped slang talk] is the first cavalry of the globe; it takes precedence over all other Harmonian formations, and the supreme authorities must salute it first. The Argot receives everywhere the honors of high sovereignty: at the approach of these hordes the signal tower owes them a carillon of supremacy, and the domes must display the flag. In addressing a *sacripan* or a *chenapan* in his costume one must use the title of Magnanimous, and one must use the title of Glorious Clouds for the hordes of the Argot. In the temple they take their place in the sanctuary.[71]

The remaining one-third of boys and two-thirds of girls in Harmony would constitute the Little Bands. Contrasting in inclinations and tastes from the members of the Little Hordes, they would adopt a different manner and dress. While the Little Hordes would affect a rough and even savage bearing, the Little Bands would display an exquisite courtesy and refinement. "Waiting for the time when it would be possible to mount the Little Bands on zebras"[72]

[71] *Ibid.*, p. 153; *Oeuvres*, Anthropos, Vol. V, p. 153. The *sacripans* and the *chenapans* were subdivisions within the Little Hordes, the first being concerned with the dangerous tasks and the second with the repugnant ones. "Glorious Clouds" was apparently derived from the cavalry formation of the Little Hordes.

[72] *Ibid.*, p. 169; *Oeuvres*, Anthropos, Vol. V, p. 169.

they too would ride ponies, but they would ride them in the modern civilized, not the Tartar, manner. They would be dressed perhaps like ancient Athenians, or like troubadours, not like Asiatic horsemen.

The Little Bands would promote the love for *parure,* appearance, ornament, dress, so characteristic of children, girls in particular. They would be concerned with the upkeep and protection of the vegetal world, just as the Little Hordes would be in charge of most of the animals. In addition, the Bands would take care of the animals which must be treated with patience and refinement, for example, the beavers, and they would deal with the bees and the silkworms. The Little Bands would specialize in flower arrangement. Their refinement would extend to language; in fact, they would supervise correct linguistic usage in Harmony. While the Little Hordes would dedicate themselves to the important negative task of removing the obstacle of repugnant work from Harmony, the Little Bands would exercise the positive function of adding in numerous ways charm and attraction to the society of the future. Or, to put it differently: the Little Hordes would proceed to the beautiful by means of the good, the Little Bands to the good by means of the beautiful.

The fourth and last phase of education in Harmony, the education of youths, encompassing young people of both sexes between the ages of fifteen or sixteen and nineteen or twenty, would concentrate on containing and channeling in a socially desirable direction the new powerful passion emerging in the pupils, the passion of love. To achieve the intended result Fourier again offered two "corporations." Although all Harmonians would start the last phase of their education in the category of vestals, half of them would gradually leave it to form the parallel group of damsels. The vestals would be composed of two-thirds young women and one-third young men; the reverse would be true of the damsels. The transfer from the vestals to the damsels would remain free at all times.

The vestals, virgin as their name implied and devoted to continence, would in fact represent the ideal of young womanhood preached, but not practiced, in Civilization: modest, studious, hard-working, and helpful. In Harmony they would promote and symbolize social virtues, continuing the work of the Little Hordes and going beyond the Hordes which developed only two such virtues, ambition and friendship. These young women—Fourier has little to say about the young men of the group—would serve as the rallying point of the society of the future, evoking in particular enthusiastic admiration from the children, especially the Little Hordes, on the one hand, and the old people on the other. And they would certainly attract young men. Indeed their specific economic function in Harmony would be to serve as the magnet for attracting youth and in effect people of all ages into the large industrial armies raised to perform important tasks exceeding local resources. In contrast to the ways of Civilization, the vestals would lead a most active and prominent economic and social life. Their chastity, in any case voluntary, would be guaranteed not by any regulations from the outside, but by the watchful eye of the corporation itself. Eventually the vestals would conclude splendid alliances with other outstanding and highly desirable Harmonians. The damsels would give up continence earlier than the vestals, choosing, so to speak, an easier, if less brilliant, way in life. They too would, of course, contribute to the economy of Harmony as well as to that graded variety in human desires and conditions which Fourier considered indispensable for the perfect synthesis.

By the age of nineteen or twenty young Harmonians would thus be fully educated for life—although, to be sure, they would continue to learn later in their groups and series

—and, what is more, ideally integrated into society. From early childhood they would have participated in a significant manner in the economic activities of their phalanx. They would have learned in theory, but especially in practice, the nature of the new order. Throughout, like the world around them, they would have advanced only at the urging of their own passions and in response to their own desires. The last phase, that of the vestals and the damsels, would have served as the natural transition to the extremely complicated sexual and social arrangements in Harmony, the arrangements to which Fourier never gave full and definitive form—in spite of many particular provisions and descriptions which can be found especially in *Le nouveau monde amoureux*—but which included whole series of finely graded marriages and liaisons of all sorts. As to specialized higher education, Fourier mentioned, for example, the splendid development of medical education in Harmony, but provided little detail. Nor did he have much to say about teachers, although he did assure them of the highest positions and honors in the new society. The utopian socialist's one constant interest in the field of education, in addition to those already discussed, referred to the structure of knowledge and, in connection with that, the correct teaching methods, a topic to be considered later in this chapter.

3. Beyond the Phalanx

THE WORLD OUTSIDE

Charles Fourier paid constant, minute, even obsessive attention to arrangements in a phalanx, but he neglected the world outside it. In a very real sense, the utopian socialist's entire teaching concentrated on the phalanx. To be sure, the father of Harmony mentioned vast associated regional units with the global capital in Constantinople which enjoyed a uniquely privileged location. He liked to sketch huge serried hierarchies of sub-rulers, and rulers, culminating in the omniarch, parallel hierarchies of female sub-rulers and rulers, and still other hierarchies of Harmonians of great prominence. With a true magnanimity he bestowed ranks and honors. Yet, as most specialists have agreed, all these positions and titles would be essentially honorific and would not provide real authority or power. Fourier himself explained them by emphasizing that humans loved distinctions. And he met the argument that so many distinctions might cheapen the honor by asserting that any elevation in Harmony would be especially prized, because of the very high intrinsic value of every Harmonian and the resulting greater glory of prominence among them. As to effective control and rule, Fourier not only never developed that aspect of his hierarchies but he could not develop it: his entire world was based not on authority, but on absolute self-expression and freedom through a formula which combined the desires of every single individual with the desires of all.

In more practical terms, the economy of a phalanx would presumably depend on trade with the outside world for the satisfaction of many of its needs. Although phalanxes would tend towards autarky in that their members would produce primarily food and other items, as well as services, of immediate use to themselves, no community would be likely to attain entire self-sufficiency. Trade, and trade on a vast scale, would take place among the phalanxes. Fourier underlined this point when he argued that no phalanx should try to produce everything, but should rather take its terrain and climate into account. But while the father of Harmony went repeatedly and passionately into painstaking detail in denouncing commerce in Civilization, he barely mentioned it in the new world. The industrial armies would also, of course, extend beyond the boundaries of a phalanx. Varying in size, they would be raised from many phalanxes and would undertake construction and other tasks benefitting localities, regions, and even the entire globe. In addition, Fourier projected smaller armies of poets, musicians, and other artists traveling all over the world and staging exhibitions and contests wherever they stopped. Each phalanstery was to have ample quarters for guests. And each phalanx was to pay royalties to these and other artists, as well as to inventors and other benefactors of Harmony. Again, in education various phalanxes would go beyond the general high level and become particularly prominent in some skill or field, attracting students from outside their boundaries. Similarly, the central location of all the records of the new world would attract researchers. Many members of a phalanx would establish important outside contacts and connections in the course of their regular education and upbringing. Thus the Little Horde of a given phalanx would often act together with the Little Hordes of neighboring communities, while the crucial economic role of the vestals would be played in the industrial armies and thus outside phalanxes. In reading about life in Harmony one is often reminded of the fact that Fourier himself liked to travel. And yet all these dispositions, industrial armies, and traveling poets, and the joint activities of the Little Hordes, appear to be much more additions to the basic structure than intrinsic parts of Fourier's formula, synthesis, and system.

It is, therefore, particularly interesting to note that the father of Harmony also suggested some steps to integrate organically a phalanx with the entire new world, although he did not pursue his suggestions very far. For example, Fourier wrote:

In this respect it [a certain kind of series] is the natural link among diverse regions; for it might happen that a series of pear raisers that people would want to form in Languedoc could not be completed without joining to it groups stationed in Spain, in Piedmont, in Liguria, in Auvergne, etc. Thus a series in [apparently fourth or higher] power, measured or not measured, establishes *natural* industrial links among different nations; and as a result passional links which, being dependent on the mechanism of the series, are unknown in the state of fragmentation where industrial relations establish among the peoples nothing but jealousies, not links.[73]

But Fourier never expatiated on these geographically dispersed series, stating that series in second and higher powers were much too difficult for his unprepared readers.[74]

Even more interesting is the possibility of integrating a phalanx with its neighbors in terms of the main line of Fourier's thought, character classification. It bears repeating that the 810 characters of a phalanx would consist of 576 solitones or monogynes, that is, people dominated by a single passion, and progressively fewer individuals dominated by an increasing number of passions, culminating in eight tetragynes, that is, people dominated by four spiritual passions, eight "trimixed" dominated by two spiritual and three sensual passions, and, finally, two authentic pentagynes dominated by five spiritual passions.[75] The regular composition of a phalanx contained no "higher" characters than pentagynes. Yet such characters, although rare, did exist and would continue to exist; indeed, the father of

---

[73] *Ibid.*, p. 319; *Oeuvres*, Anthropos, Vol. V, p. 319.

[74] *Ibid.*, p. 318; *Oeuvres*, Anthropos, Vol. V, p. 318.

[75] Fourier, *Le nouveau monde industriel*, pp. 340–341; *Oeuvres*, Anthropos, Vol. VI, pp. 340–341; "Du clavier puissanciel des caractères." This last item published after Fourier's death and of central importance for the subject under discussion is unfortunately very erratic.

Harmony wrote repeatedly of their especially important roles in the society of the future.

> The heptagynes, or characters of the seventh power which pivot on 4 affective and 2 distributive passions, are the most seductive of the entire octave; one would believe that they were more than human. Julius Caesar and Alcibiades were two heptagynes. These are souls of a marvelous flexibility and of an infinite aptitude for all kinds of studies and functions. Nature does not produce more than a couple of them for every 9,728 individuals; they regulate 12 phalanxes.[76]

Next came the omnigynes, governed by seven passions—in particular, apparently the entire four group or affective plus the entire three serial or distributive passions—so rare that Fourier knew of only one example of an omnigyne, namely himself. The omnigynes did not possess at all the attractiveness of the heptagynes, but they surpassed them in utility. A single omnigyne would operate in thirty-six or forty phalanxes. Lapsing into the first person, Fourier wrote how he would move from phalanx to phalanx "reconciling" monogynes of opposing tendencies and teaching everywhere both prodigality and economy, prodigality in building and economy in matches, these necessary characteristics of the new world.

It is such hints of series linking countries and characters bridging phalanxes that point in the direction of the ulti-

[76] Fourier, "Du clavier puissanciel des caractères," p. 26. I think that "regissent" should in this case be translated as "regulate," or perhaps "orchestrate," rather than "rule." The name of "heptagynes" and the reference to the seventh power are apparently mistakes in relation to the character dominated by six passions. Cf., in particular regarding the heptagyne and the omnigyne, the table in Fourier, *Théorie de l'unité universelle,* Vol. II, p. 338; *Oeuvres,* Anthropos, Vol. III, p. 338. See also Fourier, *Manuscrits. Années 1857–1858* (Paris, 1858), pp. 179–180; *Oeuvres,* Anthropos, Vol. XI, pp. 179–180, second pagination.

mate formula for "an orchestra arranged for five billion instruments" where "each one of the five billion individuals will be useful for the happiness of all the others." [77] To call this formula fantastic, chimeric, or even mad, is merely to describe Fourier's system.

OUR PLANET AND THE COSMOS

Fourier had little to say about the nature and structure of Harmony outside the phalanx, but he enjoyed greatly discussing another theme: the triumphant transformation of our entire planet and even other parts of the cosmos following the realization of his social ideal. As indicated in the preceding chapter, the utopian socialist's cosmology, with such related doctrines as those of multiple creation and of the transmigration of souls, together with his "analogy" which performed some of the functions of a theory of knowledge for the whole system, became the favorite targets for the attacks and ridicule of Fourier's opponents while many of his followers and other well-wishers tried to explain away or simply avoid this entire side of his teaching.

Utterly fantastic and absurd, the utopian socialist's cosmology gave expression nevertheless to a number of recurrent ideas which were at the heart of Fourier's obsession. In particular, just as Fourier's psychological, social, political, and economic theory urged the validity of Fourier's formula and the absolute necessity of translating it immediately into practice, so did his cosmology. In fact, it simply expanded the same all-important message from the merely human to the cosmic plane. Again, as with other significant aspects of his teaching, cosmology had appeared already in the utopian socialist's first major presentation of his doctrine, underwent modifications but never changed its basic nature in the

[77] Fourier, *Manuscrits* (Paris, 1851), p. 346; *Oeuvres,* Anthropos, Vol. X, p. 346, first pagination.

course of his life, and remained—in spite of the continuous objections of his disciples—a part of his thought to his very death.[78]

Fourier liked to provide astounding and precise information about planets which he considered to be living bisexual organisms engaged in procreation,[79] and other celestial bodies, about astronomic time spans and distances—which were extremely modest by modern standards—about the evolution of the universe, with a mention even of the "biniverses" and "triniverses" beyond. He dealt with the emanation of aromas that led to creations and with the appearance, disappearance, and roles of satellites orbiting around planets. He believed that Jupiter and Saturn had mishandled the important operation of soaking or tempering our planet when it had abandoned its previous existence as a comet and had joined the solar system, their mistake resulting in certain asymmetrical features in the earth's form, and that Mercury would teach earth the universal language. Yet there was a certain cohesion to this bewildering, scattered, and at times even incomprehensible information. For one thing, Fourier liked to project his series into the cosmos, organizing and interrelating heavenly bodies, although he did not sustain

[78] In fact, on the basis of Fourier's late writings, especially *La fausse industrie,* one can speak of its expanding role.

[79] Already in his first major work Fourier described a planet as "a being which has two souls and two sexes and which procreates like an animal or a vegetable by the joining of two generative substances." Fourier, *Théorie des quatre mouvements et des destinées générales,* p. 38; *Oeuvres,* Anthropos, Vol. I, p. 38. As an example of Fourier's most fantastic cosmology see Fourier, *Théorie de l'unité universelle,* Vol. III, pp. 241–265; *Oeuvres,* Anthropos, Vol. IV, pp. 241–265 and Fourier, "Cosmogonie." *La Phalange. Revue de la science sociale* (May–June 1845); *Oeuvres,* Anthropos, Vol. XII, pp. 1–34. For summary and comment see, e.g., Hélène Tuzet, "Deux types de cosmogonies vitalistes: 2.–Charles Fourier, hygieniste du cosmos," *Revue des sciences humaines,* No. 101 (January–March 1961), pp. 37–53.

his effort in that direction. Newtonian physics, it should be recalled, served as the model for his entire thought. For another thing, and more importantly, Fourier never ceased to emphasize the deficiency in the cosmic arrangement produced by the failure of our planet to perform its assigned part. Fourier's cosmology was thus earth-centered, and indeed centered entirely on Fourier's own system.

The crucial point was the existence of an intrinsic connection between the failure of man to shed the chaos, vice, and misery of Civilization in favor of the organization and blessings of Harmony, and the inability of our planet to perform adequately its cosmic function. Humanity was already several thousand years late in establishing Harmony.[80] In the meantime and in connection with the delay, the climate on our planet had been deteriorating markedly, while more and more violent and varied epidemics swept larger and larger areas. Our only remaining satellite, Phoebe or the moon, had died and went on whirling in space as a pale corpse unable to play its role in the life of heavenly bodies and even emitting poisonous emanations. Still worse, the inability of the earth to supply its share of beneficial aroma affected the sun. "As long as this aroma is not formed, the sun not only has to suspend operations, but it suffers: the equilibrium of its fluids is upset; it has now been for six thousand years in a state of slow fever, of consumption; it needs all its vigor to resist it." [81]

[80] In discussing society and history Fourier emphasized that Harmony could have been established roughly as early as the time of Solon, the delay thus amounting to something over two thousand years, but, when dealing with cosmic themes, the delay often loomed longer.

[81] Fourier, *Manuscrits. Années 1857–1858* (Paris, 1858), p. 326; *Oeuvres,* Anthropos, Vol. XI, p. 326, second pagination. Fourier went on to tell how the heavenly vault had sent a relief column to the sun, a column that had been advancing by forced marches for 1,500 years. Fourier, "Aurora borealis," *Théorie des quatre mouvements et*

The foundation of a phalanx and the resulting coming of Harmony would reestablish the cosmic balance. Enthusiastically Fourier described how in a matter of a few years, with all the aromas functioning properly, earth would be blessed with new and highly beneficial creations. It would also acquire again an aurora borealis over the North Pole, and five satellites, while gangrenous Phoebe would fall into the Milky Way and dissolve there. With the pole heated, climate would change and become magnificently temperate and warm, St. Petersburg enjoying the average temperatures of present-day Nice. Marshes would dry up, volcanoes become extinct, and oceans themselves turn into a salubrious beverage. Moreover, the return of our planet and with it the sun to full cosmic activity would lead to a realignment and a contraction of the solar system, and of the universe itself diminishing the "immense desert" in its midst. Indeed, because everything is linked, and there is an unbroken chain from man, the smallest being with a soul, to God, the greatest, the transformation of our planet would affect not only the solar system and the universe, but also the biniverse, or a mass of universes, and, apparently, still larger entities beyond.[82]

des destinées générales, pp. 41–52, and Fourier, "Concerning Northern Passages and a Triple Harvest," *Théorie de l'unité universelle* Vol. II, pp. 84–107; *Oeuvres,* Anthropos, Vol. III, pp. 84–107 and Charles Fourier, "Cosmogonie," *La Phalange; Oeuvres,* Anthropos, Vol. XII, pp. 50–51.

[82] For climatic transformation consult, e.g., Fourier, *La fausse industrie,* Vol. II, p. D2 (632); *Oeuvres,* Anthropos, Vol. IX, p. D2 (632). See especially: "Textes inédits de Charles Fourier presentés par Simone Debout Oleszkiewicz," *Revue internationale de philosophie,* Vol. XVI, No. 60 (1962), Fasc. 2, pp. 147–175, where Fourier discusses, among other things, the growth and development of universes in terms of an increase in the numbers of celestial bodies and the decrease in distances among them, or contraction, as well as the role of our planet in this process.

Fourier even claimed that, according to the law that the extremes

Of all the cosmic blessings resulting from the establishment of Harmony, Fourier liked to dwell most on the new
creations. A magnificent new creation, combining in fact
two creations, which would follow promptly the organization of the new social order would enrich enormously the
resources of our planet. Humanity would acquire huge
quantities of gold and silver located conveniently near the
surface, materials for special glass by means of which it
would be possible to observe the inhabitants of other planets
and establish contact with them, and other treasures. The
planet and the animal world would be similarly transformed. Fourier commented often and bitterly that at present the animals in particular were a faithful reflection of the
sorry state of mankind: but for a few exceptions, they were
either neutral, that is, useless to man, or more often hostile,
destroying his work, and even attacking and devouring him.
The multiform snakes alone, with the dreaded rattlesnake in
the van, went a long way towards giving a symbolic expression to Civilization, in particular to calumny which permeated it.

After the coming of Harmony everything would change:
the old vicious species would disappear, while whole new
series of wonderful servitors and friends would be created.
For example, while at present only the small domestic cat
was a friend of man, whereas all the larger felines were his
enemies, in the future superb anti-tigers, anti-lions, anti-

meet, man, or rather the phalanx, the lowest entity with a soul, is
particularly dear to God, the highest, and thus particularly influential in cosmic destiny. Although small, the earth is an important
planet, and its aromas are of great significance. And our solar system
occupies the central position in the cosmos. See the texts published by
Debout Oleszkiewicz, *passim,* and Fourier, *Manuscrits. Années 1857–
1858* (Paris, 1858), pp. 318–321, 325–326; *Oeuvres,* Anthropos, Vol.
XI, pp. 318–321, 325–326, second pagination and Fourier, *Le nouveau
monde amoureux,* pp. 465–496.

leopards, anti-panthers, and their like would appear to serve humanity. They would be about one-third again as large as their counterparts in Civilization, and they would exhibit all the marvelous agility and speed characteristic of their race. The largest one of them, corresponding to the tiger with a collar, the mightiest and the most dreaded cat in Civilization, would carry seven travellers at a time at a speed of twenty or twenty-five miles per hour, running softly, barely touching the ground and leaping ditches. A traveller would need but twelve hours to go from Paris to Lyon.[83] Less magnificent animals than the cats would also perform valuable services. If "anti-tigers" would carry men on land, "anti-hippopotamuses" would drag their boats in the rivers and "anti-whales" at sea, while "anti-sharks" would help fishermen, and "anti-crocodiles" kill crocodiles.

Fourier projected no new creations of humans. Nevertheless he envisaged their thorough transformation in Harmony. The societary system giving full expression to all passions, inclinations and talents would raise man to a new level of existence. One result would be the ecstatic happiness of mankind. Another would be its creativity. "Consequently, when the globe is organized and brought to its full complement of three billion, there will be habitually on the globe thirty-seven million poets equal to Homer, thirty-seven million geometricians equal to Newton, thirty-seven million comedians equal to Molière, and similarly with all the talents imaginable." [84]

Moreover, the theoretician of the phalanx did not limit himself to a social and cultural leap forward, but indicated

[83] This prediction of speedy travel has often been listed as one of Fourier's remarkable prophecies. For specific information on the "anti-tiger" and his performance see, for example, Fourier, *Egarement de la raison . . .* and *Fragments,* p. 113.

[84] Fourier, *Théorie des quatre mouvements et des destinées générales,* p. 84; *Oeuvres,* Anthropos, Vol. I, p. 84.

also physiological change. As we know, the Harmonians would enjoy an average life-span of one hundred forty-four years, be virtually free from disease, and display astounding vigor and energy. Beyond that Fourier was deeply concerned with such matters as skin tanning and color, and the nature and operation of the senses, presenting and resolving problems in his usual unique manner.

Man in relation to his color is in plain discord with the center of harmony or the sun. The star which colors and embellishes the entire nature obscures man and blackens his skin. It does not blacken the lilies or the tulips: on the contrary, a flower exposed to the sun is whiter, more vivid in its diverse colors than one that has been cultivated in the shade—and yet, man who is the flower of nature, the presumptive center of social harmony, is discolored, dirtied through contact with the sun, which is also the pivot of material harmony. Here you have two pivots of harmony quite obviously in discord. They will rally together in time. Man, after sixteen generations passed in the mechanics of attraction used to strengthen his temperament, will be regenerated in the material aspect, as much by acquired vigor as by the acquisition of new fluids emanating from the living moons and rings which our globe will reacquire. Man will then begin (I postpone all detail on the subject) to whiten in the sun: the inhabitant of Senegal will be whiter than the Swede and the Siberian. He will acquire the harmonic color, or reinforced white, because of contact with the star from which light emanates. He will acquire the harmonic or direct vision, or eyes able to fixate the sun, like those of the eagle and the cock; the inverse harmonic vision, or eyes which see in the darkness, like those of the lion and the cat; the mixed harmonic vision, or ambiguous vision by diverging eyes, like those of the chameleons. Finally, man will rally to harmony in his visual system, and be in concord in every respect with all possible combinations and distributions of light. This is what one must acquire in respect to one sense alone in order to reach Unity.[85]

[85] Fourier, *Manuscrits* (Paris, 1851), p. 44; *Oeuvres,* Anthropos, Vol. X, p. 44, first pagination.

Fourier also suggested that Harmonians would be amphibious. And, as already mentioned, they would eventually acquire a huge, magnificent, and most useful "archibras," or tail.

The establishment of the new social order on earth would benefit not only the cosmos but also the souls of the departed. Treating afterlife not unlike a phalanx with exceptionally great opportunities, Fourier postulated an extremely complicated system of metempsychosis. Souls kept migrating, alternating between existences in human bodies on earth and transmundane lives in the aromal sphere surrounding our planet. In one calculation Fourier listed hundreds of such migrations, with 405, 810, and 1,620 as his key figures, lives in the other world being twice as long as lives in this and thus consuming two-thirds of the total time.[86] If terrestrial bodies were composed of earth and water, the celestial ones consisted of ether and aromas. The father of Harmony disdained the common notion of the celestial kingdom as a realm of immateriality and inactivity. To the contrary, the denizens of the other world would be better equipped physically than the inhabitants of this one and thus capable of greater activity and enjoyment. They would make the best use of their senses, and they would acquire such new abilities as that of planing or moving swiftly and effortlessly through the air which humans can only experience occasionally and briefly in their dreams. Nor would equality prevail: instead the next world would retain the differentiation and gradations of a good phalanx. Moreover, all human souls were elements in a series of souls culminat-

---

[86] Fourier, *Théorie de l'unité universelle*, Vol. II, p. 319; *Oeuvres,* Anthropos, Vol. III, p. 319. See the entire discussion of "The thesis of bi-complex immortality, or of attractions proportionate to the essential destinies," pp. 304–346; *Oeuvres,* Anthropos, Vol. III, pp. 304–346.

ing in the great soul of the planet of which they were in a sense parts. And it was that great soul that inhabited the body of a child between his birth and his teething when a specific soul migrated into him. Fourier saw special wisdom in the facts that the inhabitants of earth could not communicate with the other world and had no recollection of previous existences. Otherwise, in the conditions of Civilization, they would have all committed suicide.

Yet metempsychosis too was flawed by the failure of men to establish Harmony on earth. In the other world souls were handicapped in the material sense because they had not received a full physical development, and in the spiritual sense because reincarnation in Civilization, or among savages or barbarians, presented grim prospects. More important still, as long as our globe remained in its fallen state, the souls were tied to it and could not, after a certain number of reincarnations on earth, embark on a glorious cosmic journey to other planets, the sun, the Milky Way, other suns, universes, biniverses, triniverses, etc.[87] None of our ancestors had so far been able to undertake this voyage, and their destiny rested in our hands. In its turn, the great soul of the planet itself suffered from the chaos of Civilization. As a result of it, it was treated as a pestiferous vessel by other celestial bodies, which supplied it with the necessary aromas, but kept it in quarantine and refused it other contacts.[88] Again, the only salvation lay in the foundation of Harmony.

Fourier's incorporation of both the soups and the stars, the

---

[87] Fourier, *La fausse industrie*, Vol. II, p. 457-2; *Oeuvres*, Anthropos, Vol. IX, p. 457-2.

[88] Fourier, *Théorie de l'unité universelle*, Vol. II, p. 332; *Oeuvres*, Anthropos, Vol. III, p. 332. The great soul of a planet had its own glorious journey to look forward to: after the demise of the planet, it would enter another celestial body, and eventually become the soul of a universe, a biniverse, a triniverse, and so on (*ibid.*, pp. 326–327; *Oeuvres*, Anthropos, Vol. III, pp. 326–327).

living and the dead, into his system was supported in part by what the father of the phalanx described as the new science of analogy. Fourier concluded that because unity was one of the fundamental characteristics of Divinity, because everything was linked, true knowledge of one segment of reality opened the way to knowing other segments which had to be analogous to the first. Moreover, the theoretician of Harmony turned to analogy not for illustration or suggestion, but for proof. If Y was analogous to Z, then it had to be a certain way because of the nature of Z. The problem was to establish what was analogous to what, and then on the basis of the known to decipher the unknown. It is in this manner that Fourier sought to relate his social theory to Newtonian physics or the climatic and cosmic disasters of our planet to the horror of Civilization.

Charles Fourier delighted in analogies. His writings were replete with such statements as the following:

A musician who knows the relations of a simple octave with thirteen keys will learn quickly how to form a double octave with 32 keys and the pivots: without a knowledge of this distribution one can not understand:
Either the system and relations of the known planets,
Or the location of the four which are yet to be discovered,
Or the framework of the alphabet consisting of 32 plus the pivotal ones: â, a; ô, o,
Or the organization of the human races into 32 kinds and the pivotal ones.
Thus our treatises of geography cannot get to the point of classifying human races, and even less of understanding the purpose of their varieties.[89]

[89] Fourier, *Mnémonique géographique*, p. 11. Fourier must have meant that geographers could not get to the point of classifying human races correctly, for he proceeded to indicate mistakes in their classification. For Fourier's own statement of his discovery of analogy and of its central position in his system, see Fourier, *Théorie des*

Musical analogies were especially common, but the theoretician of Harmony also liked to match, for example, passions,
colors, mathematical calculations, geometric figures, and
metals. It would seem that in Fourier's ideal view all reality
was structured as parallel series integrated into one super-
formula.

But it was in particular in commenting on Civilization, in
establishing connections between "the substances of diverse
kingdoms and the passions of man" [90] that analogy became:

the most entertaining of the sciences; it gives a soul to all nature.
In every detail of animals and plants it depicts human passions
and social relations, the interior of man, as faithfully as a painter
depicts the exterior, and these pictures cut sharply because of the
fidelity of the brush. For example, why does the *lion* have clipped
ears, as if trimmed by scissors? This is so because the lion represents the king. One does not have kings listen to truth; the courtiers would not let it approach; sovereigns are thus *morally* deprived of the use of their ears.[91]

The donkey with his long ears stood, by contrast, for the
peasant whom it was customary to denounce openly. Or to
take the remarkable case of the noble elephant. That huge
and honorable beast expressed the four group passions of
friendship, love, family feeling, and ambition in their virtuous form. The elephant was a fine, but not servile, friend,
a decent and faithful lover, and an upright parent who refused to have children in captivity. The animal was no as-
cetic, for, in addition to devouring a huge amount of food, it

quatre mouvements et des destinées générales, p. 12; *Oeuvres*, Anthropos, Vol. I, p. 12.

[90] Fourier, *Sur l'esprit irreligieux des modernes* and *Dernières
analogies* (Paris, 1850), p. 58—the analogies occupy pages 49–63;
Oeuvres, Anthropos, Vol. XII, p. 210—the analogies occupy pages
201–216 of the volume.

[91] *Ibid.*, p. 49; *Oeuvres*, Anthropos, Vol. XII, p. 201.

enjoyed a fine dress and expensive utensils. The elephant had no coat and even covered itself with dust to indicate the fate of virtue in Civilization. It was an excellent but costly laborer, in accordance with the intention of nature that laborers live well. The elephant's tusks were magnificent, while the elephant's trunk was poorly clad, because the first represented the condition of the military and the second that of the workers in our society. Its behind was ludicrous, because people laugh behind the back of virtuous men. The teeth of the elephant were arranged in four groups, two ascending and two descending, by analogy with the two ascending and the two descending passions to which the animal gave expression. The elephant's tiny eyes showed the blindness of our virtuous men, who practice virtue themselves but do not look for ways to make it dominant in the world, whereas its huge crushed ears demonstrated the sad position of a virtuous human being who hears only hypocrisy or a praise of vice around him.[92]

If the elephant represented the sorry fate in Civilization of the four group passions positively developed, his counterpart, the disgusting dog, symbolized the negative evolution of these passions.[93] Many other animals, as well as plants, added their comments on human society. In fact, God was justified in creating even the most repulsive creatures, because they merely reflected the contemporary impasse of man. Still, one could also find hope by analogy. A disgusting caterpillar became a beautiful butterfly or a most useful silkworm—just as Civilization would one day become Harmony.[94]

[92] *Ibid.*, pp. 51–54; *Oeuvres*, Anthropos, Vol. XII, pp. 203–206.
[93] *Ibid.*, pp. 54–55; *Oeuvres*, Anthropos, Vol. XII, pp. 206–207.
[94] *Ibid.*, pp. 59–60. For a rich discussion of analogies in the plant world, see "Mosaique de tableaux en règne végétal" in Fourier, *Théorie de l'unité universelle*, Vol. III, pp. 222–241; *Oeuvres*, Anthropos, Vol. IV, pp. 222–241. See also Charles Fourier, "Analogie

Analogies of different kinds would play an important role in the education and intellectual life of the Harmonians. From a very early age children would be taught to recognize series everywhere, whether in their own phalanx, in such natural phenomena as light, which—as children would easily see with the help of a prism—constitutes a fine series of seven primary colors, or in the starry sky. Other analogies would make particular branches of knowledge, such as history and geography, interesting and meaningful. For instance, instead of teaching separately reigns in their chronological order one could present a group consisting of Charlemagne as the pivot, of Clovis, Hugues Capet, Louis IX, and Louis XIV as "the quadrille," and of Napoleon as the culminating "cumulative" personality. In this manner one could develop and transcend the good but simple work of Plutarch and become "a complex Plutarch" (*un Plutarque composé*).[95] Some of the analogies which gave structure to knowledge could be seen immediately by anyone who cared to look, others required thought. A special difficulty was

et cosmogonie," *La Phalange. Revue de la science sociale* (August, September–October, November–December 1848); *Oeuvres,* Anthropos, Vol. XII, pp. 35–199.

[95] Fourier, *Théorie de l'unité universelle,* Vol. IV, p. 283; *Oeuvres,* Anthropos, Vol. V, p. 283. Cf. Fourier, *Mnémonique géographique,* p. 6, where Napoleon is the "cumulative" figure for twelve rulers, ranging from Pericles to Peter the Great, so that "thirteen monarchs and thirteen epochs" can be taught at the same time. Children would also learn the complexity, or grafting, characteristic of nature and of Harmony, as against the simplicity of Civilization. Analogy would also, for example, transform the field of medicine, making it an exact science truly effective in combating disease (see, e.g., Fourier, *Manuscrits. Années 1857–1858* (Paris, 1858), p. 186; *Oeuvres,* Anthropos, Vol. XI, p. 186, second pagination), and revolutionize the disciplines of botany, physics, and algebra (Fourier, *De l'anarchie industrielle et scientifique,* p. 17). On the entire subject of analogy in Harmony, see also Fourier, *Le nouveau monde industriel et sociétaire,* pp. 459–467; *Oeuvres,* Anthropos, Vol. VI, pp. 459–467.

provided by the fact that Fourier's favorite group of analogies, the analogies *par excellence,* that is, comparisons between animals and plants on the one hand and human society on the other, contained sexual elements. Because children were to be kept ignorant of sex until the final phase of education, these analogies could not be used in the learning process. However, they would become a leading intellectual preoccupation of mature Harmonians who would constantly discover and publish ever-new analogies for the edification and amusement of themselves and of their fellows, and also, incidentally, for a high financial reward in the nature of a royalty.

Analogy and other peculiar processes of Fourier's reasoning helped to tie his cosmology and related doctrines, such as metempsychosis, to his project of social and economic reform on earth. The link was organic in the sense that all of Fourier's reasoning and system was of a piece. In this respect, as in some others, the father of Harmony saw better than many of his admirers and detractors. Moreover, cosmology and metempsychosis raised the significance of Fourier's teaching to a still higher plane. Not only the future of humanity, but the evolution of the cosmos itself, as well as the fate of the souls of the departed hinged on the adoption of the system proposed by the humble commercial employee. While salvation and blessedness beckoned on the one side, on the other there loomed the continuing and increasing horrors of Civilization, and even, as Fourier asserted on occasion, the prospect of the perishing of our planet.

The wits of Paris and their journals which judge a novelty according to the academic standing of its author will not fail to laugh at the news which I am going to announce: and this is that our globe is in imminent peril of death, and that it has no more than 3 *siéclades* to exist (3 times 144 = 432 years), if it does not consent in the course of this respite to the easy undertaking of a

passional phalanx of 818 contrasting characters, a test on which
our advent into Harmony depends.[96]

Indeed everything depended on the Messiah of reason and
his message.

4. *Implementation*

THE MESSIAH OF REASON

As has been noted in the preceding chapter, Fourier considered himself "the Messiah of reason" at the beginning of
his didactic publishing activity. And he held to this belief for
the remaining thirty-five years of his life. "Reason" referred,
of course, to the utopian socialist's formula and system. The
precise nature of Fourier's messiahship is less clear. That
messiahship, although essentially *sui generis* like so much
else about Fourier, acquired notably a certain Christian, or
rather quasi-Christian, coloring. Perhaps unconsciously even
more than consciously Fourier was seeking the most powerful messianic tradition that he could find to support his all-
important message and purpose.

That Fourier was no Christian in any ordinary sense cannot be denied. In addition to postulating his own God, the
father of the phalanx believed in the essential goodness of
man and considered salvation, fully obtainable on earth, to
lie in the complete release and full play of all passions. He
constantly assailed "superstition," a term which apparently
included, although Fourier never spelled it out, virtually all
the dogmas of virtually all the Christian denominations. At

---

[96] "Textes inédits de Charles Fourier presentés par Simone Debout
Oleszkiewicz," p. 175. For details of the impending destruction of
the globe, see Fourier, *Le nouveau monde amoureux*, p. 490;
Oeuvres, Anthropos, Vol. VII, p. 490.

the same time he proclaimed, as we have seen, his own far-reaching doctrines on such topics as the afterlife and the transmigration of souls. The Vatican was no doubt on firm ground when it placed Fourier on the Index.

Yet it is not sufficient to state simply that Fourier's teaching was not Christian. This formulation takes no account of Fourier's Christian background and, especially, of Fourier's own view of the matter. For Fourier's doctrine, although never called explicitly "the new Christianity," proposed to translate into practice the message of the Gospels. It belonged in this respect to a whole series of early nineteenth-century ideologies which, while representing a complete break with traditional Christianity, claimed Christ and Christ's work as their own. Or, to be more exact, one must point here too to an ambiguity in Fourier: an ambiguity between fulfilling Christianity and superseding it, between the figure of Christ and the "scientific" nature of the new teaching, a matter purely of reason and demonstration.[97]

Fourier's borrowing from Christianity was reflected most fully and explicitly in his use of Biblical citations.[98] This utilization ranged from isolated references to extensive expositions and discussions from the Gospels mobilized in sup-

[97] For a striking statement of this ambiguity see Henri Desroche, "Fouriérisme ambigu. Socialisme ou religion," *Revue internationale de philosophie*, Vol. XVI, No. 60 (1962), pp. 200–220. Cf. "There are two personages from whom I cannot part without denying myself: these are *Jesus Christ* and *Newton*." Fourier, *La fausse industrie*, Vol. II, p. 463-x; *Oeuvres*, Anthropos, Vol. IX, p. 463-x.

[98] Fourier also borrowed some religious symbolism and ritual for his own system, e.g., for the Little Hordes. These latter borrowings, however, were often generally religious rather than specifically Christian; they represented on the whole convenient acquisitions by an outsider, whereas by his use of Biblical citations Fourier tried to place himself in the center of the Christian tradition. It is beyond the scope of this book to discuss the general relationship between Christianity and the Age of Reason and subsequent European thought, including that of Fourier.

port of the utopian socialist's own mission and message.[99] In fact, as was so often the case with Fourier, everything received meaning in terms of his teaching and was used, in turn, to throw light on that teaching and its destiny. Christ, Fourier repeatedly pointed out, had never ceased denouncing the sophists, the philosophes, those scribes and Pharisees who "have taken away the key of knowledge: ye entered not in yourselves, and them that were entering in ye hindered (Luke 11:52)."[100] Condemning these learned men He turned instead to children, that is, to beings "given entirely to attraction and not at all to moral philosophy." "Verily I say unto you, Whosoever shall not receive the kingdom of God as a little child, he shall not enter therein (Mark 10:15)."[101] And He urged men: *"Quoerite et invenietis."*

Now salvation has been found. Christ spoke in parables of the Kingdom of Heaven and of the Holy Ghost who would be sent to console and teach men. Harmony was the answer.

Two revelations are necessary to guide humanity: the one that relates to the salvation of souls was made by Jesus Christ and the

[99] Fourier's favorite Biblical quotations included *"Aures habent et non audient: Oculos habent et non videbunt"* which served as the epigraph for his *Théorie de l'unité universelle* and "It is the blind that lead the blind." The utopian socialist's last major work, *La fausse industrie,* opened with another Biblical epigraph: *Quoecumque ignorant, blasphemant.*

Fourier treated the subject extensively in Fourier, *Le nouveau monde industriel et sociétaire,* pp. 423–450; *Oeuvres,* Anthropos, Vol. XI, pp. 423–450 and Fourier, *La fausse industrie,* Vol. II, pp. 457-5-458-2, 461–488, 505–516; *Oeuvres,* Anthropos, Vol. IX, pp. 457-5-458-2, 461–488, 505–516. See Riasanovsky, "L'emploi de citations bibliques dan l'oeuvre de Charles Fourier," pp. 31–43.

[100] Fourier, *Le nouveau monde industriel et sociétaire,* p. 362; *Oeuvres,* Anthropos, Vol. VI, p. 362.

[101] *Ibid.*

prophets; it is in no sense an object of study, but of *simple and pure faith.* The one that relates to the destiny of societies is brought to us by attraction; it is an object of study, of *speculative faith,* of hope in the intervention of God, and of a methodical search for His societary code.[102]

"I alone followed the instructions of Jesus Christ. I sought and I found." [103] "St. John the Baptist was the prophet precursor of Jesus, I am the prophet *post-cursor,* announced by Him, and completing His work of the rehabilitation of men, solely in its industrial aspect." [104] Christ had said:

"But the Comforter, which is the Holy Ghost, whom the Father will send in my name, He shall teach you all things (John 14:26)." Well, the Holy Ghost has as His organs all those who express new ideas, proved by mathematics and experience, such as my entirely mathematical theory. . . .[105]

The sense of a supremely high mission was blended with bitterness and rage at fellow men, who rejected the message, especially at the philosophes, the intellectuals:

When finally a man has sought and has found the code, which you despaired of ever seeing, what attitude must you take in regard to this invention? Are you in your senses if you slander it before it has received a proper examination? . . . Blush for this act of vandalism: it is for you that the evangelist said: "light is come into the world, and men loved darkness rather than light, because their deeds were evil (John 3:19)." [106]

---

[102] *Ibid.,* p. 360; *Oeuvres,* Anthropos, Vol. VI, p. 360.

[103] Fourier, *La fausse industrie,* Vol. II, p. 479; *Oeuvres,* Anthropos, Vol. IX, p. 479.

[104] *Ibid.,* p. 485; *Oeuvres,* Anthropos, Vol. IX, p. 485.

[105] *Ibid.,* p. 488. *Oeuvres,* Anthropos, Vol. IX, p. 488.

[106] Fourier, *Le nouveau monde industriel et sociétaire,* p. 377; *Oeuvres,* Anthropos, Vol. VI, p. 377.

Christ Himself had declared that blasphemy against the Holy Ghost would never be pardoned either in this world or in the world to come.

These and other such citations indicate clearly that Fourier wanted to ground his messiahship in the Christian tradition and present his message as part of the Christian revelation.[107] Yet he always qualified. He was concerned solely with the "industrial aspect" of salvation. In contrast to that of St. John the Baptist, Fourier's mission was not personal, but "concurrent, a career open to all, the prize of a special study assigned to human reason, the prize appropriate to whomever would do the work of interpreting the divine code, the analytic and synthetic calculus of passional attraction.[108] Although messianic elements in the utopian socialist's psychology and teaching were very strong from the

[107] He also found numerous specific points in the Bible illustrating and supporting his teaching, and he was quick to overcome such obstacles to his views as Christ's assertion that Christ's kingdom was not of this world: certainly it was not of this world as it now stood, not of Civilization; it will become of this world when the world enters the stage of Harmony (Fourier, *ibid.*, p. 365; *Oeuvres,* Anthropos, Vol. VI, p. 365). As to the resemblances between Christ's teaching and Fourier's, perhaps most remarkable is Fourier's interpretation of Christ as a hedonist: at the wedding in Cana He changed water into "exquisite wine," He fed five thousand people with bread and fish, He complained of His hard lot when He had no place to rest his head, He reprimanded the Jews for reproaching Him His love of good meals, and He sat down for a refined dinner at a Pharisee's while a courtesan spread perfumes over Him, etc. (Fourier, *ibid.*, p. 364; *Oeuvres,* Anthropos, Vol. VI, p. 364). It should be added that this view of Christianity was unusual for Fourier. More often he argued that Christian precepts, frequently the opposite of his, were by that very token appropriate for Civilization, while Fourier's were meant for Harmony. In Civilization one was forced to restrain one's passions, one had to be modest, self-denying, and so forth. See my above-mentioned article for more detail on Fourier's use of Biblical citations.

[108] Fourier, *La fausse industrie,* Vol. II, p. 485; *Oeuvres,* Anthropos, Vol. IX, p. 485.

beginning and apparently even grew with time, becoming particularly prominent during the last years of his life, Fourier did not proclaim himself simply the Messiah. To the end he preferred to be a "hypomessiah," a "sub-Messiah," a "vice-Messiah," "the Messiah of reason." [109]

"Reason" remained essential to Fourier, standing in the way of a possible plunge into religion and the founding of a religious sect.[110] As the father of Harmony warned in the same passage in which he proclaimed himself the "post-cursor" prophet of Christianity: "Let us be careful not to link mysticism to a purely scientific matter." [111] Nor was imagination any more welcome. Writing of his message, Fourier asserted with vehemence:

Before we proceed further let us note that I have not *imagined* this light (*fanal*), I have *observed* it in nature. Many people believe that they are paying me a flattering compliment when they tell me that I have imagination. This means assimilating me to their scientific charlatans. I *imagine* nothing. I invent, I draw my theories from *observation* and experience, in accordance with the precepts of Condillac and of Descartes. This is not imagining.[112]

[109] Concerning Fourier's use of various "messianic" terms see, in addition to the material already cited, Fourier's very interesting notes to a conversation between Lamartine and Lady Esther Stanhope in Lamartine's *Voyage en Orient*. These scribbled interjections and comments were published as the eighth fragment, pp. 127–128, in Fourier, *Egarement de la raison . . .* and *Fragments*.

[110] Another obstacle to establishing a sect might well have been Fourier's determination to appeal to all men of every persuasion rather than segregate himself and his followers. This attitude of Fourier will be discussed in the next section of this chapter.

[111] Fourier, *La fausse industrie,* Vol. II, p. 485; *Oeuvres,* Anthropos, Vol. IX, p. 485.

[112] Charles Fourier, Unpublished manuscripts, Cahier 10/9, p. 137. For a more charitable treatment of imagination as an aid in scientific investigation, with a reference to Kepler, see Fourier, *Manuscrits* (Paris, 1852), p. 127; *Oeuvres,* Anthropos, Vol. X, p. 127, second pagination. Still, here too Fourier calls the praise of imagination in an inventor "a very stupid compliment."

The father of the phalanx insisted that he was a discoverer and an inventor—he used the two terms interchangeably—of the new system: nothing more, but also nothing less.[113] To elucidate his role and contribution, he liked especially to compare himself to the hypothetical inventors of gunpowder and of the compass.[114] These men too could offer humanity

[113] Fourier's characteristically careless use of "discovery" and "invention" probably relates to what he considered to be the fundamental character of his system. The system was a discovery, because it represented Fourier's penetration of the laws of nature as applied to human society. Yet Fourier drew the formula of this correct human society and offered it to his fellow-men as an invention to be put into operation.

As usual, Fourier proceeded to subdivide inventors into categories and to deal in detail with his own qualities as an inventor. Cf. one of his more interesting discussions of the matter: "1. The cultivated genre, the genius of invention. 2. The rough genre, the instinct of invention. 3. The fortuitous genre, invention by chance. Of these three genres, the intermediate, the instinctual or rough one, is perhaps the most fruitful, and, as a result, the most worthy of protection. I belong to these inventors of the rough genre who owe nothing to science and have everything from instinct. This is a rank inferior to but no less useful than genius, and it merits protection all the more because the author does not have the resources possessed by well-educated genius. It is not an obstacle to discoveries; it cannot be denied that they fall to the lot of instinct as much as to that of genius; one finds mechanics by instinct who would be able to construct a clock without ever having looked inside one; instinct is all the more prolific in discoveries, because it is stopped neither by prejudices nor by false doctrines. Condillac defined intellectual virtuosos well by saying, 'Those who will have studied nothing will understand better than those who will have received an extensive education.' He could have added, *will invent better*." Fourier, Unpublished manuscripts, Cahier 10/9, p. 132.

[114] See, for instance, Charles Fourier, "L'inventeur et son siècle," *La Phalange. Revue de la science sociale,* First Semester, Vol. IX (1849), pp. 207–211 for the compass, and p. 233 for gunpowder. In general terms, Fourier also liked to compare himself to Columbus, another discoverer of a new world, and to Galileo, as well as, of course and always, to Newton.

It is worth noting that Fourier not only considered his entire

startling and far-reaching changes and developments. Their views and promises must have sounded fantastic to their contemporaries. Yet at present no one questioned their correctness. Demonstration sufficed to make scientifically right views generally acceptable.

THE STRUGGLE FOR RECOGNITION

Demonstration thus became the heart of the matter. But demonstration, that is, the establishment of a trial phalanx, implied a certain measure of recognition and support. Yet Fourier's first statement of his teaching, his *Théorie des quatre mouvements et des destinées générales,* published in 1808, attracted very little attention, almost all of it of a critical and some of it of a derisive nature. The harsh reception probably contributed to the fact that the theoretician of Harmony did not present another full exposition of his views until 1822.[115] And even after the *Traité de l'association*

system to be a discovery, but also referred to parts of it as distinct discoveries, sometimes with particular dates. At times one discovered more than what one had been looking for. The search often took years. For instance, Fourier stated that he discovered only in 1819 the passional calculus for a small phalanx of 500 and even 200 people. Fourier, *Manuscrits* (Paris, 1851), pp. 5–7; *Oeuvres,* Anthropos, Vol. X, pp. 5–7, first pagination. See also notably Fourier, Unpublished manuscripts, Cahier 10/9, pp. 36, 75. Emile Poulat, "Le séjour de Fourier en Bugey (1816–1821)," *Le Bugey* (1956), pp. 1–25, especially p. 10, and Fourier's letter in Pellarin, *op. cit.,* pp. 197–200. In working out his calculus Fourier followed "the algebraic procedure." Fourier, *Manuscrits* (Paris, 1851), p. 274; *Oeuvres,* Anthropos, Vol. X, p. 274, first pagination.

[115] The selection from Fourier's manuscripts (pp. 193–240), "L'inventeur et son siècle," cited in the preceding footnote, the first part of which bears the title "the sphinx without Oedipus or the enigma of the four movements" (pp. 193–206), is of great value in judging Fourier's reaction to the reception of his first book and more broadly to his critics and reading public in general. But it must be used with caution. Considering the fiasco of his book with the advantage of hindsight, Fourier claimed that the fantastic selection

domestique-agricole and, seven years later, *Le nouveau monde industriel et sociétaire* came out, their author remained little known but much derided. Although a few disciples finally appeared, rival advocates of sweeping social reforms, such as Saint-Simon and Owen, acquired prominence. The Messiah of reason, with his all-embracing message of salvation, found himself in an indifferent and even hostile world.

Fourier tried to explain. He deserved consideration if only because he continued the universally accepted work of Newton, digging in the same precious mine. Anyone could find a single day to devote to an important matter. A day meant twelve working hours. Yet he offered to teach his system in just six lessons, if only people would listen. "One could even, by limiting oneself to a skimming of the [new] science, acquire in one lesson sufficient notions to be convinced that the mechanics of passions and of universal unity have indeed been discovered. . . ."[116] The crucial experiment itself would not have to last long. Once a trial phalanx was established, "six weeks of exercise should suffice for the demonstration, and should cause general imitation."[117] Moreover,

and organization of material was baffling on purpose, to confute critics and would-be plagiarists. It should be emphasized that while Fourier represented the form of the book as a device serving special purposes, he never questioned the validity of its content, "Such is the book of the *four movements,* a book which is a masquerade by its methodical violation of rules, its premature and inopportune information, and other studied bizarre features. As for the rest, I do not have a syllable in it to disavow" (p. 206).

[116] Fourier, *La fausse industrie,* Vol. II, p. E3; *Oeuvres,* Anthropos, Vol. IX, p. E3.

[117] Charles Fourier in *La Reforme Industrielle ou le Phalanstère,* No. 1 (June 1, 1832), p. 7. Six weeks was Fourier's favorite time span needed for the trial phalanx to prove itself, although occasionally he varied it. Two or three years would be required for the phalanxes to become the universal mode of life, replacing through imitation not only Civilization but also all barbarian and savage societies.

with his proposal to save mankind Fourier sought no personal profit or advantage. In contrast to other inventors, he did not ask for the highest salary, the management of finances, or other lucrative functions: he wanted to be only a simple assistant in the project, the pilot directing the mechanism.[118] Even the eternal glory and priority of his invention could in a sense be shared, for an invention, to be effective, needed not only the inventor, but also others, notably an "orator" to attract attention to it, and especially a realizer, or realizers to put it into operation. Besides, as Fourier never ceased to point out, his epoch-making discovery opened enormous new vistas where there would surely be enough creative work and fame for all. In terms of scientific fields alone, not only cosmology and analogy needed further development, but there were many other new sciences which the father of Harmony had barely time to invent and which were waiting for their ploughmen.[119] The very fact that Fourier's teaching humiliated all of Civilization, both its learned men and its ordinary citizens, had to be considered a happy augury, because it indicated that the benefits of the utopian socialist's discovery would also extend to everyone and everything.[120]

The point about benefit to all needed further elucidation. To be sure, Harmony would mean universal blessedness. Still, Fourier was concerned lest certain special groups consider his plan of reform a challenge to their well-being, and he hastened to assure them that they too would gain in every way from the change. For example, the new system would

---

[118] See, e.g., Fourier, *La fausse industrie*, Vol. I, p. ee377; *Oeuvres*, Anthropos, Vol. VIII, p. 377.

[119] Fourier mentioned the names of a few of these additional sciences, but did not elaborate. On one occasion he claimed to be the inventor of 152 sciences (*ibid.*, p. 300; *Oeuvres*, Anthropos, Vol. VIII, p. 300).

[120] Fourier, Unpublished manuscripts, Cahier 10/9, p. 113.

have no tariffs and, therefore, no customs officials. But these officials had nothing to worry about. Just the opposite, the social transformation would bring them a fourfold advantage: they would retain half their present salaries; they would receive full salaries in their new positions related to agriculture; they would exchange ungrateful and insipid work for a pleasant occupation with a guaranteed regular advancement; and they would benefit greatly from the cheapness of life.[121] The utopian socialist's most remarkable arrangement was meant to satisfy his main enemies, the philosophes, the intellectuals, the critics:

As for the rest, let the sophists be reassured: the explosion which will strike their libraries will be for them a horn of plenty. I regret to announce that an immense fortune is guaranteed them: I do not wish it to them, for I cannot like a sect that for 24 years has been riddling me with calumnies; but I must confess that, because of an extreme need of men of letters capable of directing education, the societary order will build bridges of gold for all experienced writers, good rhetoricians, good critics, and capable of teaching the young. All will obtain copious dividends from the provinces where they will accept the directing role, and they will live there splendidly without the fear of removal.

Their writings, while to be sure thrown into the river of forgetfulness from the scientific point of view, will be resurrected from the comic point of view. They will be published in several million copies for the perpetual amusement of the globe, and there will be added to each page an explicative gloss on the contradictions and absurdities with which these controversies swarm.

The glossators will be the philosophers themselves; they will parody their oracles and legislators, from Plato to Rousseau, from Minos to Target. For them it will be an entirely new and immensely lucrative occupation; a treatise of three volumes will be parodied in three months, and, supposing it is published in three million copies (about six for each phalanx), the writer, were he

---

[121] Fourier, *Manuscrits. Années 1853–1856* (Paris, 1856), p. 141; *Oeuvres*, Anthropos, Vol. XI, p. 141, first pagination.

to receive no more than a franc, will obtain a profit of three million on this parody. It is in this manner that philosophy, the new phoenix, will become, through its demise, a Pactolus for its disciples, who will clown with it and give it the immortality of ridicule.[122]

The philosophes would not understand, the critics continued to deride Fourier's teaching, and the public to neglect it. Enraged, the father of Harmony kept assailing his enemies from the beginning of his career as a writer to his very death. He was especially incensed at the men of letters and journalists who could so easily destroy reputations and against whom an author without an established position and wealth had no resort. Behind their disregard and disdain the theoretician of the phalanx saw a plot to keep his discovery and system away from the public, whether by a conspiracy of silence or by ridicule. In fact, they would do anything, from slandering him personally and classifying his teaching with the social panaceas of various charlatans to drawing attention to the alleged wisdom of India, and thus away from Fourier. At the same time they remained ready to pounce on and snatch anything Fourier did not properly secure in order to plagiarize it.[123]

In righteous indignation the theoretician of the phalanx demanded that he be given an equal opportunity to answer

[122] Charles Fourier in *La Reforme Industrielle ou le Phalanstère,* No. 6 (July 6, 1832), p. 53. Pactolus refers to a river in Lydia, in Asia Minor, which yielded gold-bearing sand. The Target in question must have been Guy-Jean-Baptiste Target (1733–1806), a prominent writer, lawyer, and member of the Constituent Assembly. Fourier made perhaps his most extensive effort to convince the intellectuals in his section on "the scholars and the artists dupes of Civilization" in Fourier, *Théorie de l'unité universelle,* Vol. II, pp. 348–451; *Oeuvres,* Anthropos, Vol. III, pp. 348–451.

[123] See, for example, Fourier's list of 32 kinds of enemies and obstacles opposing and maligning him: *La fausse industrie,* Vol. II, pp. B5(704)–C5; *Oeuvres,* Anthropos, Vol. IX, pp. B5(704)–C5.

his critics, that newspaper writers deposit money as a pledge of their honorable behavior, that journalists be held collectively responsible for prevarication and slander. Never at a loss in the matter of organizing, Fourier devised "juries for the examination of discoveries," "tribunals of counterweight and guarantee," "juries of guarantee" and other such bodies which had to be introduced in France and Europe to assure an inventor a fair hearing.[124] He insisted also that his system be given the attention of various scholarly societies sponsoring different competitions and contests, whether these dealt with questions of religion or of indigence. Fourier deserved their prizes, because his system solved their problems, although sometimes their questions were so narrowly worded as to miss the point of his answer.[125] In all his dealings with the philosophes Fourier maintained a stern dignity: "They must remember that they are the sinners and the obscurantists in social politics, and I am the Messiah, the creator of that science. In opening for them the way of salvation I acquire the right to point to them their faults and to summon them to repentance."[126]

[124] The three quoted names of projected institutions refer to three sections, pp. 34–45, 46–48, and 237–241 in: Fourier, *Théorie de l'unité universelle*, Vol. I; *Oeuvres*, Anthropos, Vol. II, pp. 34–45, 46–48, and 237–241.

[125] Witness Fourier's fury at the Academy of Moral and Political Sciences which asked in 1836 in its annual competition the idiotic question of what constituted indigence, as well as a question about its causes, but not the all-important one of its cure. See the sections entitled "winning the Beaujour prize," and "proofs of treason obtained from the Beaujour prize" in Fourier, *La fausse industrie*, Vol. I, pp. 409–411, 402–408; *Oeuvres*, Anthropos, Vol. VIII, pp. 409–411, 402–408. Cf. *ibid.*, p. 138 footnote; *Oeuvres*, Anthropos, Vol. VIII, p. 138 footnote re Fourier and an analysis of civilization proposed by the Athénée of l'Hôtel de Ville.

[126] Fourier, *Manuscrits. Années 1857–1858* (Paris, 1858), p. 91; *Oeuvres*, Anthropos, Vol. XI, p. 91, second pagination.

As years went by Fourier counted with a combination of despair and grim satisfaction the price of human folly. Would the French never learn?

France for its part has lost in the course of these seven years more than 1,200,000 to 1,300,000 men in battle, apart from the revolutionary plagues. Paying with one's head, as the French have done, is not being a smart joker. Must they not tremble at the thought that, if the calculus of attraction is correct, it could have been put into operation from the year 1808. The smarties have to reproach themselves for all the blood that has been spilled and all the plagues that have been endured since the bad reception which they gave to this discovery. I was quite certain that this insult would be washed off with rivers of French blood. . . . Since 1808 He [God] has directed events as if destiny has undertaken to punish Civilization, and above all the French. Are there any insults or scourges that have not beset them since? The French nation and the French name have become the laughing stock of mankind. French victories themselves have become crimes for those who won them. Opprobrium, ruin, public servitude, in sum all the calamities which assailed, devoured [   ] date from the time when it delivered an insult at the discovery of the calculus of attraction. The capital where this discovery was insulted has been invaded twice, defiled by the outrages of its enemies; it believed that it ruled the world, it has become its plaything. I repeat it, if I had power over destiny, could I ask for a more resounding vengeance? . . .

It was appropriate to wait for the end of this political tragedy and let the French surfeit themselves with baths of blood, and after that present to them a parallel between the benefits which they have refused and the ills which they have suffered. I made a secret resolve to wait until France loses another million heads in combat, and every time that I was asked the announced calculus of attraction I gave dilatory answers. Finally the year 1813 paid off amply the tribute of a million heads which I had imposed upon France. There is even today an excess in massacre of 300,000 or 400,000 heads. Now I can invite the French gentlemen to draw a parallel, to compare the brilliant fate which they would have enjoyed since 1808, on the hypothesis of the foundation of unity which could have taken place that same year. . . .[127]

Neither Fourier's insistent explanations nor even the dreadful lessons of history could penetrate the folly of the Frenchmen or of mankind in general. The utopian socialist's later writings fared no better than his *Théorie des quatres mouvements*. The world remained unreformed. The father of Harmony kept counting the years and pointing out to humanity the opportunities lost. If preparations for a trial phalanx had been made in the autumn of 1830, it could have been established in the spring of 1831, and could have achieved full success in June of that year; all of Civilization would have been transformed into a society of phalanxes in 1832, the barbarians would have followed in 1833, and the savages in 1834; the satellites would have returned to our planet, and new creations would have taken place in the sixth year of operation of the new system, that is, in 1838. Or, to put it differently, the war in Algeria would have ended in January, 1833, the Chinese, the Japanese, and all other barbarians would have joined the new unitary system of the globe, and, in 1834, a congress of global hierarchy would have met and proclaimed Louis-Philippe the omniarch of our planet.[128]

[127] Fourier, "L'inventeur et son siècle," pp. 223–224. The brackets enclosing an empty space stand for a word which the editors could not decipher.

[128] Fourier, *La fausse industrie*, Vol. I, pp. 436–437; *Oeuvres*, Anthropos, Vol. VIII, pp. 436–437. The volume was published in 1835. Fourier's definition and treatment of barbarians and savages will be discussed in the next chapter.

In addition to showing the advantages of Harmony, Fourier from the beginning gave advice to his readers to help them with the transition to the new system. They were not to build new buildings, not to emigrate in search of fortune, "not to sacrifice present good for future good," but to produce children, accumulate "mobile riches," such as gold and silver, and so forth. See, for instance, "Advice to the

Because no one would listen, Fourier resignedly repeated Arago's sad observation: "The man of genius is always unrecognized whenever he outdistances his age, no matter in what manner." [129] At times he tried to warn mankind that he might die suddenly, and his message disappear with him. On other occasions he seemed to accept that eventuality, looking only to a vindication after death at least two generations later, Fourier's ungrateful contemporaries having thus been deprived of the great discovery. Only after perhaps a hundred or a thousand trials based on material scattered in Fourier's writings: "Finally, when they will have fully established all the details of the mechanics of passions, they will realize, from various enigmatic sentences in my announcements, that I held the entire system in my hands. My triumph and my glory will be as complete after my death as if the trial had been made during my lifetime." [130]

Such pessimism however was the exception rather than the rule. In general, and in spite of all disappointments and obstacles, Fourier remained convinced that his priceless discovery would be adopted by mankind, and immediately rather than later. The philosophes, to be sure, showed no signs of repentance, or even of a qualified understanding, and because of them public opinion continued both its indifference and its hostility. But this could be bypassed. After all, only the founding of a single trial phalanx was necessary to assure the universal triumph of Fourier's system. Anyone with means, or even without means but with prestige or pro-

Civilized concerning the coming social metamorphosis" in Fourier, *Théorie des quatre mouvements et des destinées générales*, pp. 307–311; *Oeuvres*, Anthropos, Vol. I, pp. 307–311.

[129] Fourier used this assertion, and several others of the same tenor, as epigraphs to Fourier, *Pièges et charlatanisme des deux sectes Saint-Simon et Owen*. He also utilized it as an epigraph to the second volume of *La fausse industrie*.

[130] Fourier, "L'inventeur et son siècle," pp. 198–199.

motional ability, could provide the resources for Fourier to establish such a phalanx. Because everyone, ruler, subject, or organization, would benefit enormously from the undertaking, obvious candidates were in the hundred thousand. Only one of them had to be prevailed upon to make the attempt. "I could not repeat too often to my followers and partisans that they must devote themselves exclusively to persuading, convincing one out of a hundred thousand candidates, *one is enough.*" The utopian socialist's life became in large part a search for and an expectation of candidates, or rather the candidate, and his writing reflected the same preoccupation.[131]

[131] Fourier, *La fausse industrie,* Vol. II, p. P8 (787); *Oeuvres,* Anthropos, Vol. IX, p. P8 (787).

Cf. Fourier's daily waiting, at noon, for a visitor who would subsidize a phalanx, mentioned in the preceding chapter as an outstanding example of his persistent adherence to a rigid schedule. In his works, Fourier devoted numerous pages and sections to listing candidates and convincing them that they must support a trial phalanx. While strictly speaking these pages and sections were not part of the utopian socialist's system, they became its necessary accompaniment. Fourier himself apparently attached a great importance to them and wrote them with earnestness and even passion. The longer discussions of the matter include: Fourier, *Le nouveau monde industriel et sociétaire,* pp. 483–489 ("Candidature individuelle") (*Oeuvres,* Anthropos, Vol. VI, pp. 483–489); Fourier, *La fausse industrie,* Vol. I, pp. 210–233 ("Candidats et dupes") (*Oeuvres,* Anthropos, Vol. VIII, pp. 210–233); *ibid.,* pp. 233–247 ("Appendice") (*Oeuvres,* Anthropos, Vol. VIII, pp. 233–247); *ibid.,* pp. 337–340 ("Moyen d'en finir des conspirateurs") (*Oeuvres,* Anthropos, Vol. VIII, pp. 337–340); *ibid.,* pp. 340–344 ("Direction manquée") (*Oeuvres,* Anthropos, Vol. VIII, pp. 340–344); Vol. II, pp. E8 (778)– P8 (787) ("Candidats et disciples") (*Oeuvres,* Anthropos, Vol. IX, pp. E8 [778]–P8 [787]); *ibid.,* pp. P8 (787)–G9 (803) ("Etudes sur les candidats") (*Oeuvres,* Anthropos, Vol. IX, pp. P8 [787]–G9 [803]).

It was this belief of Fourier in a benefactor who would subsidize a phalanx and thus transform the world that evoked particular criticism from his Marxist commentators.

THE CANDIDATES

The original candidate in all probability was Napoleon. It was to him that Fourier appealed in most flattering terms in his early works, and it was the activities of the emperor that formed the immediate background for Fourier's plans and expectations.

Already a new Hercules has appeared; his immense works make his name resound from pole to pole, and humanity, accustomed by him to the spectacle of miraculous deeds, expects from him something prodigious that will change the fate of the world. Peoples, your presentiments will be realized; the most brilliant mission is reserved to the greatest of the heroes; it is he whose task it is to erect universal Harmony on the ruins of Barbarism and Civilization.

Nor apparently did anyone rival Napoleon in Fourier's eyes at that time. This belief in the French emperor, characteristic of many writers of the age, was buttressed, in Fourier's case, by some specific arguments: in particular, the theoretician of the phalanx appreciated Napoleon's drive toward European political unity and integration which he considered most propitious for the establishment of Harmony. Even after the fall of Napoleon Fourier continued to praise his bid for a unification of Europe, although he found fault with his methods and drew repeatedly a highly critical, although not entirely one-sided, portrait of his most famous contemporary.[132]

[132] Quoted from Fourier, *Théorie des quatre mouvements et des destinées générales*, p. 101; *Oeuvres*, Anthropos, Vol. I, p. 101. Fourier's comments on Napoleon are scattered throughout his writings. For a more concentrated treatment which emphasizes the problem of European unity and brings up sixteen accusations against the emperor and three "causes justificatives," see Fourier, *Manuscrits* (Paris, 1951), pp. 317–334; *Oeuvres*, Anthropos, Vol. X, pp. 317–334, first pagination.

Appealing to his own ruler and government to establish a phalanx and thus introduce the new order seemed to Fourier the natural way to proceed. After Napoleon, he turned to Napoleon's successors. In Charles Pellarin's words:

> With this goal and this hope Fourier addressed himself to all the governments which succeeded one another in France and to their ministers, as well as, without distinction, to all influential people of every nuance of opinion. After he published, in 1822, the *Traité de l'association domestique agricole,* and, in 1823, the *Sommaire* of the Treatise, the author had copies of them distributed, accompanied by extensive letters, fitting the disposition of every person whom he wanted to win for his cause. It was as much Monsieur de Villèle as the leaders of the opposition.[133]

The appeals continued, of course, beyond 1823. In fact, Fourier was convinced that Baron Guillaume-Antoine Capelle, the minister of public works in Polignac's cabinet, came to appreciate his proposal and was on the point of translating it into practice when the Bourbon monarchy fell in the revolution of July, 1830. After that, the father of Harmony concentrated his attention on Louis-Philippe, although certainly not to the exclusion of other possible candidates. The new king especially needed Fourier's invention to establish his prestige and guarantee his security. The founding of a pha-

---

[133] Charles Pellarin, *Fourier et ses contemporains. L'utopie et la routine. L'expérimentation et l'empirisme en matière sociale.* (Published together with the text of:) *Lettre de Fourier au Grand Juge* (*4 nivose an XII*) (Paris, 1874), p. 37.

It is this unceasing and indiscriminate appeal of Fourier to all shades of political opinion in France, reactionary and liberal, clerical and anti-clerical, Bourbon, Orleanist, and Bonapartist, that makes a study of his political views an unrewarding subject. Nor, given Fourier's assumptions, was his attitude at all inappropriate: only the establishment of a phalanx mattered. That establishment, it might be noted, would eliminate all politics together with the entire Civilization.

lanx would lead to his elevation to the omniarchate of the
globe, while grateful people would provide enormous dow-
ries and allowances to his numerous children whom royalty
all over the world would hasten to seek in marriage. Furthermore, the phalanx would save the king from both the
rebels of the Right in the Vendée and the terrorists of the
Left in Paris who would lose all their following to the triumphant monarch. There was no problem faced by Louis-
Philippe which Fourier could not solve.[134]

Fourier turned first to his own ruler, and he emphasized
his patriotic desire to give France a prior use of his great discovery. Still, mankind and indeed the cosmos could not wait
indefinitely for the men who guided French destinies to
make up their minds. The theoretician of Harmony, therefore, addressed also foreign potentates, as well as societies
and private individuals both at home and abroad. By the
time he published *La fausse industrie* the list of candidates
was divided into five categories: the French court, other
rulers, the ministers, the great landed proprietors and capitalists, and the scholarly world.[135] Louis-Philippe remained
the monarch most in need of Fourier's invention. Among
other things, the utopian socialist this time threatened him
with a legitimist crusade of European powers on the one
hand, while on the other he indicated that within three
months the sovereigns of Russia, England, and Austria
could be made to seek his protection, leaving only the emperor of China as his equal on the face of the globe.

[134] Fighting his endless battle against the *philosophes*, Fourier
even promised to demonstrate to Louis-Philippe "that scientific conspiracies are sisters and mothers of political conspiracies and of in-
fernal machines." Fourier, *La fausse industrie,* Vol. I, p. 401;
Oeuvres, Anthropos, Vol. VIII, p. 401.

[135] See footnote number 131 for the distribution of the principal
material on the candidates in *La fausse industrie.* I am combining
this material in my exposition.

Moreover, Louis-Philippe had to hurry also because he was not the only claimant to the French throne. "But of all the disappointments the most piquant . . . will be that of the court of France in case that the old court, which has found refuge in Prague, will have the whim to listen to sage advice and to establish, in three months, the nucleus of the universal metamorphosis." [136] And if the older Bourbons could triumphantly profit by Fourier's discovery, so could the Bonapartists.

Prince Louis Napoleon III would not have ventured the Strasbourg folly had he been informed that he can *whenever he wishes* obtain without conspiracy or commotion a throne superior to that of France, and count the king of France among his vassals, provided the king of France does not take the initiative of the attempt. Were Prince Louis to become only the Caesar of the Latin West, which will include the empires of the Latin idiom, France, Spain, and Italy in its proper limits, he will already be superior to the emperor of France.
He can, by the sole influence of his title of the direct heir of Napoleon, find in an instant subscribers for a trial attempt at unity. So many people of means hold to Napoleon's memory! [137]

They would tell Napoleon's heir that, while refusing to listen to any conspiratorial plans, they would willingly help in a beneficial undertaking which, if successful, would elevate him by acclamation of kings and peoples. But the Bonapartes seemed determined to do the wrong thing. While Prince Louis Napoleon resorted to plotting, Prince Joseph was gathering thousands of farmers in Nashville in an expensive effort to establish a useless settlement. Had he in-

[136] Fourier, *La fausse industrie*, Vol. I, p. 246; *Oeuvres*, Anthropos, Vol. VIII, p. 246. Cf. "A fine career for *Henry V*, he would be much more than king of France: his mother, the duchess, is enterprising, this idea would be to her taste," *ibid.*, Vol. II, p. 18 (781); *Oeuvres*, Anthropos, Vol. IX, p. 18 (781).

[137] *Ibid.*, Vol. II, p. E8 (778)–F8 (779); *Oeuvres*, Anthropos, Vol. IX, pp. E8 (778)–F8 (779).

stead taken half-a-dozen lessons from Fourier and founded a trial phalanx, he "would have been today the hereditary omniarch of the globe." [138]

Whereas staying behind could destroy one's chances, no one would suffer from rushing in. There would be thrones, lands, and peoples for all. If the Orleanist branch of the Bourbon family remained in France, the elder one could establish itself in Italy, with Florence as the probable capital. In the new order enormous lands would be brought under cultivation, population would be transported to till them, relieving pressure at home, and the entire planet would be rationally organized. As a result:

In sum, I can prove, dividers in hand, that, while making in full generous provision for the present titleholders, at the rate of 3 for 2 (territory with three million souls for two million brought in, and 3,000 francs of income for an eliminated position worth 2,000), in providing even better for them in accordance with the peculiarities of the locality, there will still remain to furnish and allot one hundred forty empires with surface equal to France, not counting what would be found in the austral and boreal regions after the thawing of the poles; I predict the content of at least ten empires there: a total of 150 empires to distribute, and consequently approximately 500 kingdoms, and so on down the higher and the lower ranks.[139]

All of these positions were to be doubled for women, who were to be rulers in their own right, not wives of rulers. No wonder that Fourier's rearrangement of the world could provide for all crowned heads, members of their families, claimants to thrones, and even private individuals.

Of the rulers, many had special reasons to welcome the utopian socialist's discovery. Bernadotte of Sweden needed a

---

[138] *Ibid.*, Vol. I, p. 226; *Oeuvres,* Anthropos, Vol. VIII, p. 226.
[139] *Ibid.*, Vol. I, p. 228; *Oeuvres,* Anthropos, Vol. VII, p. 228. For a more modest estimate see p. 219 of the same volume.

solid base in his adopted country—Fourier added that because of Bernadotte's sordid ingratitude to France he would be sorry to see him win the great prize. The Duke of Leuchtenberg required consolidation and a brilliant coup. Both "the Prince of Orange" and King Leopold of Belgium would be well-advised to establish a trial phalanx: the first had just lost half of his kingdom, the second was unable to obtain in full the half given to him and was uncertain of the future. Nicholas I of Russia was an outstanding candidate for a different reason. He was the only sovereign to think of succession to Napoleon and universal domination; but he simply remained unaware of the easy way to become the omniarch of the globe. Elsewhere Fourier emphasized the great advantages for Russia of the climatic changes which would follow the introduction of his system. "As to England, it could well undertake a mass suicide by hanging; its cabinet, its Parliament, its profound politicians, its subtle economists, its eager manufacturers, all these good people would be covered with jeers, and would have nothing left to do but hang themselves, if the palm of societary initiative is carried off by France." [140] Besides, England needed Fourier's invention to provide for its swarming poor and to strengthen its rule in India. Austria, in its turn, needed it to consolidate its territory. Still other monarchs, such as those of Bavaria and Denmark, had their own reasons to sponsor the new order.

Beyond Europe, Mohammed Ali faced the Turkish threat. Indeed Enfantin could not have done him a better service than to inform him of Fourier's system. Unfortunately Enfantin had "the vice of all rationalists and progressivists, he does not want to adopt a single idea of another person." [141]

---

[140] *Ibid.*, Vol. I, p. 217; *Oeuvres*, Anthropos, Vol. VIII, p. 217.
[141] *Ibid.*, Vol. I, p. 243; *Oeuvres*, Anthropos, Vol. VIII, p. 243. Owen too, Fourier argued on another occasion, should have estab-

Finally, in the new world Fourier paid particular attention to the United States. The North American republic required his assistance, because it had "many storms to conjure": the danger of a split between the North and the South, the threat of a Negro uprising, "the hatred of the hordes which have been pushed back and especially of the cannibals of the West," and the need to improve the temperatures.[142] The father of Harmony stressed repeatedly the fact that his discovery would convert the Indians into enthusiastic full-fledged members of the new system, disposing of the inhuman efforts and plans to exterminate them.

If Fourier's discovery could bring enormous advantages to the existing rulers and political entities, it could as easily create new ones. Prince Adam Czartoryski, for example, had merely to turn to Fourier to resurrect the Poland of his dreams.

Prince Czartoryski would be eminently appropriate: he would have as shareholders all those interested in Poland; he would have for himself personally the guarantee of a restitution in the possession of his domains, for all Poles the certainty of a recovery of their confiscated property and of a return of the families deported to Siberia and to the Caucasus; after this the renaissance of Poland, its erection into an empire by Nicholas himself, who will have only this means to win the favor of the congress of unity in order to obtain an augustate.[143]

Alas, victims of revolutions could think of nothing but revolutions as remedies! One could expect more sense from

lished a trial phalanx: its failure would have proved Owen's superiority over Fourier, its success would have made Owen a true benefactor of mankind. Fourier, *Pièges et charlatanisme de deux sectes Saint-Simon et Owen*, p. 66.

[142] Fourier, *La fausse industrie*, Vol. II, p. J8 (782); *Oeuvres*, Anthropos, Vol. IX, p. J8 (782).

[143] *Ibid.*, Vol. I, p. 235; *Oeuvres*, Anthropos, Vol. VIII, p. 235.

Monsieur de Rothschild who reportedly wanted "to emancipate, to reconstitute the Israelite nation, to reestablish in
Jerusalem a Jewish monarch, with his own flag, consuls, and
diplomatic ranking. He would obtain without discussion the
position of king of Judea, for one of the regal subdivisions of
the Chaldean empire, called Judea or Lebanon, will occupy
all of Phoenicia and Palestine up to the Red Sea and the por-
tion of Syria irrigated by the Orontes. He would obtain, as
the founder, the empire of Chaldea, and give the kingdom
of Lebanon or Judea to one of his brothers." [144] He would
enjoy too the fine irony of a Jew becoming a supreme benefactor of all Christians. The road open to the patriots of
Poland or Judea could certainly also be taken by those of Ireland or Italy.

Turning to ministers of state and other "superior un-
crowned candidates" Fourier emphasized that in Civilization
they had no chance to become hereditary sovereigns, even on
a petty scale. By contrast, his discovery opened for them
breathtaking vistas of serried titles, honors, and ranks. A dis-
gruntled British politician who had failed to obtain a lord-
ship could become the omniarch of the globe and thus
suzerain of his present king. To put it more modestly:

It is obvious that a minister or a capitalist or a landed proprietor
who will establish the trial phalanx will have at least one of these
empires, and perhaps a caesarate, a division containing 3 or 4 empires. Since they will be subdivided into kingdoms, califates, etc.,
these positions will be given to those who had helped the estab-

[144] *Ibid.,* Vol. I, p. 224; *Oeuvres,* Anthropos, Vol. VIII, p. 224.
Cf. E. Silberner's article on Fourier's anti-Semitism and the subsequent change in his attitude toward the Jews. The author's attribution
of the change to Fourier's desire to appeal to Rothschild to establish
a phalanx is in my opinion correct, if too cautious. E. Silberner,
"Charles Fourier on the Jewish Question," *Jewish Social Studies,*
Vol. VIII, No. 4 (October 1946), pp. 245–266. Fourier's anti-Semitism
will be discussed in the next chapter.

lishing by their confirmed services, such as those of the chief of a chancellory whose presentations contributed to the decision of the king or the minister to proceed with the establishing. A notice to the chiefs of chancellories, they can be very useful.[145]

"The candidates of the fourth class," that is private individuals with means, were very numerous indeed. "There are, as I have said, one hundred thousand Europeans or Americans, landed proprietors as much as capitalists, who can undertake the trial foundation, either by themselves or through the cooperaton of their shareholding friends and clients." [146] In fact, more expensive projects than a trial phalanx were being subsidized all the time, and Fourier had to combat the silly gigantomania of the Civilized world, ready to throw its money away at a tremendous rate, but unwilling to invest in the one project that mattered.

Of course, anyone who possessed or could raise the necessary funds would profit enormously from establishing a trial phalanx. To select some candidates rather than others, Fourier, as one approach, concentrated on those men who donated or bequeathed large sums of money to worthy causes, which, however, would be much better served by the realization of Fourier's project. A Monsieur Aligre, for example, sank two million francs into a hospital in Chartres. With that amount, he could have taken care of the health of the entire world and done much else besides. A Monsieur Dupuytren bequeathed 500,000 francs for two purposes: to establish a chair of "pathological anatomy," and to finance retirement for needy doctors. Were he to use his money to lead the world into Harmony, he would have ensured the creation of at first 40,000 and eventually 200,000 chairs of pathological anatomy, and would have provided not only a

---

[145] Fourier, *La fausse industrie,* Vol. I, p. 221; *Oeuvres,* Anthropos, Vol. VIII, p. 221.
[146] *Ibid.*

magnificent retirement but also sudden fortune for all "doctors, surgeons, and pharmacists," who would be in extreme demand in the new order. In addition, he would not have deprived his heirs of the 500,000 francs, but would have instead made a most profitable investment for them.[147] Indeed, heirs of benefactors should rally behind Fourier's project in order to avoid losing fortunes. Some men devoted their resources to promoting improvements in agriculture. Others wanted to abolish slavery. There existed numerous bureaus of charity and societies to help the poor. Yet these and so many other worthy aims could be served best not by the usual simple-minded and expensive efforts but by founding a trial phalanx.[148]

Nor was the appeal of Fourier's project limited to benefactors. Just as in the case of rulers and ministers of state, businessmen and other private individuals had everything to gain from it in terms of self-interest. For example, the banker and prominent political figure Jacques Laffitte was experiencing hard times: in fact, he had stated that he was forced to give even his daughter's dowry to his creditors; also, he had expressed the belief that he was in no position to engage in enterprises. Laffitte failed to realize that no more than 500,000 francs and three-months' time were needed, and that the mere prestige of his name as director would assure the financing of the undertaking by eager shareholders.

It is necessary to regain this dowry in three months, to have the globe provide a dowry for the daughter and the son-in-law, to give to the son-in-law the Teutonic caesarate, the supremacy over

[147] *Ibid.,* Vol. I, pp. 231–232; *Oeuvres,* Anthropos, Vol. VIII, pp. 231–232.
[148] For those preoccupied with charity at least, Fourier's undertaking should have been considered "une spécialité des fonctions" *ibid.,* Vol. I, p. 218; *Oeuvres,* Anthropos, Vol. VIII, p. 218.

three empires, those of Germany, England, and Poland, and to
the lady a dowry of a hundred *unitary* francs, a hundred francs
from every phalanx, that is, fifty million francs, to which the
globe will add the female caesarate of the same region as that of
her husband.[149]

Other businessmen could profit from the transition to the
new system by cornering the market on needed products
and making various timely arrangements, for, while there
would be no speculation or any unsavory business practices
in Harmony, transition proper provided the best opportunities for those with initiative to make fantastic fortunes. For
example, instruments would have to be found for 500,000
orchestras, while organ music would also expand on the
same tremendous scale. Great landlords, such as Monsieur
Aguado of Spain, could obtain, as their reward for founding
a trial phalanx, huge properties under the new system, with
industrial armies to turn swamps into fertile fields.

Local patriots would also make excellent candidates to im-
plement Fourier's project, because Harmony, in contrast to
Civilization, would enjoy a balanced economy and rectify
the unhealthy concentration of activities in certain cities and
areas. In France, for example, the valleys of the Loire and
the Garonne and the ports of Bordeaux and Nantes would
no longer be sacrificed in favor of Le Havre and Paris. The

---

[149] Fourier continued: "But these are gigantic dreams: that is
what makes your theory suspect, gives ground to detractors, and
alienates from you cautious people?

"Well, then! hope for less: do you want instead of the Teutonic
caesarate a small hereditary principality, like Neuchâtel given to
Berthier? Do you want instead of a hundred francs of dowry only
ten francs? This will amount to no more than five million. You have
the choice," *ibid.,* Vol. I, p. 227; *Oeuvres,* Anthropos, Vol. VIII, p.
227. This passage suggests even more than certain others the possible
influence of Napoleon's activities on Fourier's ready granting of
principalities and caesarates.

region of Bordeaux would gain greatly also because, with
the abolition of all tariffs, its superb and easily transportable
wines would win the markets of the entire world. If the
lobbyist for Bordeaux, Monsieur de Fonfrède, followed
Fourier's advice and established a trial phalanx, he would
soon be "making ministers: this is a more comfortable role
than soliciting them." [150] In France at least the rectification
of the economic structure meant primarily a challenge to the
usurpation of economic life by Paris. Yet, while repeatedly
making this point, the father of Harmony characteristically
also appealed to Parisian patriots whose city, in its turn, had
much to gain from the coming of the new order. Indeed,
until the third generation and the transfer of the capital to
its ultimate seat in Constantinople, Paris would function as
the capital of the entire reformed world. It would then be
able to build, "at the expense of the hierarchy of the globe,"
twenty magnificent and much-needed boulevards, "like
those in Washington," while at present it was mobilizing its
resources to construct a single one, from the Louvre to the
Bastille.[151]

The fifth class of candidates, representatives of scholarship
and culture in general, had obvious reasons to wish that
Harmony would replace Civilization. The new order would
resemble paradise to men devoted to the intellect and the arts.
Not to repeat the magnificent perspectives of the musicians,
the teachers, or the doctors, the architects, for example, "will
have to rebuild all the villages of the globe; to construct
500,000 great palaces and estates as a replacement for miserable huts." [152]

[150] *Ibid.,* Vol. I, p. 230; *Oeuvres,* Anthropos, Vol. VIII, p. 230.
[151] *Ibid.,* Vol. II, p. L8 (783); *Oeuvres,* Anthropos, Vol. IX, p. L8 (783).
[152] *Ibid.,* Vol. II, p. Z8 (796); *Oeuvres,* Anthropos, Vol. IX, p. Z8 (796).

The *booksellers,* worried today by the contrary fashions which diminish their sales, will empty in nine months all their stores, if French is adopted as the provisional language of unity. They will not have enough presses to republish, at the rate of two or three hundred thousand copies each, good French works in literature, the sciences, and the arts.[153]

Using a different approach, Fourier emphasized that his discovery also solved the problems of various scholarly societies. Thus the Geographic Society watched helplessly "all its voyagers" perish miserably in distant lands at the hands of the natives. The solution lay obviously in the introduction of Fourier's new order and the resulting transformation of the savages and barbarians of Africa and other continents. And how could the Society of Statistics collect its information effectively until the world was properly organized? [154]

The candidates pressed on, bursting the confines of Fourier's five categories. Without exhausting the fivefold classification, the theoretician of the phalanx sketched a new one. This time there were some two dozen groups and subgroups. Many were repetitions or elaborations of the old five; some were new and frequently overlapped them and one another, for Fourier readily admitted that a person

---

[153] *Ibid.*

[154] Fourier, *Le nouveau monde industriel et sociétaire,* p. 484; *Oeuvres,* Anthropos, Vol. VI, p. 484. Fourier, *Pièges et charlatanisme de deux sectes Saint-Simon et Owen,* p. 67. Fourier, *Théorie de l'unité universelle,* Vol. I, pp. 45–46, Vol. II, pp. 149–150; *Oeuvres,* Anthropos, Vol. II, pp. 45–46; Vol. III, pp. 149–150. "There exist in Paris more than fifty scholarly societies each of which aims at some good which can be born only from the societary linking," Charles Fourier in *La Réforme industrielle,* No. 4 (June 21, 1832), p. 38. See also, e.g., Poulat, "Le séjour de Fourier en Bugey (1816–1821)," pp. 29–45 (Fourier's appeal, dated May 28, 1820, to the Academy of Belley). Cf. Fourier's conviction, discussed earlier in this chapter, that his system was the right answer for all kinds of competitions and contests sponsored by learned societies.

could be a promising candidate on more than a single count. For instance, the *déclassés,* and their symmetrical counterpart, the *surclassés,* received the utopian socialist's attention.

I call *déclassé* a man whom Civilization places below the rank which he is worthy of occupying. In Germany such is the Prince of *Schwarzburg-Sondershausen* who, confined to a small state of 60,000 souls, has shown himself by his conciliatory spirit to be worthy of governing 60 million: he has granted to his subjects all liberal and permissible reforms in legislation, finance, administration, etc. . . .[155]
The *surclassés* are the persons who, whether because of their merit, wealth, or position, seem to be debtors in relation to their contemporaries. Opinion expects something big from them, something monumental; it accuses them and presses them down if they do not respond to its appeal; they themselves feel this duty. For example, Madame de Stael, who unites intelligence and imagination with great wealth, must render her memory illustrious by leaving behind some reminders other than the frivolities of a novel. It would be a good role for her to establish the trial essay of Harmony which she could locate in Copet. She could find even in Switzerland, and still better in Paris, 1,000 subscribers, while herself taking only a dozen shares.[156]

Similarly Lafayette's son could more than live up to the fame of his name. "If the son establishes societary unity through subscription of which he would be the head, it

[155] Fourier, *La fausse industrie,* Vol. II, p. S8 (790); *Oeuvres,* Anthropos, Vol. IX, p. S8 (790).
[156] *Ibid.,* Vol. II, pp. S8 (790)–T8 (791); *Oeuvres,* Anthropos, Vol. IX, pp. S8 (790)–T8 (791). Fourier even expressed a general belief that in working on his system he had learned more from women than from men, and that women were more likely to understand him, because they were not stuffed with philosophical prejudices and fully realized that Civilization was the opposite of nature (*ibid.,* Vol. I, pp. 236–237; *Oeuvres,* Anthropos, Vol. VIII, pp. 236–237). However, he did not pursue these interesting points.

would be possible to say: *the father evoked the dream of liberty in the two worlds, the son established its reality.*" [157] Other candidates could turn to Fourier to save their defeated parties and lost causes. This was, for instance, the opportunity missed by the recently deceased liberal publicist Nicolas-Armand Carrel who had 3,000 subscribers to his journal and thus could have easily organized the financing of a trial phalanx. Old men and women needed Fourier's discovery no less than younger ones. They had no time to lose, while their lot in Civilization was especially hard. Besides, those of them who dreaded the dissipation of their fortunes by their heirs would be fully reassured by the establishment of the scientific new order. [158]

[157] *Ibid.,* Vol. II, p. T8 (791); *Oeuvres,* Anthropos, Vol. IX, p. T8 (791).

[158] Many persons and institutions to whom Fourier appealed on particular occasions were not included in his summaries of candidates. The greatest single omission was that of the Church which he cited repeatedly elsewhere. Fourier admired the Church, because of its excellent organization, and its ability to raise funds and to get things done. He argued that the Church had to sponsor his discovery to prove once and for all the benevolence of God, and to defeat the freethinkers, the Saint-Simonians, and other challengers. Other prominent candidates, not mentioned in the summaries, included the Freemasons, who also attracted Fourier's admiration because of their organization. For a characteristic instance of Fourier's appeals to the Church, see Charles Fourier, "Revue des utopies du XIX siècle," *La Réforme industrielle ou le Phalanstère,* No. 8 (July 19, 1832), p. 67 and to the Masons, *ibid.,* p. 59. For Fourier's early estimate of the possibilities of Freemasonry, see Fourier, *Théorie des quatre mouvements et des destinées générales,* pp. 195–202; *Oeuvres,* Anthropos, Vol. I, pp. 195–202. Similarly Fourier appealed on behalf of all those Frenchmen, ranging from the royal family which did not receive its annual funds during the twenty years of exile to "capitalists paid in assignats" and war veterans, widows of veterans, and their children, who could claim and collect reimbursement once the new order of plenty became a reality. See, e.g., Fourier, *Théorie de l'unité universelle,* Vol. I, p. 17; *Oeuvres,* Anthropos, Vol. II, p. 17.

COMPROMISE AND GRADUALISM

As Fourier kept waiting for the candidate, he modified his demands. While a full-scale trial phalanx was most desirable, a more modest association might be more practicable and still serve to demonstrate the validity of Fourier's discovery and the absolute superiority of the new order over Civilization. "Because there will be found five times as many people in a position to attempt a trial with 600 [men] as with 1,200, and forty times as many able to attempt a trial with 200 as with 600, it is necessary to give ample instructions for all partial trials and all the means, essential or accidental, which the founder will have in each degree of trial. . . ." [159] In fact, a partial phalanx could operate with as few members as 144 or 150 and as many as 700, larger numbers transforming it into a small version of a regular phalanx. At its greatest strength it could develop richly the group passions of the major accord, that is, friendship and ambition, but barely touch those of the minor, love and family-feeling. As membership declined, even the passions of the major accord would obtain a weaker expression.

Because a partial phalanx lacked many of the resources and opportunities of a regular one, its members had to be very carefully selected. They had to be pleasure-loving and polite, and therefore preferably Parisian or Genevan. In contrast to full Harmony where every character could be accommodated and would prove useful, the organizers of a partial phalanx should seek especially "polygynes of a high degree, like Caesar and Alcibiades, who are individuals of

[159] Charles Fourier, "De la sérisophie ou épreuve réduite," *La Phalange. Revue de la science sociale* (May–June, July–August, September–October 1849) pp. 386–450, 5–64, 161–183, quoted from p. 388; *Oeuvres,* Anthropos, Vol. XII, pp. 217–365, p. 220. This article in three segments constitutes Fourier's fullest treatment of a "partial phalanx."

an infinite flexibility." [160] They should give preference to families with industrious and well-mannered children inclined to work in gardens and farmyards. "Look for women of every age who love good appearance and good taste. . . . Look for men who are gourmets without gluttony. . . . Look for changeable characters who are dominated by the eleventh passion (the butterfly)." [161] So-called evil characters could be properly utilized only in a full phalanx, while for a partial one choices had to be made "within the liberal nuances," that is among generous, honorable, and tolerant persons. Still, the judgment of Civilization did not necessarily apply. If a calumniator would be out of place in a partial phalanx, a miser might prove useful. And those with the gallant vices should be encouraged to join. "As to details, seek especially individuals who enjoy taking care of animals and vegetables. . . . Seek and prefer in all cases those who have a musical ear, who are suited to sing in a choir or play some instrument." [162] In addition: "A piece of advice, and among the most important, is to bring together handsome people. There is beauty for every age, even for the age of 80." [163]

The emphasis in a partial phalanx had to be not on economic success, but on associating people harmoniously, on securing a real integration. In any case, visitors, who would flock to see the new establishment in operation, would contribute their admission prices to the undertaking. Fourier was only worried lest too many outsiders be admitted at a time.[164] Because much would be lacking, the success of the

[160] *Ibid.,* p. 407; *Oeuvres,* Anthropos, Vol. XII, p. 239.
[161] *Ibid.,* p. 409; *Oeuvres,* Anthropos, Vol. XII, p. 241.
[162] *Ibid.,* p. 408; *Oeuvres,* Anthropos, Vol. XII, p. 240.
[163] *Ibid.,* p. 410; *Oeuvres,* Anthropos, Vol. XII, p. 242.
[164] Fourier often stressed this phenomenon of paying visitors, Englishmen in particular, as an additional guarantee of the financial success of a trial phalanx. See, e.g., Fourier, *La fausse industrie,* Vol.

association would depend all the more on the means available, such as the integrating influence of children and the activities of the Little Hordes.

Fourier found it possible to modify his project even further. Apparently after reading Huard's article, "Examen impartial des nouvelles vues de M. Robert Owen par Henry Gray Macnab," he decided that the crucial trial phalanx could be composed entirely of children.[165] The advantages of such a composition were obvious, because there already existed orphanages with the requisite, and indeed larger, numbers of children. Although—to the best of my knowledge—Fourier never discussed a children's phalanx in any detail, it became his standard prescription for humanity by the time *La fausse industrie* came out. The father of Harmony now begged for a square league of territory and three hundred children, promising all the caesarates and augustates of the globe in return.[166]

The success of even a children's trial phalanx would assure, through imitation, a prompt establishment of association on the entire planet. A tiny effort would bring prodigious results. Fourier liked to assert that he would reverse the adage and have a mouse give birth to a mountain. Still, as long as no candidate stepped forth other alternatives of social development had to be considered. Although the theoretician of the phalanx claimed repeatedly in bitterness and despair that the refusal to listen to him would leave Civilization in a hopeless cul-de-sac or even eventuate in a catas-

I, p. Z (372); *Oeuvres,* Anthropos, Vol. VIII, p. Z (372), where Fourier states that, at a louis a day each, these visitors would pay for the phalanx within a year.

[165] Huard, "Examen impartial des nouvelles vues de M. Robert Owen par Henry Gray Macnab, trad. de l'anglais par M. Laffon de Ladébat," *Memorial universel de l'industrie française, des sciences et des arts,* Vol. 5 (1821), pp. 241–255, referred to in the first chapter.

[166] A French league equals approximately two and a half miles.

trophe, in general he took a more hopeful view of the situation. Fourier's effort and mission was to bring mankind from the fifth stage of historical development, or Civilization, directly into the eighth, or Harmony.[167] If humanity in its blindness rejected the Messiah of reason, history would take its slow course, moving from Civilization to the sixth period, that of guaranteeism, then to the seventh, that of simple or mixed association, and only afterward to the eighth. The utopian socialist witnessed all around himself indications of this historical progression. More than that, with his usual energy, dedication, and precision he proceeded to propose measures and institutions which would accelerate the march.[168]

[167] Fourier's theory of historical stages will be discussed at the beginning of the next chapter.

[168] These "gradualist" measures and institutions of Fourier have been given detailed attention by some of the leading students of Fourierism, e.g., Charles Gide and Hubert Bourgin. Still, whatever their importance for the cooperative movement or other later developments, they were only of a secondary and highly restricted significance to Fourier himself. For a very able summary of this aspect of Fourier, see Bourgin, *Fourier. Contribution à l'étude de socialisme français,* Vol. II, pp. 305–319. I disagree, however, with Bourgin when he combines, often subtly, the foundation of the trial phalanx with the gradualist path to Harmony: in Fourier's own eyes the first would have made the second totally unnecessary. To cite only one of the numerous passages which the father of Harmony wrote on this subject: "As to period 8, which is the happiest, it will be established with the speed of lightning: immediately following the demonstration which will be carried out in six weeks, all of mankind will go to work to make the [necessary] dispositions, and the year after there will be no more Civilized, barbarians, or savages. Periods 6 and 7 will have been hurdled; it is quite unnecessary to organize them, because the ladder of progress and destinies has been discovered in its entirety. . . ." Fourier, *Pièges et charlatanisme des deux sectes Saint-Simon et Owen,* p. 35. For Fourier's treatment of "issues from Civilization," see especially Charles Fourier, "Des diverses issues de civilisation," *La Phalange. Revue de la science sociale* (September–October, 1849), pp. 184–256. Charles Fourier, "Du garantisme," *op. cit.*

At his most optimistic Fourier saw dozens of "issues from Civilization." In short, everything that diminished isolation and anarchy and increased solidarity and reason in human life helped mankind to advance to the next historical stage. The utopian socialist had a curious admiration for money as an element of rationality and organization, and a more understandable one for insurance. Once the principles behind money and insurance were extended to other elements of economy and society, humanity would abandon Civilization. Consolidations and unifications of all sorts, economic as well as political, pointed in the same direction. Napoleon came close to uniting the Civilized world and inaugurating a new age. Other attempts, for example, on the part of Russia, could well be expected. Small things, such as minor changes in architecture, could have momentous consequences, for they could promote cooperation, first among a few families and eventually in the entire society.

As for ways to accelerate progress, Fourier emphasized the need to regulate commerce, which he considered to be the quintessence of Civilized selfishness and anarchy.[169] Cooperative "communal counters" were to take charge of the local purchasing and handling of goods; once organized they could expand into agriculture and cattle raising. Moreover, the utopian socialist also envisaged a complicated state regulation and indeed nationalization of commerce, with public interest and fair prices replacing avaricious anarchy. Rural banks should be organized to provide credit to all pro-

(April 1849). (The last item was also published separately under the title *Cités ouvrières. Modifications à introduire dans l'architecture des villes* (Paris, 1849), and the 32 issues in Fourier, *Le nouveau monde industriel et sociétaire,* pp. 442–444; *Oeuvres,* Anthropos, Vol. VI, pp. 442–444.)

[169] Fourier's criticism of commerce, as well as his general analysis of Civilization and its historical and potential development, will be discussed in the following chapter.

ducers, especially to the poorer ones. Furthermore: "A rural bank does not limit itself, like a pawn-office, to lending on security; it operates actively in production; it provides occupation for the poor class and establishes an experimental farm, operating according to the instructions of a committee of specialists in agriculture located in the capital under the direction of the minister." [170] The farmers of a given area would find it extremely advantageous to deal with their rural bank, because by depositing their harvest with the bank they would assure its better preservation, would immediately receive in advance two-thirds of its value, and would be paid a salary by the bank for helping store the harvest, instead of incurring expenses while trying to do this on their own; in turn, the bank would operate on a grand scale, and therefore its storage costs would be no more than one-third the amount necessary for comparable storage among scattered individuals. But it was the model farms to be established by the rural banks which attracted Fourier's special interest and which appeared and reappeared under various names and in different guises in many of his writings. These farms would add other occupations to their basic concern with agriculture, they would make work attractive, they would enable every member to save and participate in the fortunes of the enterprise, in sum, they would serve as a direct introduction to the phalanx. Association could successfully spread in other directions as well. Notably the butchers, the bakers, the restaurateurs, and members of other occupations should form cooperatives to cut expenses, reap profits, and help mankind advance beyond Civilization.

Gradual change would thus lead to a growth of institutions and arrangements presaging the societary system, and even to the appearance of nuclei of the phalanxes them-

[170] Fourier, "Des diverses issues de civilisation," p. 196.

selves. Eventually full Harmony would be reached. Still, Fourier realized only too clearly the difference between a gradual historical process and the sudden light which he brought to mankind. His heart and hope remained in the trial phalanx. When all inducements of advantage and interest seemed of no avail, the father of Harmony remarked:

There remained one more lever to bring into play, that of curiosity, which is a resource for backward planets. Often simple curiosity can take the place of counsels of wisdom, and it can happen that a planet, which possesses neither enough faith nor enough reason to conceive that God owes us an industrial code revealed by attraction, would nevertheless devote itself to the calculus of attraction through sheer curiosity.[171]

Or, perhaps, men would develop powerful enough telescopes to see how the societary system functioned on an advanced planet, such as Jupiter.[172]

Charles Fourier was convinced that he had discovered the true social system, the correct formula, and that it would benefit mankind by eliminating the abyss between human desires and human fate. In the words engraved on his tomb: "The series distributes the harmonies. The attractions are proportionate to the destinies."

[171] Fourier, Unpublished manuscripts, Cahier 10/9, p. 7.
[172] Fourier, *La fausse industrie,* Vol. II, pp. N5–Q5 footnote; *Oeuvres,* Anthropos, Vol. IX, pp. N5–Q5 footnote.

CHAPTER III

Fourier's Critique of Civilization

Commerce is the most pernicious of all the parasitic professions, such as those of monks, soldiers, lawyers, administrators, etc., which are dead hands in the social body, gnawing ulcers the diminution of which is the constant goal of Politics.[1]

. . . for to some they give soup twice a week: and the poor, the sick, do they feel hunger no more than twice a week? [2]

Charles Fourier emphasized the positive content of his teaching. In fact, he was obsessed with what he believed to be his uniquely valid scientific solution to all the problems of the world. Still, and in part precisely because of the fixity of his vision of salvation and Harmony, the theoretician of the phalanx remained a devastating critic of Civilization, that vicious reverse image of what human society was meant to represent. Fourier's criticism evoked admiration even among many, such as Marx and Engels, who were skeptical of the constructive side of the utopian socialist's teaching. Indeed, this criticism has often been cited as his main contribution to progressive thought.[3] Fourier's critique of Civilization thus

[1] Fourier, *Manuscrits* (Paris, 1851), p. 261; *Oeuvres,* Edition Anthropos, Vol. X, p. 261.

[2] Fourier, *La fausse industrie,* Vol. II, p. T6 (744); *Oeuvres,* Anthropos, Vol. IX, p. T6 (744).

[3] Praise of Fourier's critique of Civilization has been extremely widespread. For an excellent recent summary of Marx's and Engels's evaluation of Fourier, see Zilberfarb, *Sotsialnaia filosofiia Sharlia Fure,* pp. 383–410.

deserves attention in its own right as well as because of the additional light which it sheds on Fourier's ideology.

While Fourier concentrated his critical acumen on Civilization, he considered it within the framework of a total development of humanity, past, present, and future, where it constituted one of thirty-two distinct stages. Its position was graphically presented in a chart attached to the *Théorie des quatre mouvements et des destinées générales* entitled: *"Tableau du Cours du Mouvement Social. Succession et re-lation de ses 4 phases et 32 périodes. Ordre des Créations."* (See accompanying reproduction, pp 142–143.)

Civilization thus stood as the fifth age in the evolution of mankind, preceded by the original period of "confused series," described elsewhere by Fourier as terrestrial paradise or Eden, and by the subsequent stages of Savagery, Patri-archate, and Barbarism. Moreover, these later stages, as the father of Harmony explained often and in detail, had not entirely disappeared, but remained, in their pure or mixed forms, the mode of life on much of the populated surface of the globe. More importantly, Civilization was to be followed by the more "guaranteeistic" and "societary" sixth and seventh stages, and then by the eighth, the true "dawn of happiness," marking the entry of Humanity into Harmony. Fourier's entire effort, message, and mission were, of course, to bring mankind into this eighth stage, skipping the sixth and the seventh.[4] The eighth period would introduce seventeen more periods of blessed Harmony. With the twenty-sixth stage of its development, however, humanity would return to chaos, passing in reverse order the first seven stages.

---

[4] Such an "enjambement" of stages, Fourier indicated, was usual "on the suns and on the planets with strong passions." Charles Fourier, "Des lymbes obscures ou périodes d'enfer social et de labyrinthe passionel," *La Phalange. Revue de la science sociale* (January, February 1849), pp. 5–40, 97–110, quoted from p. 15.

Civilization would thus constitute the twenty-eighth stage of the evolution of mankind as well as the fifth. Death of the planet would follow the thirty-second stage.

Fourier's characteristically precise, complex, and symmetrical scheme of the evolution of man produced a cyclical pattern and a grim conclusion. It remains unknown how he obtained the scheme or why he felt that he had to adhere to it. In any case, he refused to explore its pessimistic possibilities. Instead, and in line with his usual overwhelming optimism, the theoretician of the phalanx emphasized that man had as his destiny seventy thousand happy years of life in Harmony as against ten thousand miserable years of existence in chaotic societies, because the initial and the final seven stages of human history covered but five thousand years each out of the total of some eighty thousand. Besides, why should one worry about the decline from Harmony into chaos following the twenty-fifth stage of history when the pressing problem was to reach the eighth stage and thus rise from chaos into Harmony?

While the final transitions and stages of Human history were at present irrelevant, the initial ones deserved attention. As already indicated, they both constituted the background for Civilization and continued, in large part, to coexist with it. In his usual authoritative and striking manner Fourier proceeded to describe Edenism, Savagery, Patriarchate, Barbarism, and man's progress through these stages.

The first period in the evolution of humanity, Edenism, occupied the first two centuries after Creation, and was by far the happiest mankind had so far experienced. According to Fourier, men and women were created in the prime of their lives in a number of widely scattered locations on our planet. They went on to engage in utterly free love and to enjoy the great abundance of useful plants and animals. They even established "confused series," an early forerunner

CHAOS ASCENDANT.

Règne de l'Ignorance et de la Philosophie.
Choc des Passions par défaut d'art social.

HARMONIE ASCENDANTE.

Lumière sociale, vigueur du glob
Développement et engrenage de

Les 16 Sociétés nᵒˢ 9 à 24 seront engendrées par autant de créations, dont
et modifiera d'autant les rapports sociaux, sans rien cha

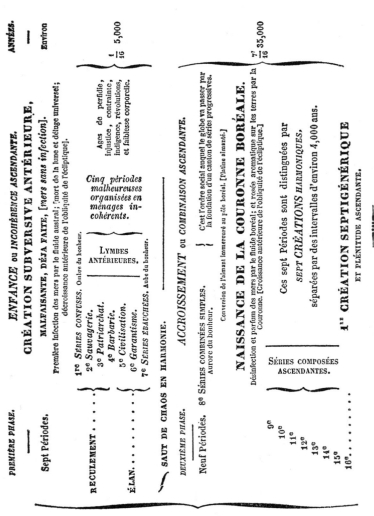

ANNÉES.

Environ

$\frac{1}{16}$ 5,000

$\frac{7}{16}$ 35,000

PREMIÈRE PHASE.

ENFANCE ou INCOHÉRENCE ASCENDANTE.
CRÉATION SUBVERSIVE ANTÉRIEURE,
MALFAISANTE, DÉJÀ FAITE, [mers sans infection].
Première Infection des mers par le fluide austral; [mort de la lune et déluge universel; décroissance antérieure de l'obliquité de l'écliptique].

Sept Périodes.

1re SÉRIES CONFUSES. Ombre du bonheur.
2e Sauvagerie.
3e Patriarchat.
4e Barbarie.
5e Civilisation.
6e Garantisme.
7e SÉRIES ÉBAUCHÉES. Aube du bonheur.

RECULEMENT......

ÉLAN..........

Ages de perfidie, injustice, contrainte, indigence, révolutions, et faiblesse corporelle.

Cinq périodes malheureuses organisées en ménages incohérents.

LYMBES ANTÉRIEURES.

SAUT DE CHAOS EN HARMONIE.

DEUXIÈME PHASE.

ACCROISSEMENT ou COMBINAISON ASCENDANTE.

Neuf Périodes.

8e SÉRIES COMBINÉES SIMPLES. Aurore du bonheur.

C'est l'ordre social auquel le globe va passer par la fondation d'un canton de séries progressives.

Conversion de l'aimant immercuré au pôle boréal. [Platine aimanté.]

NAISSANCE DE LA COURONNE BORÉALE.
Désinfection et parfum des mers par le fluide boréal; et rosée aromatique sur les terres par la Couronne. [Croissance antérieure de l'obliquité de l'écliptique.]

Ces sept Périodes sont distinguées par sept CRÉATIONS HARMONIQUES, séparées par des intervalles d'environ 4,000 ans.

1re CRÉATION SEPTIGÉNÉRIQUE
ET PLÉNITUDE ASCENDANTE.

9e
10e
11e
12e
13e
14e
15e
16e.........

SÉRIES COMPOSÉES ASCENDANTES.

"PÉRIODE PIVOTALE ou AMPHIHARMONIQUE" d'environ 8,000 ans.
[Station temporaire de l'écliptique.]

APOGÉE DU BONHEUR.

VIBRATION ASCENDANTE.

be et des créatures.
toutes les Passions.

t chacune donnera de nouveaux produits dans les 3 règnes,
anger au mécanisme des Séries progressives.

Bouleversement général par la 18e création.
Choc des Passions par défaut de luxe.

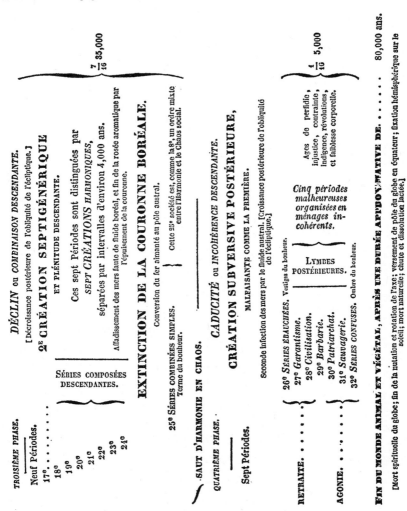

$\frac{7}{16}$ 35,000

$\frac{4}{16}$ 5,000

TROISIÈME PHASE.
Neuf Périodes.
17°..........
18°
19°
20°
21°
22°
23°
24°

DÉCLIN ou COMBINAISON DESCENDANTE.
[Décroissance postérieure de l'obliquité de l'écliptique.]
2e CRÉATION SEPTIGÉNÉRIQUE
ET PLÉNITUDE DESCENDANTE.
Ces sept Périodes sont distinguées par
SEPT CRÉATIONS HARMONIQUES,
séparées par intervalles d'environ 4,000 ans.
Affaiblissement des mers faute de fluide boréal, et fin de la rosée aromatique par l'épuisement de la couronne.

EXTINCTION DE LA COURONNE BORÉALE.
Conversion du fer aimanté au pôle austral.
Cette 25e société est, comme la 8e, un ordre mixte entre l'Harmonie et le Chaos social.

SÉRIES COMPOSÉES DESCENDANTES.

25° SÉRIES COMBINÉES SIMPLES. Terme du bonheur.

SAUT D'HARMONIE EN CHAOS.
QUATRIÈME PHASE.
Sept Périodes.

CADUCITÉ ou INCOHÉRENCE DESCENDANTE.
CRÉATION SUBVERSIVE POSTÉRIEURE,
MALFAISANTE COMME LA PREMIÈRE.
Seconde infection des mers par le fluide austral. [Croissance postérieure de l'obliquité de l'écliptique.]

Cinq périodes malheureuses organisées en ménages incohérents.

LYMBES POSTÉRIEURES.

26° SÉRIES ÉBAUCHÉES. Vestige du bonheur.
27° Garantisme.
28° Civilisation.
29° Barbarie.
30° Patriarchat.
31° Sauvagerie.
32° SÉRIES CONFUSES. Ombre du bonheur.

RETRAITE. . . . . . :
AGONIE. . . . . . :

Ages de perfidie, injustice, contrainte, indigence, révolutions, et faiblesse corporelle.

FIN DU MONDE ANIMAL ET VÉGÉTAL, APRÈS UNE DURÉE APPROXIMATIVE DE. . . . . . 80,000 ans.

[Mort spirituelle du globe; fin de la nutation et rotation de l'axe; versement de pôle du globe en équateur; fixation hémisphérique sur le soleil; mort naturelle; chute et dissolution lactée.]

VIBRATION DESCENDANTE.

of Fourier's scientific system. "These two centuries passed in a state of insouciance, in delights, in amorous festivals, in numerous and frequent meals among peoples of great vigor." [5] Life on the island of Tahiti represented a modified remnant of this happy first stage of human history.

Tahiti managed to maintain important aspects of Edenism because of its isolation and of certain practices, such as infanticide, which limited the growth of population. Elsewhere terrestrial paradise came entirely to an end. Ferocious or venomous beasts, reptiles, and insects advanced from their original location near the equator to attack man. More significantly, human societies themselves grew in numbers to overtax the available economic resources. Poverty replaced abundance; egoistic self-interest, cooperation; and Savagery succeeded Edenism. "It is always in the growth of population and of poverty that one must look for the secret of the decline of societies preceding Civilization." [6]

Savagery substituted marriage for free love. Together with the breakdown of the original passional series, the new institution gave man control over woman, relegating her to the position of an obedient servant and houseworker. In fact most economic activities and labor devolved upon women, while men preferred to spend their time in characteristic indolence, interrupted only by periodic hunting, fishing, or fighting. Fourier was of two minds and sentiments about Savagery. On the one hand, he was attracted to it, particularly by contrast with Civilization. He even declared that "the savages possess, among other enjoyments unknown to us, truth, freedom, and insouciance," [7] and he liked to list such rights characteristic of their condition and denied in more advanced societies as those of free hunting, fishing,

[5] *Ibid.*, p. 12.
[6] *Ibid.*, p. 15.
[7] *Ibid.*, p. 20.

grazing, and gathering food. No wonder that savages had no intention of joining Civilization: even guaranteeism would not satisfy them, although they would immediately adhere to Harmony. Still, on the other hand, the theoretician of the phalanx was highly critical of the state of Savagery, and he explicitly denied and denounced the Rousseauean belief in the noble savage. In economic terms, Savagery marked in a sense the nadir of human history, characterized by "inertia" or an absence of productive labor.[8] As to liberty and self-expression, all the advantages of the period belonged to men, but not to women, who found themselves in a most abject condition. Because Fourier asserted on more than one occasion that the freedom and high position of women was the best indication of the progressive nature of a society, his depiction of the state of women in Savagery was condemnation enough. If, however, more evidence was needed to destroy the myth of the noble savage it could be found in such other practices typical of Savagery as refined torture of prisoners of war. In his criticism of Savagery, as in so many of his other criticisms, the father of Harmony combined a peculiar logic of his own making with brutal realism.

With a further growth of population, Savagery evolved in its third and fourth phases into a society of wandering rapacious hordes.[9] From that condition it was but a short step to

[8] See, e.g., the summary table where Savagery is defined as inertia in Fourier, *Le nouveau monde industriel et sociétaire*, p. XI; *Oeuvres,* Anthropos, Vol. VI, p. XI. By contrast, Edenism possessed its rudimentary passional industrial series, while periods subsequent to Savagery saw a development and continuous growth of industry.

[9] Periods of human history had as a rule four phases with complex characteristics and transitions. Moreover, these phases did not necessarily occur everywhere in the usual sequence, but could, for example, reverse it. The Moors of Granada and Cordova thus belonged to the fourth phase of Patriarchate, while the modern Moors of Algeria belonged to the first.

Patriarchate and also to Barbarism. A crucial distinction consisted in the fact that savages were free men who, when necessary, elected leaders, whereas in Patriarchate and Barbarism the leaders came to dominate the followers. The transition was linked to economic change: no chief could master isolated and self-sufficient hunters and fishermen, but centralized control became possible once men shifted to group occupations, such as cattle-raising and agriculture. Barbarism in particular was also based on conquest and on the enslavement of the conquered peoples.

In contrast to his treatment of Savagery, Charles Fourier had almost no kind words to say about Patriarchate and Barbarism, his discussion of these periods rivaling in sweeping denunciation and venom his attacks on Civilization. Admirers of patriarchal relations had merely to look at "modern patriarchal peoples":

The Circassians engage in an infamous traffic of their daughters whom they fatten like the fowl of Mans to sell them to Turkish merchants. The Corsicans eternalize interfamily hatreds and wars. The Arabs live in general pederasty. These are the virtues of patriarchal peoples known in our day. They go well with those of Abraham and Jacob. The moralists must have great difficulty discovering virtues to look for them in the patriarchal state.[10]

Some peoples moved beyond Patriarchate to produce an amalgam of Patriarchate and Barbarism. This applied to the Germans described by Tacitus who combined slavery with semi-servitude or "domesticity" and Barbarian ferocity with such patriarchal characteristics as small-scale cultivation.

The most common condition on the face of the globe remained, however, Barbarism proper: "five hundred million barbarians, two-thirds of mankind, engulfed in the tortures,

[10] Fourier, "Des lymbes obscures," p. 27.

the brutalization, the slavery of the cultivators and of women, without any means of escape from this abyss." [11] If small-scale bondage distinguished Patriarchate from Savagery, large-scale slavery differentiated Barbarism from Patriarchate. The four phases of Barbarism represented different kinds of slavery. There was, to begin with, "hostile slavery," conquered nations serving their conquerors, as in the case of Jews in Babylonian captivity. There was next "confused slavery," when within a given people, such as the Chinese or the Turks, children were sold into slavery. The third phase, that of "complex slavery," occurred when one barbarian society was conquered by another, levels of slavery resulting. To illustrate it one could cite the Copts in Egypt subject to the Mameluks who were in turn subject to the Turks. Finally, there was the slavery of castes, so characteristic of India. Fourier spared no words in describing the horrors of Barbarism whether based on military aggression or, as in China, on tradition and inertia. In fact, he had a special hatred for China which seemed to him to combine utmost misery, privations, and cruelty with hypocrisy and an emphasis on commerce. Still, Barbarism had its contribution to make to the evolution of mankind. Slavery enabled economic activity to grow. If Savagery could be described as economic inertia, while Patriarchate developed small industry, Barbarism introduced middle-size industry. This was especially important because the next step, large-scale industry, was both the hallmark of Civilization and a necessary precondition for Harmony.

In economic terms, therefore, Barbarism led directly to Civilization. It would seem that in its social aspects, however, Civilization derived more from Patriarchate. The crucial issue remained as always the position of women. Civilization meant exclusive marriage and the resulting new importance

[11] *Ibid.,* p. 32.

of the monogamic wife as the sole mistress of the household. Fourier theorized that monogamy originated among small patriarchal chiefs who had special reasons to provide for the welfare and high position of their daughters given in marriage. Monogamy and a sufficiently high level of economic development produced Civilization.

The new stage of human development thus marked important economic and social advances over Savagery, Patriarchate, and Barbarism. Moreover, it held out the promise of a most sweeping and beneficial future transformation, the coming of Harmony. Nevertheless, Civilization represented a most deplorable condition of man which Fourier castigated tirelessly and without mercy. The utopian socialist's view of history combined linear progress, exemplified by his assumption of consecutive economic growth, with a more "dialectic" approach, emphasizing contrasts, breaks, and sharp transitions. He used the latter to depict Civilization in the blackest possible color, and thus in direct contrast to Harmony. And indeed Civilization was for Fourier *le monde à rebours,* the world in reverse of what it was meant to be and one day would become.

Charles Fourier's celebrated critique of Civilization was scattered throughout his writings. Except for a few minor pieces devoted largely to some specific flaws, usually of a commercial and business nature, of the contemporary world, Fourier criticized relatively briefly, if violently, in order to introduce his own solution and to assail his presumptive rivals or opponents. Prolific, as well as extremely repetitious, the utopian socialist's critique lacked general organization and integration. In reconstructing it one should keep in mind Fourier's primary concern with human passions and their social dimension as well as his interest in economic matters.

If Harmony represented the fullest expression of all the passions of every human being, Civilization stood for their wholesale suppression and perversion.[12] If a phalanx with its groups and series constituted a world of perfect integration and harmony, contemporary society had reached the extreme of isolation and hostility. Civilization was based on family feeling and the institution of the family and thus ruled by compulsion from the very start, for, one could not choose one's family, as one could choose partners to exercise the other group passions, those of friendship, ambition, and love. In his bitterness Fourier even used the science of analogy to describe family feeling as the Judas among the twelve passions. And it was this division into families that assured the utmost fragmentation of the modern social order, or, rather, according to Fourier, chaos:

To manipulate society one must begin with a study of characters and their affinities or sympathies, both among themselves and in relation to the entire society, items totally unknown to Civilized legislators, for they have brought domestic society to the highest degree of isolation and egoism by dividing it into sexual couples or exclusive married households. Would it be possible to push unsociability farther, and could one invent a domestic system reduced to less than a couple? Of course not; reproduction would become impossible if the domestic order were reduced to a single individual; by the same token proper functioning would become impossible. From which it is obvious that the life of married households, or couples, is unsociability reduced to its simplest form. A fine accomplishment for sages pretending to be philanthropists and wishing to make of mankind a single family of brothers. . . .[13]

Because of the division into families, "every father has forgotten all sentiments of charity and philanthropy to be preoccupied only with the interests of his wife and his children, a mania which makes of each father an egoist and an illib-

[12] I shall discuss further Fourier's view of passions in Chapter V.
[13] Fourier, *Manuscrits. Années 1857–1858* (Paris, 1858), p. 108; *Oeuvres*, Anthropos, Vol. XI, p. 108, second pagination.

eral person who believes himself authorized to perform every deceit and rapine under the pretext of working for *his* wife and his children, whose names he pronounces as one possessed." [14]

Since they were grounded in the family, selfishness, tensions, and clashes of interests extended to all parts of Civilized society. Professions and occupations provided excellent illustrations of this sad fact. "The procurator wishes his fellow citizens good trials, the doctor wishes them good fevers, the architect good fires, and the glazier good hailstorms which would break all the glass for the benefit of commerce. Examine one by one all the Civilized perfections: you will find nothing but intentional war of individual against society." [15] Perhaps still more importantly, Civilization exhibited deep cleavages between the strong and the weak, the rich and the poor, the exploiters and the exploited. "The mighty by means of policemen and gallows repress the passions of the people; the strong sex opposes the two weak sexes, the women and the children." [16] The poor opposed the rich, the servants the masters, the young the old, the wives the husbands.

Based on division and oppression, Civilization lived by force. "In effect, if you attempt to eliminate the executioners, the policemen, and the gallows, you will witness on the morrow how your scaffolding of perfected Civilization will be overturned by the people of whose happiness you have been boasting." [17] The lines would be quickly drawn:

[14] *Ibid.*, p. 208; *Oeuvres,* Anthropos, Vol. XI, p. 208, second pagination.

[15] Charles Fourier, *De l'anarchie industrielle et scientifique* (Paris, 1847), p. 55.

[16] Fourier, *La fausse industrie,* Vol. II, p. 470-x; *Oeuvres,* Anthropos, Vol. IX, p. 470-x.

[17] Fourier, *Manuscrits. Années 1857–1858* (Paris, 1858), p. 351; *Oeuvres,* Anthropos, Vol. XI, p. 351, second pagination. Or, to put

... an immense majority which will adhere to the movement, all the domestics, all the salaried artisans, all the military. What will remain to uphold your perfected Civilization? There will remain the orators, the spoilsmen ... but how numerous is this legion of metaphysicians and grantees? It does not rise to one-tenth of the body social. In brief, if you eliminate the gallows, the foundation of all of perfected Civilization, the edifice is overturned in an instant, and each family will reestablish the customs of Corsica and of Arabia, wars of one house against another.[18]

Executioners, policemen, soldiers, officials, law, government represented nothing but naked force, oppressing the many for the benefit of the few. No wonder that all these horrors would disappear in Harmony.

Fourier continuously challenged the credo of Civilization, for instance, in his refutation of Saint-Lambert's maxims which the theoretician of the phalanx composed as early as 1804. Saint-Lambert wrote of a community of men living under the same laws and enjoying the same benefits. Fourier retorted: "Nothing is more false; we do not enjoy the same benefits and the law treats us quite differently; it assures good revenues to some, and nothing to others; the law despoils some to enrich others." [19] Saint-Lambert praised in

it slightly differently, the entire mechanism of Civilization rested on a single accord, "that of the soldier with the king." Fourier, *Théorie de l'unité universelle,* Vol. I, p. 155; *Oeuvres,* Anthropos, Vol. II, p. 155.

[18] Fourier, *Manuscrits. Années 1857–1858* (Paris, 1858), p. 351; *Oeuvres,* Anthropos, Vol. XI, p. 351, second pagination. The break in the middle of the passage— ... —is in the original. On another occasion Fourier used his customary allowance for exception, one-eighth, to describe Civilization as "a league of 1/8 engaged in graduated spoliation of 7/8." *Ibid.,* p. 257; *Oeuvres,* Anthropos, Vol. XI, p. 257, second pagination.

[19] Fourier, *Manuscrits. Années 1853–1856* (Paris, 1856), p. 275; *Oeuvres,* Anthropos, Vol. XI, p. 275, first pagination. The entire discussion of Saint-Lambert's maxims occupies pp. 274–288; *Oeuvres,* Anthropos, Vol. XI, pp. 274–288, first pagination.

general warriors who fight to defend the community. Fourier went straight to the point: "they fight for whatever pleases their master, defense or attack. . . ."[20] Saint-Lambert instructed in lofty tones: "You owe it to your country to be just and wise."[21] Fourier exploded: "We owe it nothing, and, if one is to keep accounts, it is the country that owes us what it took away, or allowed to be taken away, from us."[22]

Saint-Lambert's maxims served as an excellent illustration of the fact that Civilization relied for support not only on the mailed fist but also on ideological drivel. Throughout his writings Fourier treated contemporary ideologies as an evil, or at best naïve, camouflage of the frightful reality.

Our politics, forced to resort to expedients to contain a famished population, inspires in it a stupid respect for its chiefs. It transforms kings into adorable and infallible divine beings; it wants one to burn with a love for them without ever having seen them; and on this point I do not see much difference between Civilized customs and those of the Tibetan Tartars who carry around their neck as a sign of honor a little sack filled with the excrements of their master, the great lama. The canaille in Civilization and Barbarism must be a thoroughly miserable lot to make it necessary to bring into play so many absurd prejudices in order to muzzle it and to prop up the bayonets which are the basis of political wisdom.[23]

Firmly grounded in eighteenth-century thought, Fourier's approach to ideologies was as reductionist as the later approaches of Marxists and Freudians.

[20] *Ibid.*, p. 277; *Oeuvres,* Anthropos, Vol. XI, p. 277, first pagination.

[21] *Ibid.*, p. 283; *Oeuvres,* Anthropos, Vol. XI, p. 283, first pagination.

[22] *Ibid.*, pp. 283–284; *Oeuvres,* Anthropos, Vol. XI, pp. 283–284, first pagination.

[23] Fourier, *Manuscrits. Années 1857–1858* (Paris, 1858), pp. 170–171; *Oeuvres,* Anthropos, Vol. XI, pp. 170–171, second pagination.

The Church also helped to support the framework and fabric of Civilization. Fourier's estimate of the Church—which almost always meant to him the Catholic Church, although the utopian socialist did make a few references to the Church of England and still other churches—has to be drawn from passing, if frequently pungent, remarks or at best brief discussions. In addition to urging the Church and its various parts and members to establish a trial phalanx and thus introduce Harmony, they follow predictable lines of criticism. From his personal experience Fourier emphasized terror associated with religion as an effective weapon to suppress man's passions and desires and to regulate human conduct. The boiling cauldrons of the next world joined the bayonets of this one in preserving Civilization. At a somewhat more sophisticated level, Christian doctrines of meekness, self-denial, and hope in the afterlife suited perfectly the desperate condition of the teeming masses in Civilization who could find no other solace. Camouflage and superstition permeated religious teachings as much as, or even more than, secular ones.[24] As a powerful institution, the Church was very much part of Civilization. It contributed heavily to the division, exploitation, cruelty, and persecution of the surrounding society, whether through the Inquisition in Spain or the role of the Church of England in Ireland. Indeed the Pope placed the works of Fourier himself on the Index, thus almost justifying Newton's charge that the Pope was Antichrist. In addition, the blind ecclesiastics had less excuse than the laymen to disregard Fourier's message: while freethinkers were not concerned with the ways of God, priests

[24] As shown in the preceding chapter, Fourier's view of historical religion as largely fabrication and superstition—a view characteristic of an important segment of thought of the Enlightenment—did not interfere with his own belief in God, his associating himself with the Christian message, or his own religious and quasi-religious doctrines.

believed in Him and were, therefore, under an obligation to be receptive to His plan for humanity which Fourier had discovered.

Indigence was the mark of the oppressed masses in Civilization. ". . . the real hell is poverty."[25] Poverty meant first of all hunger which remained the condition of much of mankind. Taste, Fourier insisted, was one of the twelve passions, indeed the most imperious of the twelve. "From which it follows that man in society has the right to *eat,* the right which Civilized philosophes and legislators have never conceded him, for they accord it only on conditions which are impossible for the poor."[26] They merely added insult and irony to the situation by talking of imprescriptible personal, political, and other rights to the famished poor who desperately needed and wanted simply a piece of bread. As to the argument that one had to work in order to eat, often there was no work, with the result that one was reduced to starving with one's wife and children to the greater glory of the ever-self-perfecting Civilization. Nor was outright starvation the only curse of the oppressed majority of humanity:

And in the places where the people does not die from *pressing* hunger, it dies from *slow* hunger, from privations; from *speculative* hunger which forces it to feed itself with unhealthy things; from *familial* hunger, by overexerting oneself at work in order to feed a family and succumbing to fevers and infirmities; from imminent hunger, by devoting oneself of necessity to dangerous occupations, work with steel, lead, vitriol, etc., which, because of the length of the working sessions and the continuity of an unhealthy occupation, destroys the worker in 10, in 6, and even in 3 years.[27]

[25] Fourier, *Sur l'esprit irréligieux des modernes* and *Dernières analogies,* p. 17; *Oeuvres,* Anthropos, Vol. XII, p. 549.

[26] Charles Fourier, *Cités ouvrières. Des modifications à introduire dans l'architecture des villes* (Paris, 1849), p. 11.

[27] Fourier, *La fausse industrie,* Vol. I, p. 406; *Oeuvres,* Anthropos, Vol. VIII, p. 406.

Repeatedly Fourier tried to draw in his characteristic manner at least a tentative summary of the miserable condition of the working masses in Civilization. In a more extensive treatment of the subject, the utopian socialist wrote:

Disfavors of the workers

NOTE. This ladder is merely a very incomplete aperçu; I am handing it over to those more experienced; they will easily be able to double the series of the misfortunes of the poor, after which the series will be classified more methodically.

Pressing evil. 1. Collection of taxes: the pursuit of fiscal agents who come to snatch from him pennies saved with so much pain for the support of his unfortunate family.

2. The necessity to expose his health to excessive and unhealthy work on which his and his children's subsistence depends.

Direct evil. 3. The counter-blow of misfortune, communicated suffering, or the ability to feel the ills of his family whose privations add to his.

4. New misfortunes which come to double his pain when he believes to have exhausted the severities of fate.

5. Unjust stigma, opprobrium and defamation which attach themselves to a poor man because of his penury, and expose him the more to disdain the more he is pressed by need.

Indirect evil. 6. A view of the favorites of fortune whom chance, intrigue or crime raise every day to affluence, as if to throw into despair the honest worker whose probity engulfs him deeper and deeper into indigence.

7. A relative decline because of the growth of luxury which, by creating each day new means of enjoyment for the rich, increases by the same token the sufferings of the multitude deprived of necessities and affected by a display of this growth of luxury, which a savage does not see.

8. Frustration of the ways of salvation provided by the law, such as legal reclamations and others, which he cannot attempt because of a lack of fortune and the impossibility of obtaining a loan.

Accessory evil. 9. Social snares, or the danger of being deceived at every step by his fellow-citizens, of meeting in the social world nothing but swarms of rascals or disguised enemies.

10. Poverty anticipated at present, or the fear to be out of work, which is a free undertaking for a savage or an animal.

11. Scientific derision, or the illusory help of literary charlatans, who, while promising the people an attenuation of their ills, crush them with new calamities.

12. The moral trap, or persecution attracted by the exercise of virtue which, by offending perverse rivals, leads them to calumny which is always well-received in Civilization.

Pivots. Y Industrial repugnance and the absence of a prerogative of animals, the beavers, the bees, etc., who, feeling attraction for work, find their happiness in that work which is the torture of the Civilized. ⅄ Betrayal of nature, or martyrdom of attraction; the goad of numerous desires which a Civilized person cannot satisfy and which lead him to his destruction, whereas nature gives to an animal only passions appropriate for its guidance and at the same time gives it a full right to satisfy them.

Transitions. Ʞ A vexing return to the past, recollection of numerous miseries already endured and still to be feared.

K Anticipated or future suffering, or the ability to foresee for one's old age, in a distant future, a growth of ills without any means of escaping them.[28]

A man's misery and alienation from his social order could hardly be greater.

While in the age of Civilization the earth groaned under the working poor, it also swarmed with parasites. To be

[28] Fourier, *Théorie de l'unité universelle,* Vol. III, pp. 191–193; *Oeuvres,* Anthropos, Vol. IV, pp. 191–193. Among other signs, Fourier frequently used a regular and an inverted Y to denote subdivisions and directions within the pivotal element, and a regular or inverted K to indicate different forms of transitions and links. For a clear, useful, but too simple explanation of Fourier's signs, see the editors' preface to *L'Harmonie Universelle et le Phalanstère exposés par Fourier. Recueil méthodique de morceaux choisis de l'auteur.* Vol. I (Paris, 1849).

See also a striking summary of growing or composite disfavors of the workers in: Fourier, *Manuscrits* (Paris, 1851), pp. 207–208; *Oeuvres,* Anthropos, Vol. X, pp. 207–208, first pagination.

sure, the numerous and varied parasitical hordes had their *raisons d'être* in the existing system: they took advantage of it, contributed to its structure, or even, as in the case of soldiers and policemen, served as its indispensable supports. Still and always they failed to produce, failed to add their share to the storehouse of humanity, and thus remained an affront to reason, a condemnation of Civilization, and a clarion call to Harmony. The parasites were of different degrees of perniciousness:

In effect, the class of merchants is clearly more deadly for industry than any other, for monks and soldiers deprive cultivation only of their hands. Lawyers add a more serious vice to the sterility of their function, the vice of distracting workers from their work in order to despoil them. Commerce, in addition to these two vices, falls into a third, that of turning against industry capital which would have been devoted exclusively to the service of cultivation and workshops, if trust and truth were established. . . .[29]

In his table of "those unproductive in Civilization" Fourier listed twelve groups of parasites, under three headings, and added to them two "pivotal" groups.[30] To begin with, there were three groups under the heading of "domestic parasites": the women, the children, and the servants. Three-fourths of the women in towns and a half of those in the countryside did nothing but housework with the result that "their day cannot be estimated in economics as more than one-fifth of a man's day."[31] Three-fourths of the children

[29] Fourier, *Manuscrits* (Paris, 1851), p. 261; *Oeuvres,* Anthropos, Vol. X, p. 261, first pagination.

[30] The table is on page 174, and its discussion occupies pages 174–183 of: Fourier, *Théorie de l'unité universelle,* Vol. III; *Oeuvres,* Anthropos, Vol. IV, pp. 174–183.

[31] *Ibid.,* p. 174; *Oeuvres,* Anthropos, Vol. IV, p. 174. One is immediately reminded of how Harmony would eliminate this waste and other parasitic wastes.

were useless in towns and of little use in the country, performing badly whatever work they did perform. Finally, some three-quarters of the servants were in fact superfluous.

Next came five groups of "social parasites." "The armies of land and sea" took away from work the most robust youths precisely when those youths should have been developing useful skills. Legions of administrators and guardians absorbed a tremendous number of people, with the customs service alone employing in France 24,000 men. A half of the manufacturers were relatively unproductive, for they fabricated inferior goods. Nine-tenths of merchants and commercial agents could have been profitably dispensed with, honest trade requiring but one-tenth or less of the personnel commercially employed in Civilization. And those occupied in transportation could be reduced by two-thirds. For good measure Fourier added smuggling to waste in transportation: it frequently utilized particularly devious and long routes to bring in merchandise. Elsewhere the father of Harmony complained that Civilization regularly employed mighty men to do jobs which women or children could easily handle, and that it engaged in still other forms of waste.

The third subheading comprised "accessory parasites" arranged in four groups. There were the unemployed of different kinds. Moreover, a realistic examination of unemployment demanded the inclusion of very numerous holidays, of workers not showing up for work 52 times a year on Mondays, of employees slackening on the job as soon as their master stopped watching them. The sophists, devoted to controversies and cabals, constituted another group. The lawyers, the economists who, parasites themselves, loved to declaim against parasites, and other members of this group not only produced nothing, but managed to bring political and other perturbations upon society. The idlers, by contrast, did nothing at all, wasting not only their own lives but also the efforts of the domestics and other men serving them. By extension idleness included the forced idle, or the prisoners, and the sick, so numerous in Civilization. The last regular group, that of scissionaries, contained people such as the beggars, the criminals, the gamblers, and the prostitutes, who were in open rebellion against Civilized injunctions and laws. The pivotal section contained two additional groups of significant parasites: "agents of positive destruction," such as speculators who brought on famine and pestilence or, again, the armed forces, this time when they were not idle; and "agents of negative creation," a very numerous category, exemplified by builders of buildings that collapse, and by people who cut down forests with dire results for the countryside or develop new methods of production which put workers out of work. Fourier noted that Civilization showed a special solicitude for agents of positive destruction.

Poverty, parasitism, and other vices of Civilization were intimately linked to commerce. While Fourier made some extremely interesting comments concerning modern industrial development and related topics, he concentrated on the middleman, the trader, the commercial agent, the stockbroker, as the most characteristic representative and the greatest evil of contemporary society.[32] This focus reflected precisely the utopian socialist's own background and experi-

[32] Most students of Fourier's thought stressed the centrality of commerce in his analysis of Civilization. For instance, Saitta wrote in reference to Fourier's analysis: "[Economic] crises are produced not by overproduction and therefore not because of the guilt of the industrialists, but by fraudulent machinations of the speculators." A. Saitta, "Charles Fourier e l'Armonia," *Belfagor,* Vol. II, No. 3 (May 15, 1947), pp. 272–292, quoted from page 284.

Fourier's treatment of industry and industrial development and crises will be discussed later in this chapter, and in the next chapter in assessing the relationship of Fourier to socialism.

ence, and, more generally, the petty bourgeois world of pre-industrial France.

At times Fourier even offered a monistic explanation in which unbridled commerce served as the reason for all the horrors of Civilization. "Thus, the displacement of a single wheel in a clock can make the entire mechanism go in the opposite direction; this is the effect that the emancipation of commerce has been producing for three thousand years in the movement of Civilization; everything is false there, essentially and systematically; everything will be brought back to truth by the single correction of the commercial system." [33] Moreover, commerce was man's "main social relation":

Each one of us is in a commercial relation every moment, to buy or to sell. We often live months, entire years, without entering administrative, judicial, or financial relations, while even the poorest one of us cannot live a day without assuming through buying or selling some commercial relation. From the fact that each one of us, rich or poor, is in contact with commerce every moment, it follows that commerce is the most widespread and the most important of our relations.[34]

Trade and traders stood as the very epitome of the fragmentation, anarchy, and utter selfishness characteristic of Civilization:

They are called *true citizens of the world,* and that with reason: for the bankers and the rich merchants have no fixed fatherland; being able to convert and transport their capital in a few days, they do not hold to a state and are always ready to abandon it if it runs into some danger. Like a band of partisans which robs

[33] Charles Fourier, "Crimes du commerce," *La Phalange. Revue de la science sociale* (July–August 1845), pp. 5–32, quoted from p. 19.

[34] Fourier, *Manuscrits. Années 1853–1856* (Paris, 1856), p. 24; *Oeuvres,* Anthropos, Vol. XI, p. 24, first pagination.

different regions alternately and stops only where it finds what to take, the merchants are ready to exploit every country, and change nations from one day to the next, to arrange a bankruptcy in Paris in order to go and make a great display of wealth a few days later in London or Berlin. There, this is what is easy for the merchants and the bankers, this is what is impossible for the clergy, the nobility, the manufacturers, and the landowners. The latter could not and would not want to be citizens of more than one country, the country to which their fortune or their political existence are linked.[35]

On another occasion, addressing especially the clergy and the intellectuals, Fourier declared:

A merchant has no god but gold and no fatherland but his portfolio; he is always ready to betray the interests of religion and of the ruler for usurious gain. Far from finding pleasure in the friends of enlightenment and in liberal ideas, he makes fun even of those good qualities which are attributed to him: he abhors and [   ] all that carries the name of a scholar; he shows a profound disdain for the philosophes who have the weakness of praising him. Similar to a reptile which lives only off polluted air, the merchant lives only off deceit and guile, dreams only disorganization, smuggling, and traps both for dear citizens and for the sovereign.[36]

In short: "Truth and commerce are as incompatible as Jesus and Satan."[37]

No wonder that merchants stopped at nothing to make their nefarious profits. Fourier liked to refer in particular to their alleged cornering of the grain market in 1812. But for this momentous action of speculators, Napoleon would have

[35] Fourier, *Manuscrits. Années 1853–1856* (Paris, 1856), p. 10; *Oeuvres*, Anthropos, Vol. XI, p. 10, first pagination.

[36] *Ibid.*, p. 104; *Oeuvres*, Anthropos, Vol. XI, p. 104. Brackets indicate that a word in the original could not be deciphered by the publishers of the manuscripts.

[37] *Ibid.*

crossed the Nieman on the fifteenth of May rather than the thirtieth of June, Turkey would have remained at war with Russia, the French would have entered Moscow on the thirty-first of July, not the fourteenth of September, at which time Napoleon would have had three more months of campaigning at his disposal as well as a full opportunity to fall back on the Ukraine if necessary—Russia would have had to sue for peace.[38] Thus, by denying timely supplies to the *grande armée* French grain speculators changed the course of history. Moreover, while these merchants themselves wanted merely to make fantastic profits by raising prices, they were probably manipulated, "as in 1789," by a hidden foreign hand, which they were only too ready to serve.[39] And in those more numerous cases where commercial activity had no epochal significance, it remained equally reprehensible and equally noxious within its limited range. Indeed merchants were worse than highway robbers: a robber, often reduced to despair by poverty, attacked at the risk of his life; a merchant despoiled his victims legally, by Tartuffe-like hypocrisy and astute machinations. In the science of analogy, commerce was represented by the ugly, dirty, and disgusting spider, spreading his web everywhere to catch flies and suck the blood out of them, just as the commercial establishment sucked gold out of its many victims.[40]

Turning to a more strictly economic analysis, Fourier was especially worried by the propensity of commerce to spread and multiply at the expense of other parts of the economy.

[38] For these calculations, see, for example, Fourier, *Analyse du mécanisme de l'agiotage* [*et*] *de la méthode mixte en étude de l'attration* (Paris, 1848), pp. 9–10.

[39] Fourier, *Manuscrits. Années 1853–1856* (Paris, 1856), p. 176; *Oeuvres,* Anthropos, Vol. XI, p. 176, first pagination.

[40] For the spider analogy, see Fourier, *Sur l'esprit irréligieux des modernes* and *Dernière analogies,* pp. 57–59; *Oeuvres,* Anthropos, Vol. XII, pp. 206–208.

"As long as the great mass of capital is directed towards busy work in preference to productive industry, as long as one sees that parasitic work is more profitable than creative labor, it can be said that industrial relations represent a repetition of the great farce of Civilization." [41] "The intermediary is thus the bloodsucker of the manufacturer and the cultivator, as well as of the consumer." [42] No successful economic reforms could be inaugurated until commerce was brought under control.

From generalities, the father of Harmony moved easily to particulars. "I was a broker and I could reveal all the scurvy tricks of the profession which are only too well known to me." [43] And in fact Fourier proceeded to describe at length the activities and the misdeeds of the brokers, an occupation for which one needed no learning, only "a good foot, a good eye, a good tongue and good fibbing," [44] and he even composed a short play on the subject.[45] Writing along the same lines, and with his usual precision, the utopian socialist addressed himself to such topics as an elaborate classification of stock exchanges,[46] a discussion of "36 kinds of bankruptcy" and other "crimes of commerce," [47] and an estimate of the

[41] Fourier, *Manuscrits* (Paris, 1851), p. 254; *Oeuvres*, Anthropos, Vol. X, p. 254, first pagination.

[42] Fourier, *La fausse industrie*, Vol. I, p. 313; *Oeuvres*, Anthropos, Vol. VIII, p. 313.

[43] Fourier, *Manuscrits. Années 1853–1856* (Paris, 1856), p. 181; *Oeuvres*, Anthropos, Vol. XI, p. 181, first pagination.

[44] Fourier, *Analyse du mécanisme de l'agiotage* [*et*] *de la méthode mixte en étude de l'attraction*, p. 56.

[45] *Ibid.* The play occupies pages 103–110.

[46] *Ibid.* A definition of the stock exchanges occupies pages 27–30, and their classification pages 30–35. Fourier's model contained five genera and twelve species.

[47] "The Crimes of Commerce" is the title of Fourier's study published in July–August 1845 in *La Phalange*. Cf., e.g., the treatment of the subject in Fourier, *Théorie des quatre mouvements et des*

annual loss to the French consumer from the adulteration of wine alone, which he put at 200 million francs.[48] These and other details served as excellent illustrations of Fourier's general evaluation of commerce. They attracted the admiration even of some of those students of Fourierism who were otherwise critical of the utopian socialist's views.[49]

Fourier's Anglophobia and anti-Semitism must also be considered in connection with his hatred for commerce, although in the case of Anglophobia residual patriotism and a natural hostility to the main enemy of Fourier's country when Fourier's ideology was being formed certainly played their part. As the theoretician of the phalanx commented bitterly on the subject of England: "It is without doubt an ignominious punishment that it inflicts on humankind, for nothing is more shameful, more productive of despair than to be subjugated without being able to fight, to be shackled, blocked and subdued politically by an unassailable enemy who does not show himself on land, except in the case of an overwhelming superiority of [his] forces."[50]

England incarnated a commercial order. Utilizing its in-

destinées générales, pp. 222–276; *Oeuvres,* Anthropos, Vol. I, pp. 222–276.

[48] The calculation was made in Charles Fourier, "Necessité d'une théorie certaine sur l'art d'associer," *La Reforme Industrielle,* No. 3 (June 14, 1832), pp. 26–31, especially p. 28. Elsewhere Fourier liked to cite a wine merchant who allegedly pointed to a well in his yard as the source of his affluence.

[49] To quote as one example M. Sambuc: "Let us confess it: if we do not always approve of Fourier when he speaks of the moralists, is is impossible for us not to applaud him when he entertains us with the abuses of Civilized commerce. At no other point of his doctrine does he merit our sympathy more." M. Sambuc, *Le socialisme de Fourier* (Paris, 1899), p. 123. Sambuc took an extremely critical view of the teaching of Fourier which he regarded as rigidly and viciously authoritarian.

[50] Fourier, *Manuscrits. Années 1853–1856* (Paris, 1856), p. 146; *Oeuvres,* Anthropos, Vol. XI, p. 146, first pagination.

sular position, it controlled the sea lanes of the globe, and thus world communications and trade. It proceeded to gain enormous wealth while checking at every point its rivals and opponents. Yet, in keeping with the nature of Civilization, these riches went to a very few, while the masses lived in utter misery. Highly profitable English factories seemed to be run by forced labor. Sailors were impressed to sustain the victorious navy. Slaves were mistreated as by no other people, except the Dutch. A most venal system of political representation assured liberties and political advantages for the rich, but only oppression for the poor. The English engaged in religious persecution, notably of the Irish Catholics. They showed extreme cruelty and perfidy in war, for example, when they bombarded Copenhagen and captured the Danish fleet without a declaration of hostilities. Indeed, stimulated by commercial rivalry, they fanned the flames of the two most tragic conflagrations of modern history, the French Revolution and the massacres of Santo Domingo. An Englishman, so Fourier asserted, could sell his wife at a market, and he received a pecuniary indemnity if she were seduced, thus obtaining a new opportunity to make money. The English developed the disastrous doctrine of *laissez-faire* which meant the subjugation of the entire world to commerce, while their efforts at association did not go beyond Owen's ignorant and hopeless schemes. It was this despicable, venal, and mercantile England that the nations of the continent were trying so hard to imitate.

If England was the country of commerce, the Jews were, perhaps paradoxically, the people of commerce. Commerce, to repeat, meant for Fourier not only trade, but more broadly the functions of middlemen in an economy: the category included not only merchants proper, but also commercial agents and employees of different kinds, brokers, speculators, and financiers of every sort. The Jews were prominent in these occupations. Claiming to speak "with knowledge, having lived a long time with them," [51] Fourier often mentioned Jews in his discussions and denunciations of commerce, and especially of brokers, speculators, usurers, and bankers. Thus, one nefarious character in the utopian socialist's short play about brokers bore the name of Israel, while Fourier's more questionable statistics included a reference to 3,000 London Jews "who urge servants to steal from their masters, children to rob their parents, and who distribute base coin." [52] Moreover, the Jews avoided productive occupations. "The Jews, to escape taxes, devote themselves everywhere to commerce, to banking, to usury, and to unproductive and deceitful activities." [53] "Nowhere does one see Jews undertaking useful services, agriculture and manufacturing." [54] Classical parasites of commercial Civilization, the Jews aimed at "invading the commerce of states at the expense of their nationals, without identifying themselves with the fate of the country." [55] As an eighteenth-century cosmopolitan rationalist, Fourier was also repelled and offended by what he considered to be the exclusiveness and prejudices of the Jews which prevented them from freely associating with Christians. In fact, he came at times to the interesting conclusion that the Jews were such an extremely undesirable people because they combined the vices of Civilization with those of Patriarchate. [56]

[51] Fourier, *Manuscrits. Années 1853–1856* (Paris, 1856), p. 34. *Oeuvres,* Anthropos, Vol. XI, p. 34.

[52] Fourier, *De l'anarchie industrielle et scientifique,* p. 18.

[53] Fourier, *Manuscrits* (Paris, 1852), p. 225; *Oeuvres,* Anthropos, Vol. X, p. 225, second pagination.

[54] *Ibid.,* p. 226; *Oeuvres,* Anthropos, Vol. X, p. 226, second pagination.

[55] Fourier, *Manuscrits. Années 1853–1856* (Paris, 1856), p. 37; *Oeuvres,* Anthropos, Vol. XI, p. 37, first pagination.

[56] See, e.g., Fourier, *Manuscrits* (Paris, 1851), p. 272; *Oeuvres,* Anthropos, Vol. X, p. 272, first pagination.

On the basis of his evaluation of the Jews, Fourier violently objected to their emancipation, advocated by the philosophes and then rapidly gaining ground in western and central Europe. Freed from all restrictions, the Jews would simply invade new areas, promoting everywhere noxious commerce and their own parasitic gains. While the father of Harmony rejected the methods of the Spanish Inquisition in combatting the Jews, he proposed to tie them to the land and make them scrape it, with no more than one Jewish family entitled to enter commerce for every fifty engaged in agriculture.[57] Fourier provided no particulars of his plan. Nor were such particulars really necessary. The trial phalanx, after all, was going to solve all the problems of mankind. This phalanx, as we know, could be established by a Rothschild as well as by another candidate.[58]

Fourier excluded no social classes or groups from his condemnation of Civilization. If the state, the church, and all other authorities and their agents concentrated on oppressing and controlling the people, if all the privileged segments of society, but especially the middle classes, exploited them and one another as best they could, the masses were not really any better. If the towns were dens of commerce and

[57] Fourier, *Manuscrits* (Paris, 1852), p. 227; *Oeuvres,* Anthropos, Vol. X, p. 227, second pagination. Or even one Jewish family in commerce for every hundred in agriculture and manufacturing. Fourier, *Le nouveau monde industriel et sociétaire,* p. 421; *Oeuvres,* Anthropos, Vol. VI, p. 421.

[58] Fourier's anti-Semitism was discussed in E. Silberner's already-mentioned article ("Charles Fourier on the Jewish Question," *Jewish Social Studies,* Vol. VIII, No. 4 [1946]) and cited in various studies of Fourier's system. Recently Zilberfarb made an unconvincing effort to absolve the theoretician of the phalanx of the charge of anti-Semitism: Zilberfarb, *Sotsialnaia filosofiia Sharlia Fure,* p. 449. Zilberfarb is, of course, correct in stating that Fourier's thinking was not based on the concept of race; unfortunately, Fourier's assumptions obviously still left room for a thoroughgoing, if less virulent, anti-Semitism.

vice, the countryside in its own way was equally despicable. In particular, Fourier rejected violently any admiration for the common man, the peasant, any cult of the people. "More than one rustic rejoices in secret over the misfortunes of his neighbors, for there is no class more jealous and full of hatred than these *good and simple inhabitants of the innocent countryside;* they detest and slander one another according to the *sweet moral brotherhood* which our philosophes place in the village, where it exists even less than in the city." [59] Fourier similarly castigated the extremely low sexual morality of the peasants, their ignorance, rudeness, and numerous other vices. The absence of a common bond, of a *lien général* permeated all of Civilization, making all of its men and all of its works turn into satanic horror. Indeed, in our society even those actions which were good in themselves produced evil results. Only Harmony could bring salvation.

And Civilization was getting progressively worse. The emphasis on the increase and acceleration of evil in contemporary society formed one of the most interesting aspects of Fourier's teaching. In England, which led the way, the utopian socialist indicated, the misery of the masses seemed to spread and deepen in direct proportion to the growth of commerce and the development of industry. Nor was this vicious evolution limited to England. In Civilization as a whole the interests of the people were separated from the progress of the system itself, and in fact came to be in an inverse relationship to it. "I call a world in reverse a methodical miscarriage of the systems which always leads to a superlative degree of ideal perfection and to a superlative degree of real degradation." [60]

[59] Fourier, *La fausse industrie,* Vol. II, p. B8 (775); *Oeuvres,* Anthropos, Vol. IX, p. B8 (775).

[60] Fourier, *Manuscrits* (Paris, 1852), p. 317; *Oeuvres,* Anthropos, Vol. X, p. 317, second pagination.

In trying to explain this paradoxical result, Fourier relied on several lines of reasoning. Civilization, to repeat, divided mankind into the few rich and the many poor, into a small group of exploiters and the exploited masses. Moreover, as already noted, the miseries of the people kept intertwining and mounting. "Our proletarians know only composite and not simple suffering; always two or three misfortunes at the same time, often half a dozen. This is evil in its composite subversive course: the destiny of humanity is double good or double evil." [61] This progression toward greater and greater evil had apparently a cumulative character for both individuals and for society as a whole. As the father of Harmony tried to explain in pseudo-scientific terms:

Let us discuss gravity: let us analyze in Y and Z two effects of a well-known falseness. In Civilization the poor class, Z, has less chance to obtain a fortune to the extent that it is more destitute: the poorer a man is, the less protection he finds, the less needed support; his indigence makes him suspect from the start, and he is refused the confidence and the employment obtained by a less penurious rival.

On the other hand, the more a man is in easy circumstances, the more lucky opportunities and employment he finds. Certain bankers live in opulence: Napoleon tosses them senatorial positions with incomes of 50,000 francs each, which they certainly do not in the least need, while so many poor and honorable families vainly solicit a modest position at 1,000 francs. . . .

Speaking theoretically: the Civilized rich obtain a greater fortune in *direct* proportion to that mass of it which they already possess, and in direct proportion to the smallness of the distance which lies between it and the greater fortune. Accordingly, they say in commerce: *"it is only the first hundred thousand francs that it takes an effort to gain."* This is true in commerce.

And the same at the court: a man already provided with a fine position quickly obtains a better one. In literature: an established

[61] Fourier, *La fausse industrie,* Vol. I, pp. s (366) – t (367); *Oeuvres,* Anthropos, Vol. VIII, pp. s (366) – t (367).

author passes off a most defective piece of work, an unknown fails to have an excellent piece accepted, not even an article for a journal.

Thus the mechanism of Civilization places for the rich a double opportunity of good on one of the scales, and no counterweight on the other; for the poor, a double opportunity of evil on one of the scales and no compensation on the other. A double subversion of justice, expressed by the two formulas Y and Z, above all by Z.[62]

A decline in the human condition in Civilization was accompanied, according to Fourier, by a climatic deterioration and by an increase in epidemics and various kinds of natural calamities.

The utopian socialist often mentioned this disastrous course of Civilization as inherent in its very structure and needing no further elaboration or explanation. On other occasions, however, he singled out certain causative factors as crucial in the decline: two especially, the growth of population, which expressed his usual predilection for Malthusianism, and an increase in the freedom, scope, and depredations of commerce, which gave him a new opportunity to vent his bias against the middleman. In addition, Fourier developed yet another closely related but distinct economic interpretation of the deepening crisis of Civilization, a variant of the overproduction or underconsumption argument.

Our destiny is to advance; each social period must advance towards a superior one. . . . The same is true of the phases: the first must move towards the second, the second towards the third, the third towards the fourth, the fourth towards the am-

[62] *Ibid.,* Vol. II, pp. X6–Y6 (748); *Oeuvres,* Anthropos, Vol. IX, pp. X6–Y6 (748). Elsewhere Fourier suggested that a social law operated here which paralleled the physical law that falling objects gathered speed.

biguous phase, and in sequence. If a society languishes too long in a given period or phase, corruption results, as in stagnant water. . . . We have been only for a century in the third phase of Civilization, but in this brief period of time the phase has advanced very rapidly, because of the colossal progress of industry; the result is that today the third phase exceeds its natural limits. We have too many materials for so little advanced a level; these materials not finding their natural employment, there is an overload and a malaise in the social mechanism. From this there results a fermentation which corrupts it; there develops a great number of noxious characteristics, symptoms of lassitude, effects of the disproportion which prevails between our industrial means and the subordinate level to which they are applied.[63]

Fourier proceeded to list and describe briefly twenty-four such disastrous effects. The split characteristic of Civilization had brought contemporary society to its ultimate dead end. "Can one see any wisdom in a social system where an idler chokes on food and laments that his granaries and his cellars are overburdened, while the mass of the working people is famished and is occupied solely in trying to ward off an appetite which it cannot satisfy?"[64] In sum, *"in Civilization poverty is born from abundance itself."*[65]

It should be added that, in line with the "dialectical" element in his thinking, Fourier asserted at times that the social deterioration which he described was desirable, that extreme evil was preferable to moderate evil, because it presaged change. It was "folly to wish to improve Civilization by any

[63] Fourier, *Le nouveau monde industriel et sociétaire*, p. 418. (*Oeuvres*, Anthropos, Vol. VI,, p. 418.) On the phases of Civilization see also *ibid.*, pp. 386–387; *Oeuvres*, Anthropos, Vol. VI, pp. 386–387.

[64] Fourier, *Pièges et charlatanisme des deux sectes Saint-Simon et Owen*, p. 32.

[65] Fourier, *Le nouveau monde industriel et sociétaire*, p. 35; *Oeuvres*, Anthropos, Vol. VI, p. 35.

kind of innovations." One was "closer to the good in the case of extreme depravity than in the case of semi-villainy." The worse, the better.[66]

Charles Fourier's analysis indicated that Civilization, with all its faults, did manage to establish a strong economic base for the happy society of the future. Indeed from about the time of Solon man was physically prepared to step into Harmony. "Large-scale industry" had been created, only correct doctrine remained to be added to accomplish the transformation. The responsibility for the tragic delay in the progress of mankind thus lay with the false prophets, the philosophes, and their 400,000 volumes of pernicious nonsense. For more than two thousand years they had been misleading humanity and turning it away from the correct path; now that the true teaching had finally appeared, their main effort seemed to be to suppress or denigrate it.

Fourier attacked incessantly these enemies of mankind.[67] Their writings showed a complete disregard of scientific method which required that investigators start from a position of "absolute doubt" and adhere strictly in their work to such principles as reliance on experience, and on observation rather than imagination.[68] Instead the philosophes merely released torrents of words signifying nothing or restating in a most complex, virtually incomprehensible form simple

[66] Fourier, *Théorie de l'unité universelle,* Vol. IV, p. 294; *Oeuvres,* Anthropos, Vol. V, p. 294. Fourier, *Manuscrits. Années 1853–1856* (Paris, 1856), p. 12; *Oeuvres,* Anthropos, Vol. XI, p. 12, first pagination. See also, e.g., Fourier, *Manuscrits* (Paris, 1851), pp. 312–313; *Oeuvres,* Anthropos, Vol. X, pp. 312–313, first pagination.

[67] The best summary of the attacks is provided in Bourgin, *Fourier. Contribution à l'étude du socialisme français,* Vol. I, pp. 165–186.

[68] Fourier was convinced that his own teaching represented a perfect application of the scientific method. For the principles to follow, see, for instance, the discussion of twelve such principles plus two pivotal ones in Fourier, *Théorie de l'unité universelle,* Vol. II, Chapter III (pp. 129–140); *Oeuvres,* Anthropos, Vol. III, pp. 129–140.

and generally known truths. Above all, they could at the most describe an evil, never show the way out. "When one is in a labyrinth the problem is to get out and not to perfect it or to keep running along its windings; one must seek and find the exit." [69]

The philosophes, represented in the science of analogy by parrots,[70] came in many categories and groups. Mention has already been made of the stalwart secular and ecclesiastical defenders of the status quo who taught the famished masses to worship their oppressors and exploiters. However, the revolutionary thinkers and doers in their turn only brought new calamities upon mankind. Fourier frequently cited the atrocities of the great French Revolution as a particularly frightening chapter in the history of humanity, as well as one with which he was personally acquainted, and he referred to Robespierre as the epitome of a bloodthirsty tyrant. Stressing his own horror of violence, he offered his key to Harmony as, among other things, the surest way to avoid the otherwise threatening bloodshed, perturbations, and revolutions.[71] The theoretician of the phalanx was clearly a man of peace. And yet it bears repeating that Fourier's main accusation against the French Revolution was that it had failed to abolish the family: rather than going too far, in one most important respect at least it did not go far enough.

[69] Fourier, *De l'anarchie industrielle et scientifique,* p. 22.

[70] "Nature depicts in parrots this mania of contradiction of the philosophic systems; one has red at the top of the wing and yellow at the bottom of the quills, another has yellow at the top of the wing and red at the bottom of the quills." Fourier, *La fausse industrie,* Vol. I, p. 330; *Oeuvres,* Anthropos, Vol. VIII, p. 330.

[71] For example, Fourier warned Louis-Philippe as he urged the king to establish a trial phalanx: "The danger persists; Fieschi's machine is in its initial stage, it will be perfected in this century of progress; other ways of assassination will be attempted; the fanatics are numerous, the hates full of poison." *Ibid.,* p. 338; *Oeuvres,* Anthropos, Vol. VIII, p. 338.

Also, there is little doubt that the utopian socialist would have accepted a trial phalanx from another Robespierre as well as from anyone else. In fact, the conservatives, the revolutionaries, the liberals, and all other kinds of political theorists and politicians were wrong and hopeless, in the opinion of Fourier, precisely because they relied on political measures and solutions when mankind needed a total abolition of Civilization together with all politics and an introduction of Harmony.

The economists at least addressed themselves to more important questions dealing with the productivity and structure of society. But they missed their opportunity. Instead of developing the promising ideas of Quesnay they surrendered to the English school which glorified free trade, free economic activity of every sort, and in effect the very anarchy of Civilization. The new false prophets of association, such as Owen and Saint-Simon, who had, to be sure, the merit of challenging the existing system, could not produce any solutions. Their views were simplistic, rather than composite, tyrannical in essence, and blind in regard to human nature. Owen in particular turned to a kind of asceticism instead of allowing human passions their full play.[72]

If the economists at least trod on crucial ground, the philosophers proper, in particular the moralists, simply could not be taken seriously. They were among the greatest hypocrites of our hypocritical Civilization, praising virtue while wallowing in vice, and eulogizing poverty while filling their coffers. Their moral disquisitions and strictures bore no relation to any kind of reality, for our society remained quite immoral. In their own way they were the falsehood of that society personified. The main mistake of the moralists was their failure to see the utter relativity and insignificance of

---

[72] See especially Fourier, *Pièges et charlatanisme de deux sectes Saint-Simon et Owen.*

all their hallowed dogmas. And yet they had merely to look around to realize their error. For example:

The Danube witnesses on its two banks a bizarre contrast of duties. On the left bank the duty is to marry but a single woman and to be faithful to her the entire life; if one marries two, that is polygamy, that is a case for the hangman. On the right bank, the duty is to marry no more than four, but, to compensate for this, there are female slaves in unlimited numbers: this is what it means to perform religious and civil duties.[73]

Developing this line of reasoning, Fourier liked to describe in detail how every vice and perversion of one society is a virtue or even a religious obligation of another.[74] Morality had no objective basis, except perhaps when it led toward the phalanx. All the sages of Civilization had to offer was a babel of opinions characteristic of the confusion and chaos of their society. "There are so many interchangeable moralities which vary with the individuals and the circumstances! I am right, therefore, to answer, when morality is mentioned, which one of the ten thousand?"[75]

Charles Fourier's critique of Civilization had sweep and power. On the basis of his highly developed, comprehensive, and original ideology, and with a vision of Harmony in front of his eyes, the theoretician of the phalanx denounced the contemporary order of existence in a fundamental and far-reaching manner. Family and society, the state and the church, economy and morals, as well as all other pillars of

[73] Fourier, *La fausse industrie*, Vol. I, p. 123; *Oeuvres*, Anthropos, Vol. VIII, p. 123.

[74] See, e.g., *ibid.*, Vol. II, pp. 566–571; *Oeuvres*, Anthropos, Vol. IX, pp. 566–572 and Fourier, *Egarement de la raison* and *Fragments*, pp. 28–30; *Oeuvres*, Anthropos, Vol. XII, pp. 569.

[75] Fourier, *La fausse industrie*, Vol. II, p. 596; *Oeuvres*, Anthropos, Vol. IX, p. 596.

Civilization, were found not merely wanting but rather representing in their essence an ultimate perversion, the direct opposite of the proper setting for human life, a world in reverse. The painter's palette had only two colors, black and white, and black alone applied to Civilization. As usual, Fourier added specific detail to broad generalization, arranging the detail in his own unique way. Thus in his treatment of "Commerce and marriage" the utopian socialist discussed jointly bankruptcy and cuckoldry and described for his readers eighty different types of cuckolds.[76] In a similar vein he offered reasoned classifications of the stock exchanges or of "the disfavors of the worker." If Fourier's presentation of the case against Civilization lacked the light touch and all humor, except bitter sarcasm, the subject was not a light one, and the sarcasm did strike time and again to support its author's violent assaults.[77]

It is important to realize that Fourier had an immense conviction about what he wrote, and that he wrote with utter sincerity. Moreover, he denounced and he preached as a prophet and a moralist. While the utopian socialist's analysis emphasized the striking relativity of moral codes, his attack on Civilization was suffused with violent moral passion aimed against a despicable society which perverted and destroyed men. There could be no compromise with evil: the issue was perdition or salvation.

Critics of Fourier have pointed out correctly that he was

[76] Fourier, *Manuscrits. Années 1853–1856* (Paris, 1856), pp. 249–273; *Oeuvres,* Anthropos, Vol. XI, pp. 249–273, first pagination. Actually Fourier described here seventy-six types of cuckoldry and merely named the last four.

[77] In perfect keeping with his general cast of mind and view of the world, Fourier's humor was limited to heavy sarcasm. Those who consider Fourier an outstanding humorist, and in particular credit him with gentle or sophisticated humor, usually read in a comic light passages that were not at all amusing to their author.

both an ignoramus and a crank. In Emile Faguet's elegant words: "He has the disadvantages of ignorance which are big, and the advantages of ignorance which are enormous." [78] A crucial advantage, no doubt, was a certain self-assurance, a readiness to judge simply and decisively, without bothering about nuances, limitations, qualifications, and contradictions. A university education or simply better knowledge of the very numerous subjects under consideration might well have hampered the utopian socialist's rough-and-ready approach. Fourier's obsession with his own solution to all the problems of mankind and his total condemnation of the surrounding world do forcefully remind the reader of various crank letters in local newspapers composed by assorted homemade discoverers of panaceas and prophets of doom.

And yet, to say the least, Charles Fourier was an unusual crank. Whether because of his education or his ignorance—and education, after all, can explain things away as well as explain them—because of his strange mentality or the circumstances of his life, the theoretician of the phalanx seemed to have time and again a strange penetration into man and the affairs of men. The most remarkable aspect of his critique of Civilization was an immediate grasp, a kind of direct vision, of oppression, exploitation, and pain, where others did not see it at all, did not see it as well, or carefully rationalized it. This oppression, exploitation, and pain applied to the relation between sexes, between generations, between classes, between countries, to the entire human condition in Civilization. Fourier refused to accept any of it. Late in life, for example, he became disturbed by the Greek war of independence and by the massacres of the Greek popula-

[78] Faguet, *op. cit.*, p. 46. Cf., e.g., Renouvier's emphasis on Fourier's limited education, described as "instruction primaire supérieure," and his daring and self-assurance. Renouvier, *op. cit.*, pp. 324–325.

tion by the Turks. He kept returning to this subject in his writings, in and out of turn, apparently simply because he could not accept it, forget it, or explain it away. Or, to end where we began our discussion of Fourier's critique of that Civilization which starved man of everything he so desperately needed: ". . . for to some they give soup twice a week: and the poor, the sick, do they feel hunger no more than twice a week?" [79] Until mankind reaches Harmony, such questions will have relevance.

[79] Fourier, *La fausse industrie*, Vol. II, p. T6 (744); *Oeuvres*, Anthropos, Vol. IX, p. T6 (744).

CHAPTER IV

Fourier and "le Mouvement Social"

I have classified the human couple in category zero, or transition, because it is but a germ of the integral man who demands 810 active characters. It is necessary to cogitate upon this assemblage to tackle the table of harmonious beings. An ignorance of this rule has misled all those who have pondered over the abovementioned table; they begin their calculations with the individual, who is an essentially false being, because he cannot either by himself or in a couple work out the development of the 12 passions, for they are a mechanism of 810 keys plus the additions. It is thus with the passional phalanx that the table begins and not with the individual who is but an embryo and particle of the integral man, as a bee is but a particle of the beehive, that is, of the passional mechanism of the bees.[1]

I alone have penetrated scientific deserts to discover there new countries.[2]

A pathetic contrast persisted between Charles Fourier's belief in the transcendent importance of his message and his circumstances. The would-be destroyer of Civilization and savior of mankind could not obtain even a modest hearing. As the theoretician of Harmony bitterly observed, appropriating a well-known text: "Light is come into the world, and men loved darkness rather than light, because their deeds were evil. *John 3: 19 III.*"[3]

[1] Fourier, *Manuscrits. Années 1857–1858* (Paris, 1858), pp. 320–321; *Oeuvres*, Edition Anthropos, Vol. XI, pp. 320–321, second pagination.

[2] Fourier, *La fausse industrie*, Vol. I, p. 300; *Oeuvres*, Anthropos, Vol. VIII, p. 300.

[3] Fourier, *Le nouveau monde industriel et sociétaire*, p. 377; *Oeuvres*, Anthropos, Vol. VI, p. 377.

Still, as already mentioned, the teaching of the Messiah of reason did not go entirely unnoticed during the Messiah's lifetime. Before his days ended, Fourier had acquired an enthusiastic, if rather small, band of disciples, had published vigorously in the new Fourierist press, and had even suffered through and condemned an abortive effort to establish a trial phalanx. The years immediately following the master's death witnessed splits and "heresies" in the Fourierist circles, but they also saw Fourierism, ably championed by Victor Considérant, rise to a considerable intellectual and momentarily even political prominence in France. Only with the June Days and the ensuing reaction, which, incidentally, sent Considérant into exile, did French Fourierism retreat to its original positions of sectarian intellectual propaganda and efforts to stage communal experiments. It maintained these positions for decades. Marx and later radicals, as well as some critics of other persuasions, accused Considérant and the Fourierists as a whole of betraying the revolutionary message of their teacher in favor of an accommodation to the dismal reality. The charge was justified to the extent that the main line of Fourierism abandoned the more eccentric aspects of the doctrine, such as cosmology, analogy, or sexology, and, much more importantly from the point of view of the accusers, to the extent that it turned to "guaranteeistic institutions" and gradualism in general in lieu of staking everything on a leap into Harmony. Indeed the Fourierism of the disciples lost comprehensiveness and vision as they busied themselves pruning certain passages of Fourier and explaining away others.

It should be kept in mind, however, that Charles Fourier himself was no proponent of revolutionary violence and, especially, that he did not readily fit into any radical scheme of history, except his own. Nor is the victory of the petty bourgeios milieu the only possible explanation for the domestication of Fourierism. One cannot help but sympathize with the followers of the master left upon his death with an all-embracing and all-important formula which could not even quite be grasped, let alone utilized to transfigure the world. To put it a little differently, the master's obsessions remained largely personal. Nor, under the circumstances, could Fourier's burning faith be easily maintained by his disciples. Even Considérant came to believe late in life that destinies may not be proportionate to attractions.

Fourier's thought expressed the cosmopolitanism of the Enlightenment, and his appeal to create Harmony was not restricted to any country, continent, or race. The theoretician of the phalanx offered salvation to all. In this respect, it was only appropriate that his message spread from France to neighboring lands and eventually to the four corners of the world. Even during Fourier's lifetime a phalanx was attempted in Rumania, while after his death many Fourierist —as well as non-Fourierist—communitarian efforts were mounted in the United States. Zilberfarb's learned and generally excellent discussion of "Fourier's ideas beyond the boundaries of France" contains sections on England, Germany, Belgium, Sweden, Switzerland, Italy, Spain, Austria including not only German Austria but also Hungarian, Slovak, and Czech territories, Poland, Rumania, the United States, Latin America from Venezuela to Patagonia, China, and certain French colonies. In addition, the Soviet scholar wrote a chapter on "the ideas of Fourier in Russia." [4]

Characteristically, the Fourierists of different lands combined the universal teaching of their master with local aspirations and demands. Thus many of the so-called Petra-

---

[4] The chapter on "Fourier's Ideas beyond the Boundaries of France" occupies pp. 253–329 and the chapter on "The Ideas of Fourier in Russia" pp. 330–382 of Zilberfarb, *Sotsialnaia filosofiia Sharlia Fure*. The book contains superb bibliographies.

shevtsy, an informal group of two score or more young men who gathered around Michael Butashevich-Petrashevsky in St. Petersburg from late 1845 until their arrest in the spring of 1849, added to Fourierism political protest, demand for change, and general opposition to the Russia of Nicholas I. They condemned the central Russian evil of serfdom and sketched projects of emancipation, while Petrashevsky himself was especially interested in a thorough reform of the judiciary. They praised the freedom of the press and objected to autocracy. In short, they embodied political protest in the specific conditions of mid-nineteenth-century Russia. Also, many Petrashevtsy disregarded or modified major parts of Fourier's teaching. For example, Petrashevsky, as well as some of his associates, championed atheism. And yet it remained Petrashevsky's hope that Nicholas I would establish a phalanx "near Paris," while he willed one-third of his estate "to Considérant, the head of the Fourierist school, for the founding of a phalanstery." [5] There is something profoundly tragic as well as strikingly ridiculous in the image of Petrashevsky dreaming about the future, dreaming how in a chain gang:

Perhaps fate . . . will put me next to a hardened criminal, on whose conscience there are ten murders. . . . Sitting down during the break for the noontime meal of dry bread, we shall start a conversation; I shall tell him how and why misfortune struck me. . . . I shall tell him about Fourier . . . about the phalanstery. . . .[6]

[5] *Delo Petrashevtsev,* 3 vols. (Moscow-Leningrad, 1937–1951). Quoted from Vol. I, pp. 183–184. There are some indications that Petrashevsky had tried to establish a phalanx on his own estate, but that its building burned down.

[6] *Ibid.,* Vol. II, p. 84. On the Petrashevtsy see Nicholas V. Riasanovsky, "Fourierism in Russia: an Estimate of the Petraševcy," *The American Slavic and East European Review,* Vol. XII, No. 3 (October 1953), pp 289–302. Young Dostoevsky belonged to the circle of the Petrashevtsy.

Nor was Fourier's influence limited to outright Fourier-ists. In fact, the relationship between the teaching of the theoretician of Harmony and the doctrines of contemporary and subsequent major and minor thinkers has remained one of the most involved and intriguing aspects of the study of Fourierism. To begin with, there was the complex connection of Fourier with Saint-Simon, Enfantin, and other Saint-Simonians, which, as already indicated, left an impact on Fourier's writings as well as on the early history of the Fourierist movement.[7] Somewhat later Marx and Engels assigned major importance to Fourier as a critic of the modern world and at the same time emphasized the "utopian" aspects of his approach which had to be overcome before a valid ideology could be created. The link to Marxism assured Fourier of a central position even in the most rigid Marxist schemes of intellectual history, and led to a thorough study of his works in the Soviet Union. French Marxists of different kinds in particular made repeated attempts not only to elucidate further the significance of Fourier in the Marxist scheme of things, but also to integrate the strange thought of the father of Harmony with that of their own master.[8]

In general many radicals, reformers, and socialists affirmed and developed various parts of Fourier's teaching.

[7] In addition to Fourier's own criticism of Saint-Simon, notably his *Pièges et charlatanisme des deux sectes Saint-Simon et Owen,* see especially Louvancour's *De Henri de Saint-Simon à Charles Fourier.* Louvancour believed that the Saint-Simonians took from Fourier "the theory of the 'rehabilitation of the flesh' and all that is related to it" (pp. 164–165).

[8] F. Armand and R. Maublanc, *Fourier. Textes choisis,* 2 vols. (Paris, 1937). M. Lansac, *Les conceptions méthodologiques et sociales de Charles Fourier. Leur influence* (Paris, 1926). An important early book on Fourier by a leading German Marxist is August Bebel, *Charles Fourier. Sein Leben und seine Theorien* (Stuttgart, 1886).

To be sure, in most cases it is difficult to draw the line between the direct influence of the theoretician of the phalanx and his school and the broader intellectual climate of the age. Thus further work is needed to establish the exact relationship between Fourier on the one hand and Moses Hess in Germany, Nicholas Chernyshevsky in Russia, or Esteban Echeverria in Argentina on the other. Still, the strange ideas of the strange thinker from Besançon kept recurring in the so-called progressive thought of the nineteenth and twentieth centuries. They also found reflection in artistic literature, notably in Zola's *Work*, as well as in other pieces by different authors. Such specialists in modern French ideologies as professors Gide and Bouglé discovered Fourierism or at least "memories" of Fourierism permeating socialism and the cooperative movement in France.[9] Indeed, in the words of Sorel, published in 1895: "The ideas of Fourier have remained fully alive in our country; it can be said that out of ten Frenchmen concerned with social questions, nine are incomplete or illogical Fourierists."[10] It should be added that a concern with social questions was not a necessary requirement for appreciating Fourier. Twentieth-century admirers of the prophet of Harmony included the surrealists led by André Breton. *"The attractions are proportionate to the destinies. In which faith I come today to you."*[11]

---

[9] See especially Charles Gide, *Fourier, précurseur de la cooperation* (Paris, 1924); C. Bouglé, *Socialismes français. Du 'Socialisme utopique' à la 'Démocratie industrielle'* (Paris, 1933). Chapters VII and VIII (pp. 93–125) of Bouglé's book deal with Fourierism.

[10] Quoted from Gide, *Fourier, précurseur de la cooperation*, p. 149.

[11] "En foi de quoi je viens aujourd'hui vers toi." Breton, *Ode à Charles Fourier*, p. 74. See also in particular Jean Gaulmier's comments to the *Ode* and Gerald Schaeffer's article "L'ode à Charles Fourier et la tradition" in *André Breton. Essais et témoignages.*

As a different example of an enthusiastic appreciation, this time with a strong pseudoscientific bent, of the more esoteric side of Fourier, see F. Jollivet-Castelot, *Sociologie et Fourierisme. Un le tout*

However, this chapter and the next will be devoted not to an investigation of Fourier's influence, either in the narrow or the broad sense, on other thinkers, but rather to a further exposition and analysis of Fourier's own teaching, this time in its relationship to some main currents of *le mouvement social*.

Following the assessment made by Marx and Engels, Charles Fourier has often been called a "utopian socialist." In fact, this has been the label most frequently applied to him. But it has not remained unchallenged. Moreover, the nature of Fourier's socialism aside, the very assertion that Fourier was a socialist has been seriously questioned. One major issue has resided in the fact that Fourier, after all, retained in his ideal society a restricted but in its own way highly developed system of private property with the result that his blueprint for the future did not entirely agree with the classic definition of socialism as public ownership of the means of production. Indeed, and much to the chagrin of many of his socialist admirers, Fourier's writings displayed a veritable passion for private property as well as for inequality. Other arguments denying Fourier's socialism have also been adduced. Thus Edmond Villey asserted that Fourier was not a socialist because he based his system on liberty and free passional attraction, while socialism, according to Villey, implied a reliance on the state and legal constraint.[12]

(Paris, 1908). Jollivet-Castelot accepted such aspects of Fourier's teaching as his cosmology, the doctrine of the transmigration of souls and analogy, but he argued that we were not yet in a position to establish specific analogies, accused the master of an overabundance of detail and classification and of a "childish" passion for new nomenclature, and expressed a strong preference for a gradual, peaceful change of the world instead of Fourier's "hurry." Cf. Jollivet-Castelot's thoroughly Fourierist "Harmonian day around the year 2,000," where marriage, nevertheless, wins out (pp. 201–209).

[12] Villey, "Charles Fourier, l'homme et son oeuvre," p. 1003.

On the other hand, some writers not only included Fourier within the socialist tradition, but also assigned to him a central position in the development of socialism. For example, Emile Faguet argued: "No one can demonstrate better than Fourier how the entire socialist movement, how all the socialist movements of the century, except Proudhon who is not a socialist, stem directly from Rousseau; Fourier is essential in order to understand this." [13]

In discussing the problem of Fourier and socialism it seems best to concentrate not on the largely semantic issue of the possible definitions of socialism and their relationship to Fourier's teaching, but rather on the fundamental contributions of the theoretician of the phalanx to the socialist mode of thought. Perhaps two such contributions stand out: the primacy of the social group over the isolated individual, and the construction of the harmonious society of the future on the basis of such groups. Moreover, as in many other instances, Fourier not only affirmed these common socialist views, but developed them to a fantastic, even insane, extreme.

To repeat one of the most important passages in all of Fourier's writing:

I have classified the human couple in category zero, or transition, because it is but a germ of the integral man who demands 810 active characters. It is necessary to cogitate upon this assemblage to tackle the table of harmonious beings. An ignorance of this rule has misled all those who have pondered over the abovementioned table; they begin their calculations with the individual, who is an essentially false being, because he cannot either by himself or in a couple work out the development of the 12 passions, for they are a mechanism of 810 keys plus the additions. It is thus with the passional phalanx that the table begins and not with the individual who is but an embryo and particle of the integral man, as a bee is but a particle of the beehive, that is, of the passional mechanism of the bees.[14]

In contrast, for example, to the tigers, who were not meant for a social "industrial" life and in whose case "two tigers, a male and a female, certainly compose the integral tiger," the integral beaver, bee, or man required a sufficient number of the species, properly organized, and provided with the setting necessary for their activities. Numbers alone, while requisite, did not suffice. Thus there could be no beehive without flowers. Human beings too required, in addition to numbers, both the necessary material means and the proper organization. A million Civilized people, with all their activities and groupings, came nowhere near forming the integral man. In fact, while Savagery provided freedom without industrial organization, and Barbarism and Civilization industrial organization without freedom, none of these conditions enabled humans to fulfil their destiny which was "the free and full exercise of all material and passional faculties." [15] One had to look to the phalanx to discover the integral man. "The nucleus or the first stage cannot be found except in a phalanx of Harmony with 810 characters, and that is truly the integral man of the first degree, and the point of departure from which we must sally to speculate concerning the relations of beings who form the complex table." [16] A phalanx thus corresponded to a beehive or to an integrated society of beavers. The difference between humans and the other two species consisted in the fact, noted

[14] Fourier, *Manuscrits. Années 1857–1858* (Paris, 1858), pp. 320–321; *Oeuvres,* Anthropos, Vol. XI, pp. 320–321, second pagination. Fourier, *Le nouveau monde amoureux,* pp. 461–464; *Oeuvres,* Anthropos, Vol. VII, pp. 461–464.

[15] Fourier, *Manuscrits. Années 1857–1858* (Paris, 1858), p. 322; *Oeuvres,* Anthropos, Vol. XI, p. 322, second pagination.

[16] *Ibid.*

by Fourier repeatedly elsewhere, that whereas the bees and the beavers, given the proper setting, formed their harmonious perfect societies automatically by instinct, man had to discover and studiously organize his.

Fourier returned to his remarkable vision of the integral man on more than one occasion. Thus he answered the Saint-Simonian assertion that the conjugal couple, man and woman, constituted the social man, by declaring that that couple constituted merely the material man, and not the social, industrial, and moral man. The latter could be found only in a societary union of different levels of characters distributed like the pipes of an organ.

Let us answer to Father Hoart that the physical man and the moral man are the two extremes: the physical or material man is the smallest combination possible, that of male and female; the moral and social man is the greatest combination possible in domestic union applying to manufacturing or agricultural work all the steps of passions, instincts, characters, tastes, accords, discords, sympathies, antipathies and other inequalities, whether of fortune or of faculties.[17]

The correct number of members for such an effective greatest possible combination was 1,620, or better 1,800 to provide for a reserve. In another passage the theoretician of Harmony followed the principle of analogy to compare the 810 characters of a phalanx to "the 810 muscles of the couple, male and female," its choirs and "quadrilles" to the teeth, and so forth.[18]

Charles Fourier kept emphasizing the true nature of the integral man because his contemporaries remained grossly ignorant of it:

[17] Charles Fourier, "Revue des utopies du XIXe siècle," *La Reforme Industrielle,* No. 6 (July 5, 1832), pp. 49–51, No. 7 (July 12, 1832), pp. 57–59, No. 8 (July 19, 1832), pp. 65–69. Quoted from p. 68.

[18] "Textes inédits de Charles Fourier présenté par Simone Debout Oleszkiewicz," p. 151.

Basing ourselves on the preceding account, we have corrected a fundamental error on the nature of the human soul: everyone believes that he has been provided with a complete and entire soul. This is a cruder mistake than would be that of a soldier pretending to constitute a regiment all by himself; he would be told that he forms but a thousandth part of it, if the regiment consisted of 1,000 men. The error of the soldier would be much less shocking than the one committed on the subject of the integrality of the soul. For the soldier is made of the same matter as the captain or the colonel; he might replace them, whereas on the passional keyboard a character of a monogyne with a single dominant passion is thoroughly different from that of a digyne, trigyne, etc. They cannot replace one another. It is even impossible to replace one monogyne by another monogyne of a different or similar title. Let us explain by an example: suppose it was the question of a game of cards and that the card-maker offered a thousand aces of hearts, only one of the thousand would be accepted, a second would be superfluous. The same is true of the passional mechanics where the 810 characters are comparable to a game with 810 different cards.[19]

Nor was it really surprising that the integral soul consisted of 810 pieces. Even the integral body demanded two individuals, one male and one female. Or, to look at it from a different angle, the integral bee required perhaps as many as 20,000 bees, all forming a single beehive. The tragedy of humanity was, of course, that the human beehive, the phalanx, had as yet never been formed. History witnessed no integral man, no integral soul, only fragments of it everywhere, like disoriented and destructive bees without a beehive.

Having postulated the absolute primacy and the supreme importance of the phalanx, Fourier proceeded to build the new world based on the phalanx. No particular illustrations

---

[19] *Ibid.*, p. 153. While Fourier divides his integral man, or soul, into 810 fragments in this passage, and apparently into 1,620, modified to 1,800, in a preceding instance, this and other such differences are not germane to the main argument.

are needed here, because Fourier's whole teaching was an illustration of this point. It is worth noting, however, that very few, if any, other writers in the entire socialist and generally collectivist tradition developed their systems to the extent and the degree of precision characteristic of Harmony. To repeat, Fourier was in an important sense not only a participant in a major intellectual trend, but also perhaps its most extreme and daring, if always idiosyncratic, theoretician and champion.

Collectivist and broadly socialist in its main assumptions and in the structure of its blueprint for humanity, Fourier's teaching included many specific views which became common in socialist writings. Thus, as we have seen, the theoretician of the phalanx emphasized the economic element in the evolution of humanity and even argued in terms of an economic determinism. Men, like bees and beavers, needed the physical means to organize an integral unit. Therefore, a sufficiently high stage of technology and economic development became one of the two prerequisites for the construction of Harmony, the other being the knowledge of correct theory. Again, a growth of population and the resulting increasing pressure on material resources served Fourier as the most important, frequently as the only, explanation of the progress of mankind through its various historical stages. In fact, in this crucially significant matter Fourier can be considered not only a disciple of Malthus, but also a forerunner of the neo-Malthusians of the twentieth century. In Harmony, it might be added, the new style of life would lead to a decline in fecundity.

The theoretician of the phalanx was also magnificently aware of oppression and exploitation. He tended to take a "realistic," brutal view of life as an arena of pitiless, egoistic exercise of naked, or more veiled, power. To be sure, it was Fourier's genius to see exploitation and oppression in family relations, in love and friendship, in groups of children or among the boarders in a boarding house, as well as in the social and economic structure of society at large. Fourier's full view of the unfortunate human lot was a nuanced, sophisticated, and penetrating one indeed. Nevertheless on many occasions he simplified it drastically and spoke merely of the exploiters and the exploited, the haves and the have-nots, the few with power and wealth and the many enslaved to them. At times the angry man from Besançon defined Civilization as a system in which the passions of one-eighth of its members were satisfied at the expense of the remaining seven-eighths, although more often and in terms of his teaching more fundamentally he stressed that the privileged themselves were also miserable, if less so than the masses, because only the phalanx could truly satisfy human passions. As has been indicated, Fourier regarded the political, social, and economic institutions, and even the ideologies of Civilization, primarily as supports of this shameless exploitation of the majority by a small minority. Few subsequent writers put the case more starkly.

The exploiters and the exploited were in effect, according to Fourier, two worlds which Civilization could not bridge. "Our social system, shot through and through with duplicity, has to have two languages as well as two educations; it is necessary to provide for the people a patois, the dogmas of hellfire; in sum, two disparate educations in the political, material, and moral sense! Ha! How can one admit unity of education into an order of things where the masses, seven-eighths of the people, are despoiled by the eighth part which laughs at their expense?" [20] Fourier's emphasis on the gulf between the rich and the poor, and his telling references to their different modes of existence were all the more impres-

[20] Fourier, *Manuscrits* (Paris, 1851), p. 189; *Oeuvres,* Anthropos, Vol. X, p. 189, first pagination.

sive because they remained free of a sentimental idealization of the masses to which some other socialists and reformers were to succumb. Although himself not an advocate of force, the prophet of Harmony observed more than once that the conditions of Civilization would lead to violent explosions and he urged the establishment of a trial phalanx in order to avert revolution.

Fourier's teaching marked a transition between the thought of the Enlightenment and the socialist and related doctrines developed later in the nineteenth century. His critique of Civilization in particular spans the two intellectual milieus and belongs fully in both contexts. Moreover, as we have seen, the prophet of Harmony presented certain approaches and arguments as fully and sharply as any of the subsequent writers. In other respects, to be sure, Fourier's works contained early and limited versions of arguments and views which were to receive a greater scope and elaboration within the socialist tradition. To quote again a passage from Fourier which has attracted the attention of more than one student of Marxism:

We have been only for a century in the third phase of Civilization, but in this brief period of time the phase has advanced very rapidly, because of the colossal progress of industry; the result is that today the third phase exceeds its natural limits. We have too many materials for so little advanced a level; these materials not finding their natural employment, there is an overload and a malaise in the social mechanism. From this there results a fermentation which corrupts it; there develops a great number of noxious characteristics, symptoms of lassitude, effects of the disproportion which prevails between our industrial means and the subordinate level to which they are applied.[21]

---

[21] Fourier, *Le nouveau monde industriel et sociétaire*, p. 418; *Oeuvres*, Anthropos, Vol. VI, p. 418.

One should be promptly reminded, however, that this was an exceptional analysis in the work of Fourier who generally interpreted economic crises in terms of an unbridled exploitation by middlemen. Another foreshadowing of a later development might be provided, for instance, by the fragmentary and disorganized "dialectic" found in a variety of places in Fourier's writings.[22]

Other specific doctrines of Fourier deserve attention with special reference to Marxism. In an excellent recent treatment of the subject, Zilberfarb dwelt on the very high appreciation by Marx and Engels of Fourier's magnificent critique of Civilization, then continued:

But the value of Fourier's teaching is not limited to the power of his criticism. In the "Manifesto of the Communist party" are noted valuable assertions concerning the society of the future which can be found in the teachings of critical-utopian socialism,

---

[22] In the words of Talmon: "Fourier's dialectics of history foreshadow Marxist dialectics." J. L. Talmon, *Political Messianism, the Romantic Phase* (London, 1960), p. 144. Pages 125–156 are devoted to "Individual and Organization in Utopia (Fourier, Considérant)."

For a sweepingly high appraisal of dialectical thought in Fourier, see Ark. A-n (Anekshtein), "Elementy dialektiki i ekonomicheskogo materializma v vozzreniaikh Sharlia Fure," *Pod Znamenem Marksizma*, No. 3 (March, 1924), pp. 202–229. Anekshtein asserts the dialectic nature of Fourier's fundamental dichotomy between Harmony and Civilization, the correct world and the world in reverse where the human passions have the opposite impact, as well as the dialectical character of his historical analysis which traces the evolution of mankind from simple series through individualism to complex series. Even Fourier's particular illustrations, notably his analogy between Civilization reaching its apogee and turning into Harmony and a silkworm entering the stage of chrysalis, are entirely dialectic. Another extreme case for Fourier and his series is presented along somewhat similar lines in the chapter on "Dialectique hégélienne et Séries de Fourier" in Raymond Queneau, *Bords. Mathématiciens. Précurseurs. Encyclopédistes* (Paris, 1963), pp. 37–51.

in particular, concerning the elimination of family and hired labor, concerning the establishment of social harmony, concerning the transformation of the state into a simple management of production. All this is most applicable to the teaching of Fourier where these assertions are most strikingly presented. We find still other mentions of the positive ideas contained in his teaching in the works and letters of Engels who made a special study of Fourier: concerning the right to work, concerning work as a natural need of man, concerning free work as pleasure, concerning competition in work; concerning the economic advantages of association and the affluent living in the society of the future; concerning the correct organization of human activity which leads to the creation of a whole man; concerning the new relations between the sexes in connection with the complete freedom of women; concerning education, based on the linking of learning and productive labor to form fully rounded and developed members of a socialist society.[23]

More connections between the views of the theoretician of the phalanx and the founders of Marxism could be added to the list. For example, Fourier pointed out that "every political invention must come from corporate bodies interested in making it." [24] In any case, Lenin stood on firm ground when he judged Marxism to be a continuation of three main trends of thought, "philosophy, political economy, and socialism," or "German philosophy, English political economy, French socialism." [25] Whether one of the three sources of Marxism be defined as socialism, French socialism, or utopian socialism, Fourier indubitably occupied a central position in it. In fact, in many analyses this source is reduced

[23] Zilberfarb, *Sotsialnaia filosofiia Sharlia Fure,* p. 407. Chapter nine, pp. 383–410, is devoted to "Fourier's social philosophy—an essential part of one of the sources of Marxism."

[24] Fourier, *Egarement de la raison,* p. 47; *Oeuvres,* Anthropos, Vol. XII, p. 633.

[25] Zilberfarb, *Sotsialnaia filosofiia Sharlia Fure,* p. 463 provides page references to Fourier in Lenin's writings.

to the works of three men: Saint-Simon, Fourier, Owen. More doubtful is the standard assertion of Marxist writers that Marx and Engels dialectically incorporated and surpassed Fourier, overcoming his deficiencies and lifting his insights to a new level of thought. To an outsider the process looks more like simple borrowing combined with borrowing from other sources and in particular with a radically different view of how theory was to be transformed into practice. But this issue belongs properly to a study of Marxism, not of the teaching of Charles Fourier.

The fathers of Marxism had to "overcome and surpass" Fourier because his socialism pointed in a number of directions unacceptable to them as well as in some which they could follow. Frequent reference has been made to Fourier's emphasis on the benefactor who would establish the trial phalanx and thus, through imitation by others, transform the world. It was for this reason in particular that the theoretician of Harmony was declared to be utopian by later proponents of the proletarian revolution or other ways of violence. The important point again is to appreciate the connection between Fourier's belief in a peaceful palingenesis and his views in general. To repeat, the new society was to include all. "The error into which all our Civilized philanthropists have fallen is to believe that one must work for the happiness of the poor without doing anything for the rich. One is far from the ways of nature when one does not work for all." [26] And even: "they ignore that it is necessary to begin with men with property: it is necessary to emancipate the masters before emancipating the slaves, emancipate the proprietors before the proletarians, the husbands before the wives, the children before the mothers, the government before the people, the progression which is the very opposite of

[26] Fourier, *Manuscrits* (Paris, 1852), p. 24; *Oeuvres,* Anthropos, Vol. X, p. 24, second pagination.

the one which our inept reformers want to follow. . . ." [27]

The issue was not the unequal hierarchic structure of the present society—indeed, humans loved and admired hierarchy—but the indigence of the masses. "There is thus but a single problem for the social science to resolve: it is to put into operation a graduated metamorphosis, elevating each class into the condition of the class immediately superior to it, elevating the poor to a middling level, the condition of the bourgeois into that of opulence, that of opulence into that of splendor, and so on all along the line." [28] Fourier liked to present tables indicating by what factor the lot of different economic groups would improve when they move from Civilization into the phalanx. The poor were to gain the most, but a pronounced difference in wealth and living standards would nevertheless characterize the new society with its three classes. And even in a more distant future when all human passions and desires would receive their fullest expression within a perfect social system, the inequalities and the hierarchies would, of course, remain.

Another peculiarity of Fourier's socialism was its agricultural character. Moreover, it was an agricultural character of a highly specific kind: the father of Harmony loved and emphasized for his society of the future horticulture—appropriately defined in the Webster dictionary as "cultivation of a garden or orchard; art of growing fruits, vegetables, ornamental plants"—while he disliked and minimized the significance of a large-scale production of cereals, *les grandes cultures.* Never at a loss to buttress his views, the theoretician from Besançon explained that human diet would change,

---

[27] Fourier, *La fausse industrie,* Vol. I, p. 421; *Oeuvres,* Anthropos, Vol. VIII, p. 421.

[28] Fourier, *Manuscrits. Années 1853–1856* (Paris, 1856), p. 290; *Oeuvres,* Anthropos, Vol. XI, p. 290, first pagination.

and that, for example, people would delight in eating fruit where they had been eating bread. The climate would, of course, also change, becoming much warmer and generally more favorable for the cultivation of fruits and flowers.

As outlined in a preceding chapter, agriculture, or rather horticulture, would form the basis both of individual phalanxes and of the entire society of the future. "There must be at least three manufacturing establishments in each phalanx, but of limited activity; for in the combined order factories are attractive only in proportion of ¼, ⅕, [or] ⅙ to the dosage of agriculture. From this it follows that it would be impossible to accumulate many factories in a land which would have little agriculture, or to dispense with factories in a land which would have much agriculture." [29] Elsewhere Fourier proposed other proportions, notably one to three. But in every case manufacturing, while unmistakably represented, remained definitely subordinate to agriculture. Because manufacturing had a highly limited power of attraction, manufactured goods would be relatively scarce, and the Harmonians would have to treat them with their characteristic meticulous care and parsimony. These goods, to be sure, would be of excellent quality and superb durability.

Even more revealing than the quantitative superiority of agriculture over industry in the phalanx, was its so-to-speak qualitative predominance. Commentators have pointed out that almost all of Fourier's examples of groups and series were taken from the realm of horticulture, not manufacturing.[30] More importantly, the theory of groups and series

[29] Fourier, *La fausse industrie,* Vol. I, p. 229; *Oeuvres,* Anthropos, Vol. VIII, p. 229.

[30] The only substantial exceptions to this domination of horticulture that come readily to mind are in the realm of gastronomy: groups or series of soups, or of lovers of soups, etc. Fourier also mentioned frequently such activities as hunting, fishing, and raising

itself seemed to be intrinsically connected to horticulture. In Professor Janet's perceptive words:

In fact, in Fourier examples of groups and series are always taken from agriculture, and above all from gardening. It is always the series of pear cultivators, of rose cultivators, etc., which are offered to us as models. It has not been sufficiently realized that the socalled passional series was very simply copied from plant series provided by natural history. Nature and art having created varieties of roses, varieties of pears, it was assumed (arbitrarily, to be sure) that the passion for roses and for pears divides itself into as many subdivisions as there are varieties. But is it the same way in industry? Can a passion be divided in proportion to the division of labor? Are there people who love the head of a pin and others who love its point? Furthermore, does industry lend itself to brief sessions, to alternation, to all this play of attractive labor, which is to make, according to Fourier, a veritable paradise out of a phalanstery, in any case if perpetual change is as pleasant as he calculates it to be? Industry demands, on the contrary, continuity, incessant repetition. Extreme ability stems in it from extreme specialization.[31]

Charles Fourier rarely missed an opportunity to champion agriculture. The celebrated industrial armies of Harmony, often cited as evidence of a close connection between Fourier's thought and the industrial and technological mobilization of societies characteristic of the twentieth century, bore in fact a more direct relation to horticulture. Their most frequently stated purposes were to drain the marshes, establish systems of dikes, and in other ways win more land for suitable cultivation by the phalanxes. These armies could also, for example, plant trees or build major canals to assist com-

domestic animals and birds, but very rarely discussed them in any detail. And he wrote enthusiastically on occasion about the practice of such arts or crafts as embroidery in Harmony.

[31] Janet, "Le socialisme au XIX⁰ siècle. La philosophie de Charles Fourier," p. 641.

munication, while Fourier's most detailed description of their activities concerned an enormous competition to produce the best *paté*. And in general Fourier was determined to improve land where necessary, so that every unit of the new society could participate in the characteristic activities of a phalanx. Again, when discussing the reduction of commerce to its correct modest size, the theoretician of Harmony emphasized that as a result 400,000 men and huge capital would be released for employment in agriculture, although occasionally he mentioned the workshops as another beneficiary of the forthcoming change.[32] Agriculture deserved priority over other occupations at the Bourse and elsewhere in the society of the future. "There is given to groups and series authority proportionate to their importance, as there is given to the cards a superiority of one over another, according to their rank. An agricultural group prevails over a manufacturing one, and the latter over a group of science and scholarship [*un groupe de sciences*]." [33]

Fourier's heart belonged to the ideal countryside of the new order, dotted with phalanxes. In contrast to Civilization, in Harmony country life would be much preferable to city life, for only in the countryside would human passions find their full expression "through active participation in ag-

---

[32] On this point see, e.g., Fourier, "Des diverses issues de civilisation," p. 220; Fourier, *Manuscrits. Années 1853–1856* (Paris, 1856), p. 135—*Oeuvres*, Anthropos, Vol. XI, p. 135, first pagination; Fourier, *Manuscrits* (Paris, 1851), p. 261—*Oeuvres*, Anthropos, Vol. X, p. 261, first pagination. The workshops are mentioned only in the last instance. The figure of 400,000 probably refers to France alone.

For the *paté* competition, see Fourier, *Théorie de l'unité universelle*, Vol. IV, pp. 352–361; *Oeuvres*, Anthropos, Vol. V, pp. 352–361 and, in full, with love as well as taste satisfied, Fourier, *Le nouveau monde amoureux*, pp. 342–386; *Oeuvres*, Anthropos, Vol. VII, pp. 342–386.

[33] Fourier, *Manuscrits* (Paris, 1851), p. 111; *Oeuvres*, Anthropos, Vol. X, p. 111, first pagination.

riculture of which the city is deprived." [34] Only in a phalanx, in a rural setting, would man discover his true happiness:

It consists of enjoying each day a variety of thoroughly plotted
sessions to the number of at least twelve, with a pivotal one:
7 *composite* pleasures for the senses *and* the soul
5 *simple* pleasures for the senses *or* the soul
1 pivotal or *parcours*
1 *transitional*
NOTE. The parcours is an enjoyment of several cumulative pleasures appearing consecutively in the course of a brief session and
joined to a continuous pleasure which reigns throughout the entire session. [35]

The cities of the new order, with all their advantages over
the present ones, would be able to offer but half the pleasures of the country. As a result, the rich would avoid towns,
except on special occasions, such as periodic fairs. City children would pass their summers in the country. Moreover, at
any given time as many as a quarter of the inhabitants of
cities would be on leave to the countryside to taste there real
happiness. Fourier even suggested that in Harmony a stay of
one, two, or three months in a city might be inflicted as
punishment. Charles Fourier's fascination and delight with
the rural life in a phalanx is all the more striking because it
is entirely one-sided: there is no counterbalancing enthusiasm for or interest in industry, urban life, technology, or
science. To repeat, industry in Harmony would apparently
consist almost entirely of arts and crafts, conveniently ac-

[34] Fourier, *La fausse industrie*, Vol. 1, p. 178; *Oeuvres*, Anthropos,
Vol. VIII, p. 178.

[35] *Ibid.*, p. 180; *Oeuvres*, Anthropos, Vol. VIII, p. 180. For a fuller
treatment of the *parcours* see Charles Fourier, "Du parcours et de
l'unitéisme," *La Phalange. Revue de la science sociale*, Vol. V (January–February 1847), pp. 21–46, 97–132; *Oeuvres*, Anthropos, Vol.
XII, pp. 475–536.

commodated in individual phalanxes. Fourier left us descriptions of a cooperation of many phalanxes to provide magnificent illumination at night, and of all the phalanxes to sing at equinox a hymn to the new order, which would thus roll around the globe with the rising sun, but he did not write in any detail of direct industrial, technological, or scientific cooperation among them.[36]

On the whole, therefore, one has to agree with E. S. Mason and other writers who have emphasized the pre-industrial nature of Fourier's socialism:

The industrial revolution passes Fourier by; he failed completely to appreciate its significance. . . . He was an economist in that older sense of the word meaning economizer. He advertised the economics of the division of labor with the enthusiasm of Adam Smith; but division of labor meant to him the simple form well illustrated in market-gardening, not the complex form associated with the machine technique. His phalanstère was based squarely on an agricultural régime and hand labor. In these respects he is exactly the opposite of his contemporary Owen, who did understand the significance of the Industrial Revolution, and who attempted to include the advantages of the new industrial methods in his community schemes.[37]

It is worth noting that Fourier himself recognized, in a sense, the more progressive nature of the views of his other

[36] For the illumination see p. 89, and for the hymn see p. 347 of Fourier, *Manuscrits* (Paris, 1851); *Oeuvres,* Anthropos, Vol. X, p. 89 and p. 347, first pagination.

Characteristically, Fourier's partial phalanx was to start with agriculture alone, some manufacturing activities being added later. Characteristically too, Fourier would not discuss these additions. Fourier, "De la sérisophie ou épreuve réduite," p. 179; *Oeuvres,* Anthropos, Vol. XII, p. 361.

On Fourier's treatment of industry see also, e.g., Gide, who writes of Fourier's hatred of industrialism and identifies industry in Harmony with the work of artisans in a village or a small town. Gide, *Fourier, précurseur de la cooperation,* pp. 79–84.

[37] E. S. Mason, "Fourier and Anarchism," p. 261.

great rival, even more "modern" than Owen, Henri de Saint-Simon. Fourier's repeated vituperative attacks on Saint-Simon, which accuse the Count of many faults and inequities including a desire to have humanity retrogress to a particularly oppressive form of the theocratic state, contain nevertheless the suggestion that Saint-Simon's doctrines pointed to the next stage of the evolution of society, the stage of economic bigness, quasi-monopoly, organization, and hierarchy.[38] If Civilization represented the fifth period in human history, Saint-Simon was moving into the sixth; Fourier, to be sure, wanted to fly into the eighth. Or, to put it differently, Saint-Simon had historical evolution on his side, while Fourier retained unchallenged the kingdom of dreams.

One contrast among many that have been drawn between the teaching of Saint-Simon and that of Fourier is that the first emphasized production and the second consumption. And it is this stress on consumption and the interests and organization of consumers that especially connects Fourier to another major modern development in Europe and elsewhere, the cooperative idea and movement. Professor Charles Gide who made a study of this connection even asserted:

There is something truly new in these protests of Fourier, for before him history had known but one ceaseless protest, that of

[38] For Saint-Simon, in addition to his own works, read especially Frank Manuel, *The New World of Henri Saint-Simon* (Cambridge, Massachusetts, 1956). A particularly sparkling and sharp, if somewhat oversimplified, contrast between Fourier and Saint-Simon is provided in Janet, "Le socialisme au XIX\e siecle. La philosophie de Charles Fourier," pp. 621–622.

On Fourier and Christian socialism, see in particular Jean-Baptiste Duroselle, *Les débuts du catholicisme social en France (1822–1870)* (Paris, 1951), notably Chapter II, pp. 80–153, "La Naissance du socialisme chrétien."

workers under the regime of slavery, under that of serfdom, under that of wage labor—and also the protest of debtors against usury—but it had not heard the complaint of the consumer: this had never made itself heard before Fourier![39]

To be sure the state had intervened, in Rome and elsewhere, to hold down prices, but there had been no understanding of the exploitation of the consumer comparable to that of the exploitation of the worker, no general theory to explain it and propose a remedy. In fact, consumers themselves, in contrast to workers, needed Fourier to see the light, to appreciate the very fact of oppression. The sage from Besançon began developing his theories when he was struck by the outrageous price of an apple, and he did not stop until he created a world of small producing and consuming groups, the phalanxes, that were not subject to anyone's exploitation. "In reality the phalanx, if it were realized, would have been quite simply a cooperative association of production and consumption."[40] A number of other specialists have expressed opinions similar to Gide's, although usually with somewhat more reserve. For example, Professor Bouglé wrote: "And in effect, technical details aside, struggle against parasitism and defense of the consumer, these two slogans which were to arouse long echoes, were thrown out without any doubt by the inventor of the phalanstery."[41]

As usual, Fourier combined principle and theory with practical prescriptions. Gide noted correctly that, in addition to the phalanx itself with its quasi-cooperative nature, the theoretician of Harmony produced blueprints for a whole flock of cooperative institutions which were to be utilized by

[39] Gide, *Fourier, précurseur de la cooperation*, p. 15.
[40] *Ibid.*, p. 31.
[41] Bouglé, *Socialismes français*, p. 134. Cf. Morris Friedberg, *L'influence de Charles Fourier sur le mouvement social contemporain en France* (Paris, 1926), pp. 129–157, especially pp. 154–157.

humanity in its forward march if it failed to achieve immediately a perfect social order.[42] These institutions, notably the remarkable "communal counters," would function as societies of consumers, rural banks, savings banks, stores providing loans for security, employment offices, insurance companies, and in particular as associations which would guarantee the interests of sellers on the market and would expand into production. To put it differently, Fourier was a true forerunner of both the consumers' and the producers' cooperatives, and of many other forms of cooperation besides. Of course, the fact that the prophet from Besançon was linked directly to cooperative thought did not mean that the cooperative thought and movement simply derived from him. Gide himself recognized that their connections with Owen were stronger than their connections with Fourier, and that Fourier's insistence on profits and his amoralism clashed with later cooperative trends. More demanding critics, such as Bouglé and E. Poisson, pointed out in considerable detail that Fourier did not know the concept of rebate, that he stressed the inequality rather than the equality of members, and that in other ways too the arrangements which he proposed were very different from the later cooperative arrangements. But while such arguments are important in tracing precise connections and influences, they do not affect the fact that Fourier was basically affiliated with cooperative thought. Even so severe a commentator as Poisson concluded on the subject of Fourier and the cooperative movement: "In the end, there is nothing in common except the associationist character, if one is to omit all sec-

[42] Gide neglected the fact that all these institutions represented at best a *pis-aller* for Fourier, who really wanted none of them. Instead he wished a trial phalanx and an immediate transformation of Civilization into Harmony. Nevertheless Gide is right in emphasizing that Fourier did sketch out these cooperative institutions which he considered preferable to the arrangements in contemporary society.

ondary matters where it is easy to draw connections which have no deep significance. But this common character, there you have a big thing, a very big thing, and, ultimately, this is sufficient." [43]

Charles Fourier clearly belonged to the socialist and generally collectivist school of thought which has become so prominent in the world in the nineteenth and twentieth centuries. But this was not his only allegiance. The prophet of Harmony was equally strongly affiliated with another major intellectual tradition, that of anarchism. With reference to the earlier description of Fourier's system as a combination of absolute order and absolute freedom, it would be appropriate to add that the order was socialist and the freedom anarchist. Of course, not all commentators and critics of Fourier recognized freedom in his world. Complex, carefully organized, and minutely graded order stood out in sharp relief. Some observers believed that it would stifle freedom, imposing the tyranny of the omniscient inventor of the phalanx, of the discreetly mentioned but nevertheless present potentates and hierarchies, or at least of public opinion. Yet, if Fourier is to be taken at his word—and a basic assumption of this entire study is that he should be so taken—his formula provided for perfect liberty and perfect self-expression for all humans: each and every social and economic arrangement assisted the free self-fulfillment of human personality, and could in no way hinder it. True, if the formula failed, there would be no absolute freedom for the humanity of the future to enjoy. There would be no absolute order either. Nothing.

Taken at his word, Fourier was certainly an anarchist. If

---

[43] E. Poisson, editor, *Fourier* (Paris, 1932), p. 13. Poisson's introduction, entitled "Fourier . . . à travers notre génération" occupies pp. 1–13 of this volume of *Réformateurs sociaux, Collection de textes dirigée par C. Bouglé.*

anarchism is a view that all government is an evil, few writers stated the anarchist position as sharply and as persistently as the father of the phalanx. The point of Fourier's attack on Civilization was that it oppressed and exploited man, regardless of the political structure or the specific historical attributes of a given regime. Government utilized every means, from the rationalizations of the philosophes and the priests to the appropriations through taxation of the individual's possessions, to maintain its control of the masses, but in the last analysis it relied on the soldier, the policeman, the jailer, and the executioner. Harmony would eliminate all political systems, and it would eliminate the state. There would be no wars, no tariffs, no crime, no political curruption, and no politics. Not only would man find himself living wholly within small groups and series with no leviathan to command or threaten from the outside, but even within these groups and series he would merely follow his own inclinations. His peers would offer stimulation, assistance, cooperation, and intrigue, but no one would order him about.[44]

Fourier's rebellion against authority was by no means limited to the state. In line with the so-called progressive thought of the Enlightenment, he had a special hatred for theocracy, and for the temporal power of the Church in general. The Church as well as the state exploited and oppressed the people. It tried to silence Copernicus and Galileo, and it created the Inquisition. A grave danger lurking in the teaching of Saint-Simon and like-minded men was precisely a penchant for a new theocracy.

If a tyrannical state and an oppressive church were among the usual targets of the Age of Reason, Fourier's sweeping

---

[44] Characteristically, Fourier generally preferred local government to central government, although he considered local government too as hopelessly deficient and corrupt in Civilization.

attack on virtually all intellectual and scholarly authorities was more original. As has been indicated, Fourier came to denounce vehemently all intellectual, scientific, and scholarly leaders of every persuasion, with the exception of Newton, some other central figures in astronomy and physics, and a very few individuals in other fields, for example Quesnay. And even these select thinkers, Fourier often asserted, proved to be in many ways blind men, who merely adumbrated the field for Fourier. In the kingdom of the intellect, the theoretician from Besançon was an extravagant iconoclast and anarchist who believed that he could sweep the slate clean, or almost clean, and start virtually anew with his own all-important formula. Interestingly enough, Fourier's pedagogical views were also in a sense anarchist: the prophet of Harmony stressed emulation, guidance by peers, intrigue, not authoritarian instruction. And in other realms in Harmony authority disappeared to be replaced essentially by free play.

Fourier rivaled the most outspoken among anarchists in his determination to destroy civilization, root and branch. Still, this was not his main concern. Of the later apostles of anarchy a Kropotkin resembled him more than a Bakunin, for in Fourier and Kropotkin, in contrast to Bakunin, the positive element prevailed over the negative, creation over destruction. Fourier's anarchism was above all a passionate belief in the absolute and perfect self-expression and self-fulfillment of every human being, entirely untrammeled and unobstructed. Nothing else really mattered, and everything had to be bent to this end. The full play of all the passions in each individual was the essence of Fourier's formula, of the phalanx, and of Harmony. Kropotkin and most other libertarians look timid and pale compared to Fourier's utterly sweeping and uncompromising demand for human personality. To put it differently, Fourier looks insane. As in the case of other anarchists, the theoretician of Harmony buttressed his views with beliefs in the goodness of man and in the natural law which governs the universe and produces beneficial results for all from the liberty of each. Only as usual Fourier went farther than these others. Every detail from the children's love of sugar to their dissimilarity from their parents pointed for him to the future transformation when, instead of producing a jarring note as at present, it would fall harmoniously into place.

Fourier's feminism can be profitably considered as one aspect of his unremitting demand for total freedom and self-expression for all human beings. For this reason it stood at the center of his teaching, and was consistently championed by the theoretician of Harmony throughout his life. Charles Fourier was both a very early and a very extreme feminist. He has even been credited with coining or giving currency to the term itself. Professor Gide wrote: "Fourier was the first 'feminist' in the sense of an absolute equality of the sexes, not only before the law, but before morality. On this subject he proclaimed some maxims which are wholly remarkable, if one thinks of the date on which they were written, and which were of such a character that nothing more daring has been said [on the subject] as of today." [45] Nor, one might add, has Fourier's feminism become at all passé since Gide made this statement. Rather it represents one of the many striking and strange links between Fourier and the concerns of today and, presumably, tomorrow.

As has been indicated, Fourier measured historical progress by the degree to which women acquired rights in a given society. This gage followed naturally from his overwhelming emphasis on human freedom and self-expression, and it attracted unstinting admiration and praise from many

[45] Gide, *Fourier, précurseur de la cooperation*, p. 162.

later champions of the cause of women.[46] To repeat, according to the theoretician of Harmony, the initial period of the evolution of humanity, that of Edenism, was characterized by free love, an equal status of women, and general happiness. It was Savagery that made women servants of men, and Barbarism that brought their condition to a nadir. In a different line of development Patriarchate established the privileged position of some women as unique wives, bequeathing monogamy to Civilization. Civilization thus represented a great progress in the condition of women over the immediately preceding stages. Nevertheless Fourier was only too well aware of its remaining failings and deficiencies in that respect. His bitter critique of the position of women in contemporary society became as important and striking a contribution to feminism as his emphasis on the emancipation of women as the *leitmotiv* of human progress. This critique was very much in the air in the last decades of Fourier's life, although the thinker from Besançon stood out, as so often, as an early, extreme, and highly idiosyncratic exponent of a common point of view. Finally, and certainly, in Fourier's own world, in Harmony, women were to have all the rights, and to enjoy perfect freedom and self-expression. At the same time as he championed feminism, Fourier did not share the outlook of those proponents of the emancipation of women who argue their case on the basis of the similarity of women and men. Instead he laid stress on the enormous variety of psychological and physical gradations, of

[46] E.g., of E. Dessignole who wrote the only special study of Fourier's feminism: E. Dessignole, *Le Féminisme d'après la doctrine socialiste de Charles Fourier* (Lyons, 1903). This useful doctoral dissertation has a certain grotesque quality because the author urges us "to obtain by Fourierist means the development of the personalities and of freedom of women within the context of well-constituted and prosperous families" (p. 141).

differences in inclinations, interests, and tastes which women will contribute to the free synthesis of perpetual enjoyment which will bear the name of Harmony.[47]

Fourier's links to different major modern trends in education were as basic as his relationship to feminism, although still more complicated. Again, it is easier to observe similarities in ideas and participation in a common current of thought than direct influences, although specialists have pointed out that, for example, the first modern preschools in France, the celebrated *écoles maternelles,* were initiated by "Elisa Lemonnier and her friends of Fourierist inspiration." [48]

The theoretician of Harmony started from the positions of the Age of Reason, "directly from the Encyclopedia of Diderot and D'Alembert," [49] and from his conviction of the fundamental importance of education.

Man without education is a being inferior to brutes. A lion, without other education than nature, becomes equal to another lion; he is not at all ridiculous in the eyes of his peers, he is on a par with them in dexterity, in instinct, and in all the qualities which constitute the perfection of a lion. It is by no means the same in the case of a man who, deprived of educational lessons, does not at all become equal to other men like him. . . . Therefore, after subsistence, there is no more urgent need for man than education.[50]

[47] These differences would often be statistical, rather than absolute —i.e., two-thirds of the boys and one-third of the girls would join the Little Hordes, while one-third of the boys and two-thirds of the girls would join the Little Bands—but this does not make them unimportant for Fourier's formula. See also the next chapter for Fourier's psychology.

[48] Dautry, "Fourier et les questions d'éducation," p. 245, footnote 35.

[49] *Ibid.,* p. 241.

[50] Fourier, *Manuscrits* (Paris, 1852), p. 246; *Oeuvres,* Anthropos, Vol. X, p. 246, second pagination.

Fourier, of course, resolved the problem through his unique and elaborate scheme of universal education in the society of the future. This scheme—outlined in an earlier chapter of the present work—has continued to attract attention and comment in the communist as much as in the Western world, and among scholars in different disciplines.

Thus, a Western writer, concerned primarily with Fourier's anarchism and modernity, asserted: "But there is another and more important sense [than examples of foresight] in which Fourier is modern. I have referred to it above as consisting in his emphasis on self-expression. It appears in his ideas on education, and takes the form of the adaptation of the subject-matter to the interests of the learner rather than the adaptation of these interests to the subject-matter." [51] A careful Soviet scholar drew the following balance:

Fourier's pedagogical system suffers from certain substantial defects which are explained by the conditions of the age and the personal peculiarities of the great dreamer. These include, for instance: an overestimation of the working and intellectual capabilities of a child, an insufficient attention to academic education, a failure to understand the role in education of factory production as the leading kind of work, an overemphasis in education of the importance of the passion for change, the fiction concerning the role of gastronomy and, in connection with that, the transformation of the kitchen into one of the fundamental institutions in education and upbringing, and so forth. However, the above-mentioned and other defects, peculiarities and even absurdities cannot conceal from us that which is fundamental in the system of socialist education developed by Fourier: the postulation and proof of the role of a social education of all children which gives every child the opportunity to develop completely all his abilities on the basis of a combination of productive labor with education, with the physical and aesthetic development; the demand for a

[51] Mason, "Fourier and Anarchism," p. 260.

total education of many-sidedly developed people, permeated by the socialist morality, self-sacrificing members of a free workers' collective. It is precisely this in the system of 'education in the order of Harmony' that constitutes the immortal contribution of Fourier to the pedagogy of socialism.[52]

It might be added that Fourier wanted not only to combine education with productive labor but also in effect to abolish the difference between mental and physical work, a development not unrelated to the virtual elimination of the distinction between town and country in the new world of happy phalanxes. Other aspects of Fourier's educational system which have attracted attention included the teaching by means of peers or of slightly older children, the early assignment to children of important responsibilities in the life of the community, and the emphasis on education as play.

Fourier has also been praised, and with some justice, for his contributions to pacifism and to internationalism, indeed to the concept of one world. The theoretician of the phalanx was not at all a typical pacifist, for he served in the army, enjoyed military pomp and display—which, in the opinion of some commentators, reappear only too often in Harmony —and emphasized the potentially beneficial historical role of great conquerors. Still, on the other hand, he joined the thought of the Enlightenment in condemning war as idiotic barbarism and proposed to transform the world by entirely peaceful and happy means. Moreover, soldiers, wars, and in fact all physical conflict was to be totally excluded from Harmony. As to internationalism, the sage from Besançon again reflected the best cosmopolitan traditions of the Age of Reason. Fourier's formula applied to all mankind, and it could be put into operation by any man of means who would subsidize the translation of theory into practice. And, of course, in the one world of Harmony there would be no

[52] Zilberfarb, *Sotsialnaia filosofiia Sharlia Fure,* p. 164.

Hellene and no Jew, no international struggle, no power politics, and no powers. It is interesting to observe that Fourier's French patriotism intruded at times into his picture of the new world. It is equally interesting to note that these intrusions were always limited and kept in check. Thus, Paris was to become the global capital of Harmony, but only temporarily until Constantinople with its uniquely advantageous location would be ready to assume permanently that position. Similarly, French was to serve as the universal tongue of the transformed world, a point which Fourier stressed to his compatriots in urging them to establish a trial phalanx. But, as Paris was to cede to Constantinople, French was to cede eventually to the perfect unitary language—to be taught to us by the planet Mercury.

Fourier's relationship to *le mouvement social* was not limited to his contributions to socialism, the cooperative idea, anarchism, feminism, educational reform, pacifism, and internationalism. Yet enough has already been said to indicate in very broad terms that Charles Fourier participated in important and often original ways in much modern intellectual development. In conclusion, the manner as well as the substance of this participation bears recalling. Fourier can be considered as one of the great prophets and yea-sayers of *le mouvement social* because of the sweep and the strength of his affirmations. Like such other towering figures as Saint-Simon, Owen, Comte, Marx, and Engels, Fourier had and loudly proclaimed an absolute conviction in the complete scientific validity of his own teaching. Together with some of these figures, and other reformers of his time besides, the father of Harmony added a quasireligious tone and fervor to his pseudo-scientific message. A sarcastic enemy of all moralizing, he nevertheless suffused his entire teaching with moral passion. Even in explicit terms, if on the one hand morality as such had no meaning for Fourier, on the other it could signify only a contribution to the advent of Harmony. "There is no virtue except that which promotes the movement of social progress."[53] A continuous road stretches from this original affirmation, magnificent in its sweep and power, to numerous innovations, reforms, and revolutions of the nineteenth and twentieth centuries, down to Labor Britain, and the Soviet Union of Brezhnev and Kosygin. It took at least initial faith to move mountains.

In an essay published in 1932 E. Poisson recollected how as a boy he learned about Charles Fourier from a fanatical minor employee who insisted on reading to him the writings of the sage from Besançon.

And thus Fourier gave to this boy, who was I, without my understanding it, and perhaps in part even because of the incomprehensibility, a kind of 'religion,' a religion which condemns the society of today and expects the realization of a new world.
Is it not there that you have the profound feeling which is the basis of the socialist conscience and by this very fact the origin of the entire immense movement at its disposal? . . . if he still lives among us is it not because he was the creator of a social 'mysticism'? All those who read him were impregnated with his thoughts, for he revealed the necessity of a new city of harmony. And the newer and simpler the soul is, the greater remains the power of Fourier.[54]

[53] Fourier, *Manuscrits* (Paris, 1851), p. 140; *Oeuvres,* Anthropos, Vol. X, p. 140, first pagination.
[54] Poisson, "Fourier . . . à travers notre generation," p. 4.

CHAPTER V

Fourier's Psychological Vision

While the heavens proclaim the glory of God, earth proclaims the absence of the divine compass in human relations.[1]

It is easy to repress passions by violence: philosophy suppresses them with the stroke of a pen; latches and the sword come to the support of gentle morality. But nature makes an appeal against these judgments, it regains its rights in secret: passion stifled at one point breaks out at another, like waters blocked by a dike; it reverberates like the fluid of a prematurely closed ulcer.[2]

Charles Fourier contributed in many ways to *le mouvement social*. Yet his contributions were usually peculiar, highly idiosyncratic, not to say heretical, different from the main current of progressive thought. More often than not there lay behind the differences Fourier's particular psychological vision, which constituted, in the last analysis, both the essence and the main thrust of his teaching.

To repeat, Fourier believed that the misery of mankind resulted from the suppression of man's passions and that he had found salvation: a formula, a system which would combine perfect self-expression of every individual, a complete gratification of each one of his passions, with a similar gratification and the resulting happiness of all human beings. Passions, in Fourier's view, were immutable and absolute.

[1] Charles Fourier in *La Reforme Industrielle ou le Phalanstère*, No. 6 (July 5, 1832), p. 58.
[2] Fourier, *Le nouveau monde industriel et sociétaire*, p. 403; *Oeuvres*, Edition Anthropos, Vol. VI, p. 403.

As the theoretician of the phalanx wrote in 1820 in his "Colloquy between men and God": *"The mortals.* We shall change the passions. *God.* What dare you propose! This change is not in My power; the 12 passions are eternal, unalterable, like the three principles of nature from which they derive. I do not possess, God that I am, the ability to change the passions. . . ." [3] It was a measure of the madness of men that they rejected the divine verdict and proceeded to suppress, fight, deflect, and attempt in every way to transform or abolish the passions.

Fourier's critique of Civilization was primarily a critique of this disastrous effort. To take a look at the central institution of Civilization, the family, so much praised by so many moralists:

I have witnessed closely many families. I have not found a single one joyful on the inside. . . .
In general, every family seems to say, like Dido:
I want to flee, I want to escape from myself.
The father escapes to the housekeeper, who spoils him with food, he runs to the cafés, to the circles and meetings of men; sometimes to those of women. The mother escapes her conjugal Argus by arranging for him distractions which keep him out while she receives her supplicant. The children at the age of puberty think only of escaping the insipidity of the household: the young girl lives only for an evening when she is at a ball; the young man, preoccupied with parties, returns to his paternal home as to a place of exile. As to the children below the age of puberty, they are not satisfied except when they manage to escape the eye of the father and the eye of the tutor to enjoy everything that is forbidden to them.
Thus individuals, considered separately, seek nothing but to escape the sweet household or to break its moral laws. As to the family taken collectively, it has no gaiety, no happy moments, except as it succeeds, aided by its means, *to escape from itself* by

[3] Fourier, *Manuscrits* (Paris, 1852), p. 341; *Oeuvres,* Anthropos, Vol. X, p. 341, second pagination.

receiving different friends and transforming, now at the table, now in a circle, now in the countryside, the family group into the group of external friendship, and often into the group of illicit loves, in accord with morality. But nothing is more mournful, more gloomy than a family, which, without the means necessary to receive or visit people, finds itself reduced to the monotonous pleasure of familial association, where the moralists want to locate happiness.[4]

In short, the family in Civilization represented an unnatural arrangement which stifled men, women, and children, and destroyed their happiness. Civilized schooling was no better. In particular, Fourier maintained, it relied on theory rather than practice, on pedantic academism, monotony, and compulsion, and it failed totally to appreciate the interests and abilities of its pupils.[5] No wonder that children were happy and active only on vacation. Other civilized institutions contributed their share to the suppression and the thwarting of human passions. As indicated earlier, Fourier sometimes described Civilization as an arrangement whereby the passions of the dominant one-eighth of the population were satisfied at the expense of the passions of the exploited seven-eighths. More frequently, however, the prophet of Harmony emphasized that in the contemporary world even the exploiters, while in every sense privileged compared to the rest of mankind, remained frustrated and miserable, for they too had no real outlet, or at best a thoroughly insufficient outlet, for their passions. It should be stressed that, in the opinion of Fourier, this frustration and clash of passions constituted the very essence of Civilization:

[4] Fourier, *Manuscrits* (Paris, 1851), p. 64; *Oeuvres*, Anthropos, Vol. X, p. 64, first pagination. A word or words missing in the published text.

[5] See, e.g., Fourier, *Le nouveau monde industriel et sociétaire*, pp. 218–221; *Oeuvres*, Anthropos, Vol. VI, pp. 218–221.

They attribute social misfortunes to this clash. Answer them that this clash is the protection of Civilization. It would decline and burn out, if passions were deprived of the objectives of luxury and of the functions, the coveting of which produces both social fury and social marvels. Man, denied this stimulus, would fall back into the pastoral stage. The Civilized state has as its essence a universal clash of passions. To want to repress or reconcile them means to want to overturn the Civilized order: if they are repressed, one falls back into patriarchal life; if they are reconciled through development by means of new measures, such as the elimination of marriage, the Civilized order is overturned, that order which has marriage, the true kernel of all social discords, as its pivot. It is therefore necessary for the good of the Civilized order that passions clash violently, because, if they are ever repressed or reconciled, Civilization will be destroyed.[6]

In the contemporary world, the frustration and violation of human passions could be easily seen all around us. The legions of the hungry testified to the tragic denial of the passion of taste to so many on our planet. The hopeless condition of the poor made any display of ambition on their part a bitter mockery. Other passions fared no better in Civilization. In addition, the constant carnage of war, sweeping epidemics, and other disasters contributed to the wholesale elimination of human beings, passions and all.

Furthermore, Fourier maintained with a striking originality, there was also the invisible toll to be added to the visible. "Passion stifled at one point breaks out at another, like waters blocked by a dike; it reverberates like the fluid of a

---

[6] Fourier, *Manuscrits. Années 1853–1856* (Paris, 1856), p. 313; *Oeuvres,* Anthropos, Vol. XI, p. 313, first pagination. This remarkable passage, written in 1806, represents very early Fourier. It is doubtful, for example, whether he would have later drawn quite that sharp a difference and quite that kind of a difference between Patriarchate and Civilization. But the view of Civilization as a clash and a thwarting of passions remained.

prematurely closed ulcer." [7] Unable to take a constructive course, passions turned to destruction, bringing added misery to humanity, misery which was no less real because it was not understood. Fourier's most famous example of repression and unconscious motivation dealt with "a princess of Moscow, lady Strogonoff" and "one of her young slave girls."

A princess of Moscow, lady Strogonoff, seeing that she was getting old, was jealous of the beauty of one of her young slaves; she had her tortured, herself pricking her with pins. What was the real motive for this cruelty? Was it really jealousy? No, it was Lesbianism. The lady in question was, without knowing it herself, a Lesbian and inclined to love this beautiful slave whom she had tortured, participating herself in the torture. If someone would have spoken of Lesbianism to Madame Strogonoff and would have managed an arrangement on that basis between her and her victim, the two would have become very passionate lovers. But the princess, not having thought of Lesbianism, fell into a counter-passion, into the subversive movement: she persecuted the object which she should have enjoyed, and her fury was all the greater because the blockage came from prejudices which hid from this lady the true nature of her passion and prevented her from taking the ideal course. A blocking of violence, which is the case in all forced privations, does not lead to such fury. Others perform in the collective sense the atrocities which Madame Strogonoff performed individually. Nero loved cruelties which were collective or of a general application; Odin made of them a collective system and Sade a moral system. This taste for atrocities is nothing but a counter-passion, a result of a blockage of certain passions. In the case of Nero and of Sade, it was the composite and the butterfly that were blocked; and in the case of Madame Strogonoff it was a branch of love.[8]

[7] Fourier, *Le nouveau monde industriel et sociétaire*, p. 403; *Oeuvres,* Anthropos, Vol. VI, p. 403.

[8] This text was published in a modified form in *La Phalange*. Emile Lehouck restored the original reading. I am using Lehouck,

Fourier proceeded beyond such particular examples to reach general conclusions. He decided that whereas one was usually aware when one's sensory or one's group passions were frustrated—a man knew when he was hungry, or when an object of his ambition eluded him—the same did not apply to the three serial or distributing passions, the cabalist, the butterfly, and the composite. Human beings in Civilization had no knowledge of these passions, discovered only by Fourier; they merely felt at their frustration a certain pressing boredom, a certain anxiety, like Caesar who seemingly possessed everything he could wish, without being able to explain the malaise.[9] They were waiting, without being aware of it, for the calculus of attraction "and in the meantime they are all more or less afflicted with a secret impatience, with a spiritual malady or void, an absence of purpose, which was deplored already by Horace. *'Post equitem sedet atra cura.'* "[10]

Blatant or hidden, the thwarting of human passions and the resulting misery pervaded all of Civilization. Nor was

Fourier aujourd'hui, pp. 33–34. I also consulted the original in Fourier, Unpublished manuscripts, Cahier 50, p. 31. It seems unkind to note that the Stroganovs, not Strogonovs, were counts, not princes, and had serfs, not slaves. Also, I know no Stroganov to whom Fourier's story would readily apply.

[9] Fourier, *Théorie des quatre mouvements et des destinées générales,* pp. 82–83; *Oeuvres,* Anthropos, Vol. I, pp. 82–83. Here, as on some other occasions, Fourier added the thirteenth passion, that of unityism, to the three distributing passions. But cf. the Stroganov example where a form of the passion of love wreaked havoc without receiving conscious recognition. At times Fourier argued that hidden love, in contrast, for example, to taste, generally acted in this hidden manner. It was no less deadly for being hidden. Fourier, *Le nouveau monde amoureux,* pp. 442–443; *Oeuvres,* Anthropos, Vol. VII, pp. 442–443.

[10] Fourier, "Du clavier puissanciel des caractères," p. 18. Cf. the third chapter of: Charles Fourier, "Du parcours et de l'unitéisme," *La Phalange. Revue de la science sociale* (January, February 1847); *Oeuvres,* Anthropos, Vol. XII.

the constant effort to change or eliminate passions of any help. Salvation could come only from a change in the social environment, from a utilization of the passions: "But there is a shift which you could utilize, that of characters. Without changing them as to their germ or radical, their development can be modified as that of a tree, the branches of which are directed at will." [11] Or as the theoretician of Harmony put it on another occasion after asserting once again that neither God nor men could change the passions themselves: "One can only change the course of the passions without altering their nature." [12] Fourier was the first man to offer humanity the only possible way out of its tragic cul-de-sac: "My claim is to have followed the road opposite to that of your legislative charlatans, such as Plato and Voltaire, Owen and St. Simon, who want to change human nature, change the springs which God put in our souls in order to direct them. I am the first, the only one, who has sought and found the art of utilizing these springs, without changing anything in them." [13]

Fourier's solution was, of course, the phalanx and the entire social order of Harmony. We have seen how the new system was designed to replace the despotism and drudgery of the family by the sparkling, passionate dance of multiform temporary liaisons. Similarly in education, pedantry and boredom would be changed into enthusiastic play under the guidance of somewhat more advanced children. Similar metamorphoses would take place in other aspects of human existence. Happiness would indeed replace misery on the face of the earth.

[11] Fourier, *Manuscrits* (Paris, 1852), p. 341; *Oeuvres,* Anthropos, Vol. X, p. 341, second pagination.

[12] Fourier, *Manuscrits* (Paris, 1851), p. 67; *Oeuvres,* Anthropos, Vol. X, p. 67, first pagination.

[13] Fourier, *La fausse industrie,* Vol. I, p. 165; *Oeuvres,* Anthropos, Vol. VIII, p. 165.

As it has been so often reiterated in this study, everything depended on the efficacy of Fourier's formula. Nor is there any obvious way to go beyond this statement. Still, the elements of the formula, the passions, are important even in isolation for one interested in Fourier's psychological views. Charles Fourier's system of passions has been criticized on many grounds. It has been pointed out, for example, that the first five in the group were really senses, not passions, and that they could not be logically classified with the others. More broadly speaking, the entire threefold listing appeared to many readers as disparate, incongruous, and strange, without clear derivation or affiliation in the history of thought. The thirteenth passion, that of unityism, seemed only to complicate matters.

Many students of Fourier also complained that his doctrine of passions was utterly immoral. To quote Edmond Villey's angry lament: "But man, what happens to him in Fourier's teaching? A perfected animal! The theory is not only *immoral;* it is, what is worse, *amoral,* which means that it does not admit any kind of *morality;* it suppresses entirely what for man is the sign of his election: the conscience! May they never again offer us the phalanstery!" [14] Or, in Gaston Isambert's more temperate and searching words:

He could have at least placed altruistic inclinations above all the rest and thus presented a concept of the human soul, which might have been debatable, but which would have been very "social," very "sympathetic." But no, he gives first place to his three bizarre inclinations: the *cabalist,* which he could have called simply ambition; the *butterfly,* which is nothing but a taste, often troublesome enough, for change; the *composite,* which is perhaps enthusiasm, but which in any case defies all precise analysis. This passional trinity definitely designates only secondary forms of activity; how many men lack one or more of these inclinations?

[14] Villey, "Charles Fourier, l'homme et son oeuvre," p. 59.

This psychology cannot serve as a foundation for morality. Accordingly Fourier has not formulated any moral theory properly speaking. Much more than that, he boasts of not having a moral theory. . . .[15]

And it has been repeatedly asserted that the prophet of Harmony simply failed to comprehend the warmth of family life, the joys of motherhood, or the beauty of a constant marriage. Occasionally the argument that Fourier's system of passions debased humanity took a more original turn. Thus Ch.-M. Limousin declared: "But there is room for a stronger criticism: Fourier forgot a whole order of passions, that of intellectual and metaphysical pleasures."[16] On the other hand, and by contrast with this entire school which accused the theoretician of the phalanx of a wholesale denigration of mankind, a number of critics have pointed out that Fourier's system appeared attractive and workable only because he arbitrarily excluded all the evil passions of man from his joyful world: the inhabitants of Harmony had no hatred, no jealousy, no envy, only taste, love, or enthusiasm.

Some commentators discussed Fourier's set of passions in terms of their function in his total system and their suitability for that system. Emile Faguet concluded that the theoretician of the phalanx was guilty of a fundamental *petitio principii*: his new order promised to produce concord among men, but unfortunately it first needed that same concord to go into operation.[17] Several critics have emphasized that Fourier in fact failed to provide a theoretical justification for the promised enthusiastic work of his groups and

[15] Isambert, *Les idées socialistes en France de 1815 à 1848*, p. 129.

[16] Limousin, "Le Fouriérisme, bref exposé. La prétendue folie de Fourier," p. 14.

[17] Faguet, *Politiques et moralistes du dix-neuvième siècle*, pp. 68–69.

series, that in particular he confused consumption with production:

There is much psychological truth in Fourier's views about attractive work; nonetheless his proof remains very vague, and in particular one can mark in it a perpetual and singular ambiguity between the tastes of production and the tastes of consumption, and an illegitimate conclusion from the one to the other. He believes that because one has the taste for enjoying something, one has by this very fact the taste for producing it. He chooses as an example the taste some have for salted bread, others for semi-salted bread, still others for bread without salt. So be it; let us accept these three kinds of taste; does it follow that there are people who experience pleasure in making bread with salt, and others without salt? The presence or absence of salt has importance for those who enjoy bread, but none for those who make it; and in general, from the fact that I enjoy something it does not follow that I take pleasure in producing it. To have a good meal is not the same as to cook; the best gourmet will not necessarily be the best chef. When it is a matter of enjoying, only pleasure is to be taken into account; when it is a matter of producing, one must take difficulty into account. There are even tastes which it is impossible to satisfy by oneself: for example, he who loves good verses or good paintings will not be for this reason a great painter or a great poet. Thus the two series, of the consumers and of the producers, do not correspond to each other, while Fourier nevertheless chooses almost always as examples consumer groups, because in their case it is indeed much easier to compare graded series. What he had to prove was not that all tastes are good, but that there are tastes and even passions for all the kinds and all the subdivisions of work necessary for man, and that these tastes are more numerous in proportion to the utility or the necessity of an occupation. But Fourier never turned his attention to this side of the question.[18]

In general Charles Fourier's promise of most enthusiastic and most fruitful work by all in Harmony has aroused

[18] Janet, "Le socialisme au XIXᵉ siècle. La philosophie de Charles Fourier," p. 643. See also, especially: Jean Dautry, "La notion de travail chez Saint-Simon et Fourier," *Journal de Psychologie normal et pathologique*, Vol. LII (1955), pp. 59–76.

much skepticism. Critics have pointed out that the theoretician of the phalanx unfortunately omitted the desire to work from his list of passions, and had, therefore, to rely on the satisfaction of such posited urges as the butterfly to obtain the promised results. But switching in rapid succession from one unpleasant job to another would hardly improve anyone's productivity.

Most of the lines of criticism of Fourier's system of passions were expressed during his own lifetime. The prophet of Harmony disdainfully dismissed or disregarded some, but he was concerned with others. He took special pains to explain how and why none of the aggressive and generally evil urges, so widespread and destructive in Civilization, would disturb the society of the future. That society, to repeat, would be a mirror image of Civilization, but with a plus rather than a minus sign. In effect, then, man possessed not twelve, but twenty-four passions, or, better, twelve passions each of which could take two opposite forms, the positive and the subversive, the first characteristic of Harmony, the second of Civilization.

Our passional alphabet is composed, like that of grammar, of 24 keys, for the 12 radical passions have a subversive course, which produces 12 other passions which are as distinct as a caterpillar is from a butterfly, or as the minor scale is from the major. We thus have in passional grammar, as in vocal grammar, 24 fundamental signs.[19]

In the abstract, then, Civilization represented the logical development of the negative versions of the twelve passions,

[19] Fourier, "Du parcours et de l'unitéisme," p. 130; *Oeuvres,* Anthropos, Vol. XII, p. 534. To the best of my knowledge Fourier never defined or described precisely the twelve subversive passions. Perhaps he felt that no description was necessary, because they were the same original passions of his system, only on a subversive course. Cf., Fourier, *Manuscrits. Années 1857–1858* (Paris, 1858), p. 299; *Oeuvres,* Anthropos, Vol. XI, p. 299, second pagination.

whereas Harmony would give full expression to their positive forms. No wonder that the two societies would no more resemble each other than night does day.

More concretely, Fourier proceeded to indicate how in the world of the future presently vicious passions would be absorbed into the total system and would contribute to desirable ends. This absorption would apparently take different forms, depending on the particular situation. For example, in an interesting passage the theoretician of the phalanx explained how the seven cardinal sins would be transformed into virtues in Harmony: (1) pride would inspire competing groups to perform superior work, erect fine buildings, and so forth; (2) avarice, as already explained, would become a truly precious mania when exercised in the interests of a phalanx; (3) lechery would prove most useful at the "court of love"; (4) envy would lead to fruitful emulation; (5) gluttony would form the foundation of education and wisdom; (6) anger in the form of an honorable anger would insist on high standards of performance and repudiate mistakes; (7) laziness, finally, or rather its disappearance, would serve to demonstrate the attractiveness of work in the new society, for laziness was a natural reaction of a human being to undesirable labor.[20] Some urges, to be sure, could not be utilized in their direct form, but it would be possible nevertheless to absorb them into the world of the future.

The theory of attraction utilizes all the passions stemming directly from natural impulses: as to *reflected or rebounding* passions, such as gambling, it absorbs them, opens to them other careers, but does not utilize them in their present state.
This is a distinction which the detractors do not want to mention; they accuse me of wishing to utilize reflected and odious

---

[20] Fourier, *Analyse du mécanisme de l'agiotage* [*et*] *de la méthode mixte en étude de l'attraction,* pp. 113–114.

passions such as that of assassination; they know only how to slander, how to make a travesty of the proposed theses.[21]

The urge for gambling would indeed find many venues in Harmony, through absorption in the cabalist passion. And, as Fourier explained repeatedly elsewhere, a murderer in contemporary society would make an excellent butcher in the world of the future.

In his struggle to absorb destructive passions into the harmonious world of his own making, Fourier also came to the conclusion that passions caused trouble not because they demanded too much, but because society offered them too little. In perfect agreement with the main line of his thought, the thinker from Besançon proposed once again to change the environment. As usual, he presented his solution in a precise and pseudo-scientific manner:

In the meantime it is the taste for pleasure that pushes the Neros and the Tiberiuses to crime. How to correct them by means of the [   ] which leads them into evil? This will be done by offering them hyperattractive pleasures, or joys of a period superior to Civilization.

Thus for the loves of a family [*ménage*] the hyperattraction is the loves of the sixth period or Guaranteeism. If a man is bored by conjugal love and if he is not offered any love of the kind characteristic of the sixth period, he will turn to adultery, fornication, debauchery, orgies and other illegal voluptuousness. He is easily corrected if it is possible to offer him loves arranged in the

---

[21] Fourier, *La fausse industrie*, Vol. II, p. G4 (684); *Oeuvres,* Anthropos, Vol. IX, p. G4 (684). The original French *"répercutées ou récurrentes"* is here translated as "reflected or rebounding." Fourier apparently took this term from Horace's lines: "Si furca naturam expellas, tamen usque recurret"—"Let us analyze the baleful results of this compressed passion and of its countermarch or *recurrence* (an expression of Horace which should be adopted for this effect of a passion)," Fourier, *Manuscrits* (Paris, 1852), p. 133; *Oeuvres,* Anthropos, Vol. X, p. 133, second pagination.

manner of the sixth period, which manner is much more seductive and yet legal. The same is true of the vices of ambition, such as the ravages of the conquerors. Their natural corrective is to be found in composite conquest, which is a method of the sixth period. Before explaining these [   ] let us postulate a principle, namely that every noxious passion has as its natural antidote the application of an attraction of a superior order, that is to say that if a noxious passion is of the Civilized order, of the fifth period, it must be treated by means of an attraction of the sixth period or Guaranteeism.

The rule does not extend to the inferior periods. One would not treat a passion of the Barbarian order by means of a Civilized one, because Civilization, while superior in degree, is not attractive. Social attraction starts only with the sixth period. Thus it is impossible to employ in the utilization of hyperattraction about which we have spoken Civilized customs which are not attractive. A Barbarian prince would prefer his seraglio to our life of households and exclusive wives, but he would choose over his seraglio the amorous customs of the seventh period.[22]

Philosophers, Fourier continued, were therefore entirely wrong to have taught moderation to princes. Instead they should have applied Fourier's treatment "to every ambition of a prince which took a vicious course," deflecting and absorbing it by the attraction of a pleasure of a superior order.[23]

Aggressive urges of all sorts created the greatest problem for Fourier. As we have seen, he was well aware of this problem, and tried to resolve it in several ways. To begin with, the liberation of passions in Harmony would eliminate a tremendous amount of hostility. Free to express her love, Princess Strogonoff would not develop hate and resort to

[22] Fourier, *Manuscrits. Années 1857–1858* (Paris, 1858), pp. 110–111; *Oeuvres,* Anthropos, Vol. XI, pp. 110–111, second pagination. Words missing in the published text.

[23] *Ibid.,* pp. 111–115; *Oeuvres,* Anthropos, Vol. XI, pp. 111–115, second pagination.

torture. Many other people would presumably experience a similar, if often less dramatic, transformation. In connection with that, Fourier indicated that even such a violent and apparently fundamental urge as jealousy was most closely linked to the social environment. While Europeans jealously insisted on exclusive marriage, the Tahitians enjoyed free love, and the Turks their seraglios. Jealousy and various related hostilities could, therefore, be exorcised from the scientifically organized world of the future with its magnificent amorous and other opportunities. To help matters, Fourier devised a special order of fakirs and fakiresses whose function it would be immediately to console rejected lovers. Other aids would include the already-mentioned confessors who would advise the inhabitants of a phalanx on how to form the happiest liaisons. Fourier was determined to provide a fully satisfying love life to every man and woman in Harmony. And while jealousy and other disturbing emotions related to love at least required continuous planning and vigilance, most contemporary sources of hatred and hostility would totally disappear, once the new society were established. Thus pain and rage produced by such obvious denial of passions as hunger, oppression, and exploitation would have no place at all in the world of the future.

Perhaps still more interestingly, Fourier, of course, provided outlets for aggression in the society which he constructed with such meticulous care. To repeat, he took a positive view of discords as ties and mechanisms in the ideal world. Assailing the Owenites and the Saint-Simonians, the theoretician from Besançon declared:

They want also to wipe out the discords, egoisms and antipathies, ignoring the fact that in an association of 1,800 persons, in full scale [*en grande échelle*] of three united classes, there will be required at least thirty thousand antipathies, sixty thousand egoisms, six hundred thousand discords, and many other means proscribed by our self-styled associationists, who do not know even how to answer elementary questions about association.[24]

Fourier's own utopia, as we know, teemed with competing and victorious or defeated groups and series. To put it a little differently, it is worth noting that while Fourier refused to consider outright hatred or rage as basic to human character, he did include ambition and the cabalist among his twelve passions and made every arrangement to permit their full play.

The magic of Fourier's formula would coordinate all the antipathies, egoisms, and discords, directing them to the good of both every individual involved and of society as a whole. Once applied it would convince all participants and observers, and provide the ultimate answer. In the meantime, however, the father of Harmony was willing to expatiate on at least some aspects of this coordination and direction. In particular, we saw, in the course of our analysis of Fourier's system, how social antagonisms would weaken and eventually disappear through the operation of groups and series and of the entire model social order. Yet the new rivalries, those of groups and series themselves, would never exceed their proper limit. Indeed, groups would always remain fundamentally linked by the interest of their common series, and the series by that of their common phalanx. Moreover, antagonisms would not be personal, because within a phalanx each individual would meet every other in many roles, most of which he would find highly attractive. Friendship would prevail over rivalry in the proportion of seven to one. As usual, Fourier liked to present his views in the manner of pseudo-scientific formulas. Thus he wrote as follows on combating egoism, with a special reference to a great enlargement of the family:

[24] Fourier, "Necessité d'une théorie certaine sur l'art d'associer," p. 30.

For minor groups, to absorb them outside themselves; for major groups, to absorb them within themselves.

That is to say that it is necessary to give so great an extension to minor groups that their egoism will be absorbed in numerous combinations with major groups; then those latter should be similarly given an extension so great that they would become philanthropic through activities [*speculations*] applicable to the entire globe. Such will be the procedure in Harmony to drown familial egoism, amorous jealousies and other vices of the four present-day groups, to absorb them in a sequence of limitless developments.

Let us apply this principle to the group of family-feeling, presently reduced to the smallest development by means of the exclusive conjugal bond. Nothing will be changed in this system in limited Harmony or the seventh period. But in composite Harmony at the end of several generations a phalanx of 1,500 inhabitants will all be interrelated in different degrees, and it will be possible to say of it: if they are not all brothers, they are all cousins. Once this familial bond is extended to the entire phalanx, the egoism which it inspires today will be transformed, without changing its nature, into communal philanthropy. This is one of the brilliant operations of Harmony; it justifies my frequent criticism of the egoism and of the vices of the present familial bond.[25]

To illustrate his successful treatment of destructive urges, Fourier liked to indicate how vicious individuals, even monsters, of the unregenerate world would become well-adjusted and useful inhabitants of Harmony. Nero served as the utopian socialist's favorite example. The celebrated Roman emperor was born with sanguinary tastes. "Nature wanted that he would, from the age of three, take part in some butchery groups of his phalanx."[26] But Agrippina would not think of such a lowly occupation as butchering for her

[25] Fourier, "Des trois groupes d'ambition, d'amour et de familisme," pp. 151–152. "Minor" refers to the passions of love and family-feeling, and "major" to the passions of ambition and friendship.

[26] Fourier, *Manuscrits* (Paris, 1852), p. 132; *Oeuvres,* Anthropos, Vol. X, p. 132, second pagination.

son. Instead she handed him over to Seneca and other false teachers, who did their best to suppress natural impulses in him, ultimately in vain and even with disastrous results. Denied his natural occupation, Nero remained cramped and thwarted in every other way too. "Nero was one of those souls whose desires are too vast, too sensitive to be sated by the puny and monotonous joys of the existing order. Such men, tired of having so quickly exhausted the narrow limits of Civilized voluptuousness, throw themselves into crime solely for the pleasure of variety, to obtain violent excitement which is necessary for them, excitement which is so rare in our societies that one goes to find it in the tragic scenes of a theater." [27] Nero was in fact a tetragyne, whose four dominant passions were ambition, love, the composite, and the cabalist.

These are the four passions the combined course of which is the most difficult. Nero, despite the help of education, could not arrive at a complex development of his four passions. He vegetated for a time in a simple or bastard manner, appearing to incline to tenderness, but once his ardor [*fouge*] took hold of him, he entered the complex subversive course and spread out his wings in crime in a grand manner, throwing diamonds to the people and slaughtering the great. One always finds on his crimes the stamp of the composite. If he has the city of Rome set on fire, he adds to this spectacle dramatic illusions by declaiming from the top of a tower verses concerning the burning of Troy. If he has senators slaughtered, this is to make them recognize him as the greatest singer. If he has his mother disemboweled, he brings into this undertaking views considered philosophical and wants to contemplate in this open body the place where he took birth.[28]

By contrast, had unfortunate Nero only been born in Harmony, he would have become "one of the best butchers in

[27] Fourier, *Manuscrits. Années 1853–1856* (Paris, 1856), pp. 314–315; *Oeuvres,* Anthropos, Vol. XI, pp. 314–315, first pagination.
[28] Fourier, "Du clavier puissanciel des caractères," p. 106.

the phalanx of the Tiber." [29] His desire to slaughter animals would have led him to an interest in their forage, in various ways of fattening them, and on into other fields of knowledge. In the sparkling world of Harmony, Nero's passions, composite and all, would have been given full play, and therefore they would have taken their natural, not their subversive, course. Nero would have developed into a most happy and most useful member of society, not the embodiment of vice of history books. Fourier emphasized that Nero's character, while relatively rare, was in no sense unique. In fact, in the world of the future every phalanx would have four tetragyne couples, one of which would be called, because of the passional correspondence to the Roman emperor, *le Néron et la Nérone,* just as another one would be named *le Henri et la Henriette.*[30] To conclude in the words of Fourier:

Thus in Harmony our characters will be utilized such as they are and without any change. There is not a single one that does not have the quality of double development. Nero was during the first years of his reign the hope and the love of the Romans. When he was given the death verdict of a criminal to sign, he regretted that he knew how to write. He followed the path of virtue up to the age of eighteen, and became soon after the most notorious of villains. All characters are subject, like Nero, to a vicious or subversive development and to a virtuous or harmonious one; they are susceptible to the *caterpillar* course and to the *butterfly* course. If then the social mechanism which I call passional series has the property of developing every character in a harmonious and virtuous manner, it will change nothing in the passions or in the characters, but only in the direction of their course, by providing the means of arriving at riches and happiness

[29] Fourier, *Manuscrits* (Paris, 1852), p. 133; *Oeuvres,* Anthropos, Vol. X, p. 133, second pagination.

[30] *Ibid.,* p. 135; *Oeuvres,* Anthropos, Vol. X, p. 135, second pagination. The Henry in question was King Henry IV of France.

through the practice of justice and truth, which today, being a way to certain ruin, has to be despised by the masses and is suspect even to the sages who commend it to us without wanting to practice it [themselves].[31]

Charles Fourier's drastic theory of passions resulted in a sharply focused and rather stark view of the human condition. For example, the utopia of the future aside, the sage from Besançon showed little or no sentimentality with regard to human urges and inclinations in the unregenerate world. Thus the great constructive role which he assigned to children in Harmony served in a sense as a counter-point to their destructive potential in Civilization. Just as the oppressed masses were restrained from bloody anarchy only by the soldiers and the gallows, children were restrained by their parents and guardians.

A child has the same quality. The first use that he would make of his liberty would be to rise against the social order and to form veritable hordes which would begin by minor pillaging, breaking shopwindows and grills, attacking with stones, maltreating, killing anyone who displeased them. There would be rapid intervention to stop them. It is no less true that these hordes of children would have finished with devastation and fire.[32]

Or, to repeat a point, Fourier showed concern for the common people and proposed to save them from their present lamentable condition without ever idealizing these people. As he liked to remark, he no more believed in the virtue of rustic shepherds and shepherdesses than in that of their literary sponsors.

Because only passions, common to all human beings,

[31] Fourier, *Manuscrits* (Paris, 1851), pp. 70–71; *Oeuvres,* Anthropos, Vol. X, pp. 70–71, first pagination.

[32] Fourier, *Manuscrits* (Paris, 1852), p. 302; *Oeuvres,* Anthropos, Vol. X, p. 302, second pagination. I happened to read this passage when newspapers were narrating the activities of the Simbas in the Congo.

really mattered in Fourier's system, very much else did not. The problem of race, for one, was to disappear in the world of the future. Fourier wrote with heavy sarcasm about "white nations which persuade themselves that the Negro is inferior to them, because of his color, which is true only with respect to his unfortunate lot." [33] The ultimate dismissal of race as a meaningful category did not prevent, as we have seen, the theoretician from Besançon from harboring all kinds of ethnic prejudices, whether against the English, the Jews, or the Chinese. But these were limited to their social structure and roles in the unregenerate world. In the fulfillment of Harmony race, caste, social antagonisms, and all other barriers between human beings would vanish without a trace. Fourier liked to point out that even in the sorry human past and present supposedly insurmountable barriers have been bridged by such fundamental passions as love, friendship, or ambition.

It should be noted that Fourier's rigid system of twelve fundamental passions allowed nevertheless, in its own way, considerable variety and flexibility in character structure and analysis. As we have seen, human beings differed, according to Fourier, in the first place because they had a different dominant passion or passions. Thus Louis XIV "was a digyne with ambition and love as pivotal," the villain Robespierre and the great statesman Lycurgus were both trigynes dominated by the composite, the cabalist, and ambition, while Henry IV represented "a magnificent tetragyne with friendship, love, ambition, and the composite as pivotal." [34]

[33] Fourier, Unpublished manuscripts, Cahier 10/9, p. 28. It should be repeated—perhaps to complicate the issue of Fourier and racism—that in Harmony all inhabitants would gradually acquire a white skin, with the sun, in harmonious rapport with mankind, bleaching rather than tanning it.

[34] Fourier, "Du clavier puissanciel des caractères," pp. 24–25. And, for a wild, although always measured, glance at a great expansion

To repeat, in terms of the number of dominant passions human beings ranged from the usual domination by a single passion, in 576 cases out of each 810 to be exact, to domination by two, three, and more passions, until in the person of Fourier himself we had the unique example of an omnigyne, a man dominated by all seven group and serial passions. Those with a greater number of dominant passions represented a higher character development and one more useful in Harmony; they were to play particularly important roles in stimulating and unifying the activities of a phalanx and even, as has been indicated, in tying phalanxes together.

While passions were basic, they were naturally subdivided into different accents or "tonics," encompassing a variety of human urges and traits. For example, Silenus was "a monogyne dominated by taste, tonic of drinking," and Harpagon another monogyne "dominated by ambition, tonic of avarice." [35] Moreover, in addition to the dominant passion, of whatever tonic, every monogyne possessed "four other subdominant passions, which exercised by degrees the principal influence, and which were to be distinguished, according to their amount of influence, into sub-dominant passions of the first, second, third, and fourth degrees." [36] To be sure, highly important as these classifications were, they referred ultimately to emphasis: fundamentally, every human being needed full freedom for every one of his twelve passions. In particular, although the more highly developed characters were dominated by the passions of the group and the series, rather than of the senses, this did not mean that their sensi-

in the number of passions as they are considered in higher powers. Fourier, *Le nouveau monde amoureux,* pp. 454–457; *Oeuvres,* Anthropos, Vol. VII, pp. 454–457.

[35] Fourier, "Du clavier puissanciel des caractères," pp. 23–24 for Silenus and p. 13 for Harpagon.

[36] *Ibid.,* p. 14.

tive passions required anything less than complete opportunity and satisfaction.

Further variations in human character were provided by the *polymixtes,* or the ambiguous ones:

> There remains to us to speak of the *polymixtes* or the ambiguous ones, who possess no dominant passions, but only rallying passions [*raliantes*], that is, passions which dominate merely accidentally and not in a fixed manner. In this case, an individual is of a vague character, and generally very false in Civilization. These characters compose more than one eighth of the 810: they include 80 *dimixtes* with two rallying passions, 16 *trimixtes* with three rallying passions, 8 *tetramixtes* with four rallying passions. They are very useful in Harmony, but very dangerous in Civilization, where they produce, in the superior genre, protean individuals and chameleons, in the inferior genre, inconsequential people, contradictory spirits, scribblers or people without character, always in docile agreement with whomever spoke to them last.[37]

The polymixtes played a crucial role in political assemblies, constituting the middle and making it possible to incorporate both extremes, which would otherwise fight, into the work of a legislative body. They included very many outstanding political figures, such as Pope Sixtus V, Cardinal Mazarin, and Alcibiades, who "was in Athens the most refined of the gourmets, and in Sparta a model of sobriety." [38] Yet Civilization was extremely cruel to the polymixtes. Typically, it suppressed one of their two lines of development, leading to its violent explosion later in life. "How often one has seen members of society move suddenly from the bosom of pleasures to monastic austerities, courtiers,

---

[37] *Ibid.,* p. 15.
[38] *Ibid.,* pp. 99–100. Fourier also recognized, and in his system provided for, people with so-called "vile," that is bizarre or unusual, preferences in regard to taste, love, or other passions. Such preferences, he explained, were in fact very common, but those who

sybarites retire to the Carthusians and the Trappists and give there examples of a complete denial of the self?"[39] In fact, "the greater part of vicious people are the ambiguous ones of the fifth degree, and become vicious because of circumstances. . . ."[40]

Fourier's treatment of the passion of love deserves further notice. As indicated in our earlier analysis, love occupied an extremely important position in the father of Harmony's system. In fact, some critics have treated the entire teaching of Fourier as essentially a plea for free and varied love. And while this approach does not do justice to Fourier's other passions, nor indeed to his entire formula and theory, one has to recognize a certain ambivalence in the theoretician of the phalanx: an ambivalence between the usual complexity, balancing, and precise proportioning characteristic of his thought, and his willingness at times to emphasize love above all. The first was the major tone of his teaching, the second the minor—but at least in respect to this minor tone Fourier can be considered to be a predecessor of Freud and the libido doctrines of the twentieth century.

However, precisely because Fourier was a brilliant forerunner of later intellectual developments, it is important not to make him too modern. As a rule, love represented for Fourier only one of twelve, or thirteen, passions—although to be sure, some of the other passions could also be linked to the concept of libido—and, compared to the contemporary concept, it was limited in other ways besides. Notably, the theoretician from Besançon considered children, until their

possessed onè of them, looked with characteristic surprise and disparagement at those possessing others. Fourier, *Théorie de l'unité universelle*, Vol. IV, 332–351; *Oeuvres*, Anthropos, Vol. V, pp. 332–351.

[39] Fourier, "Du clavier puissanciel des caractères," p. 101.

[40] *Ibid.*, p. 98. Fourier apparently meant here very vicious people, people notorious in history for their extravagant vice.

adolescence, to be a neuter sex, without the passions of love and family feeling, and he therefore postulated three, rather than two, sexes in his teaching. It is interesting that Fourier wanted to prolong this "neutrality" as long as possible. He criticized study by children of the Bible and other material which would give them premature sexual information, withheld from them for the same reason in the world of the future the great science of analogy, and took particular pains to arrange things so that the young inhabitants of Harmony would not observe intercourse among animals. Whether because of Fourier's upbringing and environment or for deeper psychological reasons, even Fourier's presumably total liberation of the passion of love among grown-up men and women contained its ambiguities. While Fourier mentioned incest as part of the free sexual practices characteristic of Edenism, and in *Le nouveau monde amoureux* of Harmony, and while he liked to project different kinds and combinations of sex relations, he scorned and condemned pederasty in classical Greece and sometimes criticized other sexual deviations.[41]

Some hundred and thirty years after the death of Charles Fourier, his psychological vision deserves attention for a number of reasons. The thinker from Besançon concluded that the all-pervasive misery of mankind stemmed from the suppression of passions. Although interested in the economic structure of society and in very much else besides, he used his insight as an essentially monistic explanation of the human predicament: the repression of passions produced pain and sorrow, their liberation would bring happiness. The thwarting of passions meant not only a denial of obvious human needs, but also the kind of frustration which

[41] See, e.g., Fourier, "Des trois groupes d'ambition, d'amour et de famillisme," p. 139. But cf. note 38 above and the emphasis on sexual deviations as vital social links in Harmony in *Le nouveau monde*

the sufferer could not explain or understand. Moreover, refused their natural outlet, the passions took a subversive course, filling the world with antagonisms, hatred, and destruction. Love stood out as a particularly important passion, while the family, as presently constituted, represented both the foundation of our entire civilization and the greatest obstacle to the freedom of the passions.

Fourier's psychological approach pointed in more than a single direction. For one thing, the father of Harmony's obsessive psychological counting and classifying was to enjoy a great future. Broadly speaking, the theoretician of the phalanx can be considered a precursor of all modern psychological testing and counseling, from standard job tests for all applicants to complicated techniques used by psychiatrists in diagnostic work with mental patients. Fourier would have been delighted with the number and variety of tests available in our world in the mid-twentieth century, although he would probably have objected to the lack of organization and coordination in the business of testing. He would have, no doubt, welcomed the computer. In the enthusiastic words of a specialist in the field, Robert Pagès, in regard to Fourier: "But he is also and above all the precursor or inventor of a series of psychological techniques and knowledge, starting still from intuitive and descriptive inner-psychology, but subject to a program of sociotechnical validation." [42] It is

amoureux. Also, that volume establishes Fourier's special liking for Lesbianism, a feeling which Fourier claimed to have discovered in himself at the age of 30 or 35 (pp. 59, 122, 163, 197, 206, 389–393); *Oeuvres,* Anthropos, Vol. VII, pp. 59, 163, 197, 206, 389–393.

[42] Pagès, "Quelques sources, notamment fourieristes, de la sociologie experimentale," p. 139. Cf. e.g., Fourier, *Le nouveau monde amoureux,* pp. 397–400; *Oeuvres,* Anthropos, Vol. VII, pp. 397–400.

Fourier's determination to put every person into his precise niche appealed to some ideologists of the Right as well as of the Left. As Charles Maurras put it: "I cannot rank myself among the disciples

the direction of Fourier's thought, not the particular classifications and techniques he proposed, nor the continuity or lack of continuity between him and later champions of testing, that is especially important here.

Even more centrally in terms of Fourier's teaching, his psychological theory led not only to the emancipation of women, and to "the rehabilitation of the flesh," but to a complete liberation of all human passions and the entire human potential. Therefore, the prophet from Besançon can be considered a patron saint of all those who have inscribed total human freedom and self-expression on their banner. It is interesting that Fourier postulated, at the beginning of the nineteenth century, a society of affluence and of leisure. The problem was to make human life intriguing and absorbing in a world unconcerned with economic survival, self-defense, or disease. No wonder that Fourier's contemporaries failed to understand him, or criticized him bitterly, often both. No wonder too that the father of Harmony has recently received lavish praise, as the creator of "a philosophy of happiness," [43] as "the moralist of the future." [44]

[*adeptes*] of Charles Fourier. How is it possible not to be among his admirers? The thing that is truly admirable in this great man, is the marvelous instinct, and one that never abandoned him, for the division of labor in nature and, therefore, in the human species. Nothing is useless, he said, and everything can be of service. It is enough that everyone be in his place and that each instinct find somewhere its satisfaction. Our entire conception of Monarchy is grounded too thoroughly on the law of the division of labor to permit us to address to Charles Fourier the slightest reproach." Charles Maurras, "La doctrine sociale de la Royauté, (Deuxième article)," *La Gazette de France* (June 16, 1901).|

[43] "A philosophy of happiness" is the title of a major part of Lehouck, *Fourier aujourd'hui*, pp. 17–129.

[44] To be sure, Madame S. Debout Oleszkiewicz refers to Barrès in using this phrase, but the endorsement is her own: S. Debout Oleszkiewicz, "Introduction," *Oeuvres complètes de Charles Fourier,*

Still, although the Freudian and the post-Freudian perspective has certainly enhanced the stature of Fourier, his thought remains, as ever, heretical. Significantly, the admirers of the theoretician of Harmony have been not Freud's orthodox disciples, but rather such neo-Freudian dissidents as Norman Brown who rebelled against the restrictions on man recognized, indeed often formulated, by their master. Brown's affirmation of life as passionate play does correspond remarkably well to Fourier's vision of human activities as a web of passionately pursued hobbies.[45] As Professor Frank Manuel remarked about Fourier and other "prophets of Paris," their blind spot was "the absence of a tragic sense."[46] More broadly, it was a refusal to recognize any, or almost any, limitations on man and human happiness. Fourier wrote, introducing the subject of education:

For thirty centuries the question has been raised whether man is born vicious or virtuous, and as usual the only result has been to confuse the issue. One will be convinced through this brief account of natural education not only that man is born virtuous, inclined towards justice, truth, and unity, but also that all the social vices with which he has been reproached are impulses of virtue, perverted by the Civilized regime, a regime contrary to the injunction of attraction, which travesties these impulses by means

Tome I (Paris, 1966), p. II. The entire interesting Introduction occupies pp. I–XXVII.

Moreover, the decoding of the genetic message apparently opens tremendous possibilities of future change in another area particularly dear to the strange thinker from Besançon, that of biological transformation.

[45] Norman O. Brown, *Life against Death: the Psychoanalytical Meaning of History* (New York, 1959). Direct references to Fourier are on pages 34, 53, and 318.

[46] Frank E. Manuel, *The Prophets of Paris* (New York, 1962), p. 314. The excellent section on Fourier occupies pp. 195–248, and the Epilogue pp. 296–315 of the book.

of obstacles which it poses from an early age to the course of the passions.[47]

Not only man was good, but God and nature also conspired to bring a perfect fulfillment to humanity. Charles Fourier's fascinating genius and abiding appeal consisted in a combination of great psychological insight and reckless optimism. His solution to the human condition which he penetrated so remarkably well was immediate paradise.

If only the destinies were proportionate to the attractions!

[47] Fourier, *Manuscrits* (Paris, 1852), p. 103; *Oeuvres,* Anthropos, Vol. X, p. 103, second pagination.

BIBLIOGRAPHY

BIBLIOGRAPHICAL NOTE

An excellent recent bibliography on Fourier and Fourierism may be found in I. I. Zilberfarb, *Sotsialnaia filosofiia Sharlia Fure i ee mesto v istorii sotsialisticheskoi mysli pervoi poloviny XIX veka,* Moscow, 1964. This bibliography lists the titles of the works in the original languages and, therefore, can be used to a large extent by those who do not read Russian. It occupies pages 460–532 of the book and is carefully divided into subsections, ranging from Fourier's own writings and those of his followers to "works touching in part on Fourier and Fourierism." E. Poulat's monograph *Les cahiers manuscrits de Fourier. Étude historique et inventaire raisonné,* Paris, 1957, remains indispensable for those interested in Fourier's unpublished legacy. Fourier's writings remain scattered, but by far the fullest and richest edition is the one being at present published by Edition Anthropos, Charles Fourier, *Oeuvres complètes,* vols. I-XII, Paris, 1966–1968. References to this edition are given in footnotes wherever appropriate.

The list below is meant simply to give full references to the works specifically mentioned in the present book, in the version and edition which I used. Because of its very nature, it does not include some material on which the study is based.

WRITINGS BY CHARLES FOURIER
MENTIONED IN THIS STUDY

Fourier, Charles. "Analogie et cosmogonie," *La Phalange. Revue de la science sociale* (August, September–October, November–December, 1848).

———. *Analyse du mécanisme de l'agiotage* [*et*] *de la méthode mixte en étude de l'attraction,* Extract from *La Phalange. Revue de la science sociale* (1848).

———. *L'Avenir. Perspective d'un phalanstère ou palais sociétaire dédié à l'humanité.* (D'après le plan de Ch. Fourier. Accompagné d'une déscription signée: Victor Considérant.) Anon., n.d.

———. *Cités ouvrières. Modifications à introduire dans l'architecture des villes.* Paris, 1849.

Fourier, Charles. "Cosmogonie," *La Phalange. Revue de la science sociale* (May–June, 1848).

———. "Crimes de commerce," *La Phalange. Revue de la science sociale* (July–August, 1845), 5–32.

———. *De l'anarchie industrielle et scientifique.* Paris, 1847. (Also known as *Anarchie industrielle et scientifique.*)

———. "De la sérisophie ou épreuve réduite," *La Phalange. Revue de la science sociale* (May–June, 1849), 161–183.

———. *Dernières analogies* (also known as *De l'analogie*). (Published in *Sur l'esprit irréligieux des modernes* and *Dernières analogies,* Paris, 1850.)

———. "Des diverses issues de civilisation," *La Phalange. Revue de la science sociale* (September–October, 1849), 184–256.

———. "Des lymbes obscures, ou périodes d'enfer social et de labyrinthe passionnel," *La Phalange. Revue de la science sociale,* IX (January–February, 1849), 5–40, 97–100.

———. "Des trois groupes d'ambition, d'amour et de familisme," *La Phalange. Revue de la science sociale* (January–March, 1846).

———. "Du clavier puissanciel des caractères," *La Phalange. Revue de la science sociale,* VI (July–August, 1847), 5–47, 97–135.

———. "Du garantisme," *La Phalange. Revue de la science sociale* (April, 1849).

———. "Du parcours et de l'unitéisme," *La Phalange. Revue de la science sociale,* V (January–February, 1847), 21–46, 97–132.

———. *Egarement de la raison démontré par les ridicules des sciences incertaines* and *Fragments.* Paris, 1847.

———. *Fragments.* (Published in *Egarement de la raison démontré par les ridicules des sciences incertaines* and *Fragments.* Paris, 1847.)

———. "Harmonie universelle," in *Manuscrits.* Vol. I. Paris, 1851. (First published in *Bulletin de Lyon,* December 3, 1803.)

———. *La fausse industrie morcelée, répugnante, mensongère, et l'antidote, l'industrie naturelle, combinée, attrayante, véridique, donnant quadruple produit et perfection extrême en toutes qualités. Mosaïque des faux progrès, des ridicules et cercles vicieux de la Civilisation. Parallèle des deux mondes industriels, l'ordre morcelé et l'ordre combiné.* 2 vols. Paris, 1835–1836.

Fourier, Charles. Brief contributions to *La Reforme industrielle ou le Phalanstère* (July, 1832–February, 1834).

———. *Le nouveau monde amoureux. Oeuvres complètes.* Vol. VII, Paris, Edition Anthropos, 1967.

———. *Le nouveau monde industriel et sociétaire ou invention du procédé d'industrie attrayante et naturelle, distribuée en séries passionnées.* In *Oeuvres complètes* de Charles Fourier. Vol. VI, 3rd ed. Paris, 1848.

———. "Les trois noeuds du mouvement," *La Phalange. Revue de la science sociale,* IX (February, 1849), 111–169.

———. "Lettre au Grand-Juge," in Charles Pellarin, *Fourier et ses contemporains. L'utopie et la routine.* Paris, 1874. (First published in *Bulletin de Lyon,* 4 nivôse, an XII.)

———. "L'inventeur et son siècle," *La Phalange. Revue de la science sociale,* IX (March, 1849).

———. *Manuscrits. (Publication des manuscrits de Charles Fourier.)* 4 vols. Paris, 1851–1858. (Vol. I – 1851; Vol. II – 1852; Vol. III – 1853–1856; Vol. IV – 1857–1858.)

———. *Mnémonique géographique, ou méthode pour apprendre en peu de leçons la géographie, la statistique et la politique.* Paris, n.d. [1824].

———. "Necessité d'une théorie certaine sur l'art d'associer," *La Reforme Industrielle,* No. 3 (June 14, 1832), 26–31.

———. *Pièges et charlatanisme des deux sectes Saint-Simon et Owen qui promettent l'association et le progrès.* Paris, 1831.

———. "Revue des utopies du XIXᵉ siècle," *La Reforme Industrielle,* No. 6 (July 5, 1832), 49–51; No. 7 (July 12, 1832), 57–59; No. 8 (July 19, 1832), 65–69.

———. *Sur l'esprit irréligieux des modernes* and *Dernières analogies* (also known as *De l'analogie*). Paris, 1850.

———. "Textes inédits de Charles Fourier présentés par Simone Debout Oleszkiewicz," *Revue internationale de philosophie,* No. 60 (1962), 171–174.

———. *Théorie de l'unité universelle.* In *Oeuvres complètes.* Vols. II–V. 2nd ed. Paris, 1841–1843.

———. *Théorie des quatres mouvements et des destinées générales.* In *Oeuvres complètes.* Vol. I, 3d ed. Paris, 1846.

———. *Traité de l'association domestique-agricole,* also known as *Théorie de l'unité universelle.* In *Oeuvres complètes.* (See above.)

Fourier, Charles. "Triumvirat continental et paix perpetuelle sous trente ans," *Bulletin de Lyon,* 25 frimaire, an XII. (Reproduced in *Oeuvres complètes de Charles Fourier.* Vol. I.)

———. Unpublished manuscripts. Cahier 10/9.

———. Unpublished manuscripts. Cahier 50.

OTHER WORKS MENTIONED IN THIS STUDY

"A propos d'un talisman de Charles Fourier. Analyse critique et essai de reconstitution," *La Breche* (February 4, 1963), 18–23.

A-n, (Anekshtein), Ark. "Elementy dialektiki i ekonomicheskogo materializma v vozzreniiakh Sharlia Fure," *Pod Znamenem Marksizma,* No. 3 (March, 1924), 202–229.

Armand, F. and Maublanc, R. Editors of *Textes choisis.* 2 vols. Paris, 1937.

Beecher, J. "L'archibras de Fourier. Un manuscrit censuré," *La Breche,* No. 7 (December, 1964), 66–71.

Bebel, A. *Charles Fourier. Sein Leben und seine Theorien.* Stuttgart, 1886.

Bouglé, C. *Socialismes français. Du 'Socialisme utopique' à la 'Democratie industrielle.'* Paris, 1933.

Bourgin, H. *Etude sur les sources de Fourier.* Paris, 1905.

———. *Fourier. Contribution à l'étude du socialisme français.* 2 vols. Paris, 1905.

Breton, A. *Ode à Charles Fourier.* Paris, 1961.

Brown, N. O. *Life against Death: the Psychoanalytical Meaning of History.* New York, 1959.

Dautry, J. "Fourier et les questions d'éducation," *Revue internationale de philosophie* (Bruxelles), No. 60 (1962), 234–260.

Debout Oleszkiewicz, S. "Introduction," pp. I–XXVII in *Oeuvres complètes de Charles Fourier.* Vol. I, Paris, Edition Anthropos, 1966.

———. "L'analogie ou 'Le poème mathématique' de Charles Fourier," *Revue internationale de philosophie* (Bruxelles), No. 60 (1962), 176–199.

———. (Ed.) "Preface." VII–CXII in *Le nouveau monde amoureux. Oeuvres complètes de Charles Fourier.* Vol. VII. Paris, Edition Anthropos, 1967.

———. (Ed.) "Textes inédits de Charles Fourier," *Revue internationale de philosophie,* No. 60 (1962), 171–174.

Dessignole, E. *Le Féminisme d'après la doctrine socialiste de Charles Fourier.* Lyons, 1903.

Delo Petrashevtsev. 3 vols. Moscow-Leningrad, 1937–1951.

Desroche, H. "Fouriérisme ambigu. Socialisme ou religion?" *Revue internationale de philosophie,* XVI, No. 60 (1962), 200–220.

Duroselle, J.-B. *Les débuts du catholicisme social en France* (1822–1870). Paris, 1951.

Faguet, E. *Politiques et moralistes du dix-neuvième siècle.* Paris, 1898.

Friedberg, M. *L'influence de Charles Fourier sur le mouvement social contemporain en France.* Paris, 1926.

Fromm, E. *Marx's Concept of Man.* New York, 1961.

Gaulmier, J. "Notes," in André Breton, *Ode à Charles Fourier.* Paris, 1961.

Gide, C. *Fourier, précurseur de la cooperation.* Paris, 1924.

Gromier, M.-A. *La vie, les oeuvres, les disciples de Charles Fourier,* Paris, 1906.

Hémardinquer, J.-J. "La 'découverte du mouvement social,'" *Le Mouvement Social,* No. 48 (July–September, 1964), 49–70.

Huard. "Examen impartial des nouvelles vues de M. Robert Owen par Henry Gray Macnab, trad. de l'anglais par M. Laffon de Ladébat," *Memorial universel de l'industrie française, des science et des arts.* Vol. V (1821), 241–255.

Ioannisian, A. "Istochniki proektov assotsiatsii Fure," *Istorik Marksist,* No. 1 (1939), 101–124.

———. *Genezis obshchestvennogo ideala Fure.* Moscow-Leningrad, 1939.

Isambert, G. *Idées socialistes en France de 1815 à 1848.* Paris, 1905.

Janet, P. "Le socialisme au XIXᵉ siècle. La philosophie de Charles Fourier," *Revue des Deux Mondes,* XXXV (1879), 619–645.

Jollivet-Castelot, F. *Sociologie et Fourierisme. Un le Tout.* Paris, 1908.

L'harmonie universelle et le phalanstère exposés par Fourier. Recueil methodoque de morceaux choisis de l'auteur. Vol. I. Paris, 1849. (See Editor's Preface.)

Lafontaine, A. *Charles Fourier,* Paris, 1911.

Lansac, M. *Les conceptions méthodologiques et sociales de Charles Fourier. Leur influence.* Paris, 1926.

Lehouck, E. *Fourier aujourd'hui.* Paris, 1966.

Limousin, Ch.-M. *Le fouriérisme. Bref exposé. La pretendue folie de Fourier. Réponse à un article de M. Edmond Villey intitulé: "Fourier et son oeuvre."* Paris, 1898.

Louvancour, H. *De Henri de Saint-Simon à Charles Fourier. Etude sur le socialisme romantique français de 1830.* Chartres, 1913.

Manuel, F. *The New World of Henri Saint-Simon.* Cambridge, Massachusetts, 1956.

———. *The Prophets of Paris.* New York, 1962.

Mason, E. "Fourier and Anarchism," *The Quarterly Journal of Economics,* XLII, No. 2 (February, 1928), 228–262.

Maurras, C. "La doctrine sociale de la Royauté. (Deuxième article)." *La Gazette de France* (June 16, 1901).

Michelet, J. *Histoire de la revolution française.* Vol. VI, Paris, 1869.

Nicolai, J. *La conception de l'évolution sociale chez Fourier.* Paris, 1910.

Pagès, R. "Quelques sources, notamment fouriéristes, de la sociologie expérimentale," *Archives internationales de sociologie de la cooperation,* No. 4 (1958), 127–154.

Pellarin, C. *Fourier et ses contemporains. L'utopie et la routine. L'expérimentation et l'empirisme en matière sociale.* Paris, 1874. (Published together with the text of "Lettre de Fourier au Grand Juge," *Bulletin de Lyon,* 4 nivôse, an XII.)

———. *Charles Fourier, sa vie et sa théorie.* 2d ed. Paris, 1843. (English translation of the first part, *The Life of Charles Fourier.* New York, 1848.)

Poisson, E. (ed.) "Fourier . . . à travers notre génération," in *Fourier.* Paris, 1932, 1–13. A volume in the series *Réformateurs sociaux, Collection de textes dirigée par C. Bouglé.*

Poulat, E. "Le séjour de Fourier en Bugey (1816–1821)," *Le Bugey* (1956), 1–25.

———. *Les cahiers manuscrits de Fourier. Etude historique et inventaire raisonné.* Paris, 1957.

Queneau, R. "Dialectique hégélienne et Séries de Fourier," in *Bords. Mathematiciens. Précurseurs. Encyclopédistes.* Paris, 1963, 37–51.

Renouvier, Ch. "La philosophie de Charles Fourier," *La Critique Philosophique, Scientifique, Littéraire* (Paris), (1883). (No. 14 [May 5], 209–220; No. 16 [May 19], 241–251; No. 21 [June

23], 321–333; No. 28 [August 11], 23–32; No. 29 [August 18], 33–40.)

Riasanovsky, N. "L'emploi de citations bibliques dans l'oeuvre de Charles Fourier," *Archives de Sociologie des Religions,* No. 20 (1965), 31–43.

———. "Fourierism in Russia: an Estimate of the Petraševcy," *The American Slavic and East European Review,* XII, No. 3 (October, 1953), 289–302.

Saitta, A. "Charles Fourier e l'Armonia," *Belfagor,* II, No. 3 (May 15, 1947), 272–292.

Sambuc, M. *Le socialisme de Fourier.* Paris, 1899.

Schaeffer, G. " 'L'ode à Charles Fourier' et la tradition," *André Breton. Essais et temoignages.* Neuchatel, 1950, 83–109.

Seillère, E. *La philosophie de l'impérialisme. Vol. IV: Le mal romantique. Essai sur l'impérialisme irrationel. Première partie. Le romantisme des pauvres. Charles Fourier.* Paris, 1908.

Silberling, E. "Composite," *Dictionnaire de sociologie phalanstérienne. Guide des oeuvres complètes de Charles Fourier.* Paris, 1911, 93–94.

Silberner, E. "Charles Fourier on the Jewish Question," *Jewish Social Studies,* VIII, No. 4 (October, 1946), 245–266.

Talmon, J. L. *Political Messianism, the Romantic Phase.* London, 1960.

Tuzet, H. "Deux types de cosmogonites vitalistes: 2. – Charles Fourier, hygieniste du cosmos," *Revue des sciences humaines,* No. 101 (January–March, 1961), 37–53.

Villey, E. "Charles Fourier, l'homme et son oeuvre," *Revue d'économie politique* (Paris), 11ᵉ année (1897), 999–1017; 12ᵉ année (1898), 30–59.

Volgin, V. P. "Sistema Fure" in *Sharl Fure, Izbrannye sochineniia,* Vol. I. Moscow-Leningrad, 1951, 5–79. (Also an earlier and somewhat different version published as "Sistema Fure" in *Pod Znamenem Marksizma,* No. 7–8 [July–August, 1929], 102–126.)

Wilson, E. "Origins of Socialism. III: The Communities of Fourier and Owen," *The New Republic,* LXXXXI, No. 1178 (June 30, 1937), 213–217.

Zilberfarb, I. "L'imagination et la réalité dans l'oeuvre de Fourier," *Le Mouvement Social,* No. 60 (July–September, 1967), 5–21.

Zilberfarb, I. *Sotsialnaia filosofiia Sharlia Fure i ee mesto v istorii sotsialisticheskoi mysli pervoi poloviny XIX veka.* Moscow, 1964.

——. "Tvorcheskii put Sharlia Fure," *Frantsuskii Ezhegodnik, stati i materialy po istorii Frantsii.* Moscow, 1959.

INDEX

Age of Reason. *See* Enlightenment
Agriculture, 69-70, 146, 196-199
Agrippina, 231-232
Alcibiades, 85, 132, 237
Alembert, Jean le Rond d', 210
Analogy, science of, 95-99, 109, 162, 173
Anarchism, 205-208
Anti-Semitism, 124, 124 n., 164, 165-167
Argentina, 184

Bakunin, Michael, 207
Baudet-Dulary, A. F., 13. *See also* Fourierists
Beecher, Jonathan, 72 n.
Belgium, 181
Bernadotte, Jean (Charles XIV, King of Sweden), 121-122
Bouglé, C., 203, 204
Bourgin, Hubert, 27, 27 n., 135 n.
Bourse, 49, 53, 199-201
Breton, André, 184
Brillat-Savarin, Anthelme, 25 n.
Brown, Norman, 242
Bulletin du mouvement sociétaire, 12
Business. *See* Commerce
Butashevich-Petrashevsky, Michael, 182

Caesar, Julius, 85, 132, 220
Capelle, Guillaume-Antoine, 118
Carrel, Nicholas-Armand, 131
Catholic Church, 131 n., 153-154, 206
Charlemagne, 98
Chernyshevsky, Nicholas, 184
Childhood and youth, Fourier on, 70-81, 134, 234, 238-239
China, 181

Christianity in Fourier's thought, 100-105
Church of England, 154
Class, social, 46, 60-65, 167, 196
Collectivism, 186-190
Columbus, Christopher, 106 n.
Commerce and merchants, 3, 6, 24, 82-83, 136-137, 139, 157-167, 168-169, 176, 197
Comte, Auguste, 213
Condillac, Etienne Bonnot, Abbé de, 105 n., 106 n.
Considérant, Victor, 12, 180, 182. *See also* Fourierists
Constantinople, 82, 213
Convention, the National, 5, 58
Cooperation and cooperatives, ix, 24-25, 144, 184, 204
Copernicus, Nicholas, 206
Cosmology, 38-40, 86-89, 89 n., 99-100, 109
Cosmopolitanism, 181
Cuisine. *See* Gastronomy
Czartoryski, Prince Adam, 123

Dautry, Jean, 30
Deism, 34-36. *See also* God, Religious Views
Descartes, René, 105 n.
Diderot, Denis, 210
Directory, the, 6, 10
Dostoevsky, Feodor, 182 n.

Echeverria, Esteban, 184
Ecology, 187-188, 198-200
Economic determinism, 190
Economists, the, 174
Education, 70-81, 191, 194, 207, 210-212, 217, 232
Enfantin, Barthélemy Prosper, 122, 183

253